# Better Homes and Gardens®

# Christmas-Time
## Cook Book

# Contents

BETTER HOMES AND GARDENS BOOKS

Editorial Director: Don Dooley
Managing Editor: Malcolm E. Robinson      Art Director: John Berg
Asst. Managing Editor: Lawrence D. Clayton      Asst. Art Director: Randall Yontz
Food Editor: Nancy Morton
Senior Food Editor: Joyce Trollope
Associate Editors: Sharyl Heiken, Rosemary C. Hutchinson, Elizabeth Strait
Assistant Editors: Sandra Mapes, Elizabeth Walter, Catherine Penney
Designers: Harijs Priekulis, Faith Berven
Contributing Editor: Patricia Brooks

Our seal assures you that every recipe in *Christmas-Time Cook Book* is endorsed by the Better Homes and Gardens Test Kitchen. Each recipe is tested for family appeal, practicality, and deliciousness.

# Christmas

Anyone with a sweet tooth will appreciate these Christmas treats—(clockwise from left): *Quick French Chocolates, Dark Fruitcake, Almond-Coconut Bars, Light Fruitcake Ring, Cherry Christmas Pie, Buttery Peanut Brittle, Dutch Letters, Candy Window Cookies* (see index for recipe pages).

# Getting Ready for Christmas

Golden brown roasted turkeys carried steaming to the table, red-cheeked carolers munching cookies and sipping hot punch, and joyous revelers nibbling New Year's snacks—they all mean the holidays are here. Get into the swing of celebrating by paging through the *Christmas-Time Cook Book*. You'll find this exciting book includes hundreds of ideas for entertaining at Christmas, Thanksgiving, and New Year's. It focuses especially on celebrations found throughout North America.

In the first part of the book, explore the wonders of Christmas. Start by spending Christmas at home with the folks in New England, the Midwest, or Williamsburg. Or drop in on a typical Christmas get-together of the Italian-Americans, Canadians, Hawaiians, and many others. At the beginning of every feature you will find the fascinating story of how each of these groups spends Christmas. You also will find menus and interesting historical tidbits about many of the recipes.

Then browse through the delightful sections of cookies and candies, main dishes, salads and vegetables, breads, desserts, and beverages. Among these pages discover a variety of stuffings to use with your choice of poultry. You also will find a handy poultry roasting chart which lists times and temperatures for roasting a variety of holiday birds. Choose from a festive array of traditional as well as modern recipes such as Beef Wellington, Cranberry-Pear Coleslaw, Christmas Kringle, Buche de Noel, or Parsonage Punch. If you have trouble using up holiday leftovers, the recipes based on leftover cooked meat will be a real boon. Be sure to watch for helpful preparation tips that accompany many of the recipes.

At Thanksgiving enjoy the warmth of families together at a hearty feast. In the Thanksgiving for Everyone section, you'll find out how to re-create an Early American Thanksgiving menu. Or, for an unusual meal this year, join the residents of warm weather states in an Outdoor Thanksgiving. Just imagine savoring Hickory-Smoked Turkey, right off the grill. Finally, if you enjoy planning your own Thanksgiving menus, try substituting Turkey Breast Italian-Style or Pheasant with Wild Rice for the traditional turkey and round out your meal by selecting recipes such as Raisin-Filled Sweet Potatoes, Whole Wheat-Pumpkin Seed Muffins, and Grandma's Pumpkin Pie.

When New Year's comes around, turn to the *Christmas-Time Cook Book*. Ring in the new year with a flourish. Plan an informal buffet and include Creamy Chive Dip, Appetizer Beef Patties, Pickled Shrimp Appetizer, and Deviled Popcorn.

For the last of the Christmas season's holidays, bring your family good luck by having Ham Hocks and Black-Eyed Peas or Scottish Oatcakes. Hearty soups such as Shrimp and Rice Soup are perfect to serve while the family watches the New Year's Day bowl parades and games on television.

Looking for party ideas that will start the year off right? You'll find them in the tempting New Year's recipe section. Try an assortment of appetizers and snacks for munching, hearty sandwiches to serve at midnight, and a collection of easy-to-make salads and desserts.

Break up the winter wearies by celebrating the Chinese New Year. This exotic holiday, often in the middle of January, provides a natural theme for a party. Charm your guests with such oriental specialties as Tea Leaf Eggs, Stir-Fried Pea Pods, Grand Old Man, or Eight-Treasure Pudding.

Part of the fun of the holidays is putting yourself into the season. In the Make Your Own Christmas section, you will discover a series of gifts and decorations to make for Christmas. Solve your Christmas shopping woes by creating food gifts for those on your list. Choose from jellies, homemade liqueurs, candies, cookies and seasoned nut mixtures. Then, think up festive and useful containers to put them in. You also can add glamour to your holiday tables by creating your own centerpieces. There's everything from tabletop Christmas trees to wooden crèches to choose from.

The *Christmas-Time Cook Book* is full of helpful ideas for the holidays. Let it make Christmas-time easier for you.

# Christmas at Home

Christmas in America is a joyous mixture of old world traditions and contemporary habits — of regional and ethnic customs enriched by favorite recipes lovingly transported from one place or country to another.

In this section we have put together a collection of these family recipes as well as menus, and customs.

Start by reading the feature that highlights your national background or locality. Then turn to stories about other countries. You'll notice that foods from Germany, Italy, and Scandinavia still are honored any place these groups settled. But in areas such as the Southwest and Hawaii climate as well as national background influences the tantalizing blend of new and old traditions.

Down South where camellias bloom in December, there's *Turkey with Cornbread Dressing* and a *Southern Giblet Gravy* made with chopped eggs. *Scalloped Oysters* are a must for dinner as are *Pecandied Yams* and *Ambrosia*. (See complete menu on page 15.)

# Christmas in New England

## Menu

*Oysters Elegante*
*Standing Rib Roast*
*with*
*Stuffed Mushroom Crowns*
*Swiss Potatoes au Gratin*
*Creamed Onions*
*Oven-Cooked Cranberries*
*Holiday Fruit Salad*
*Fluffy Graham Muffins*
*Squash Pie*
*or*
*Boston Cream Pie*
*Beverage*

Currier-and-Ives scenes of tranquil village churches etched in snow, children with red cheeks flying through the landscape on sleds or skating on frozen ponds, carolers bundled up outside an old clapboard farmhouse—these are images that evoke the spirit of a traditional New England Christmas.

Christmas in some parts of New England was not always the happy time it is now. The General Court of Massachusetts in 1659 enacted a law by which "anybody who is found observing, by abstinence from labor, feasting, or any other way, any such days as Christmas day, shall pay for every offense five shillings." Anyone suspected of celebrating was called a "Christmas keeper."

But for other New Englanders, Christmas was and is *the* big winter holiday, a time of feasting, celebrating, rejoicing, and reuniting one's family. All the immigrants who snuggled into the New England coastal towns and inland hills brought their own customs which eventually became New England's own: the Germans' Christmas tree, the Dutch St. Nicholas and love of hearty feasting, the Scandinavians' love of evergreens and mistletoe, the English traditional holiday fare and fondness for caroling.

A New England Christmas is traditionally a time of plenty. The summer and fall harvests contribute to the rich assortment of fresh foods on the holiday table. While mid-afternoon dinner on Christmas day is the big feast of the season, the entire week before and after Christmas are times of parties, visits, and the exchange of gifts. Many families still enjoy cutting their own Christmas trees while others enjoy buying living trees which can be planted outside after the holiday is past.

Many of New England's old country inns continue the hospitable Christmas traditions—borrowed largely from the English—of wassailing and elaborate Christmas dinners, sleigh-riding, and seasonal festivities.

Private celebrations are not so elaborate, but Christmas is, nevertheless, a time of super-abundance. Even frugal Yankees spare no expense at Christmas-time. It is a generous time of giving and neighborly sharing. Outdoor trees are lighted nights before Christmas, and spruce or holly wreaths are tacked to front doors. Inside, the heady aroma of gingerbread, spices, mince and pumpkin pies baking, and other compelling oven lures vie with the fragrance of Scotch pine and fir that fill New England houses at this most hospitable of seasons.

## Squash Pie

*New Englanders always have eaten much more squash than other Americans do, and they serve it in a variety of ways—none more popular than this pie! Hubbard squash, with deep orange meat, is the New Englanders' choice for this tasty Squash Pie.*

| | |
|---|---|
| 2 cups mashed cooked Hubbard squash | ¼ teaspoon ground ginger |
| ½ cup sugar | ⅛ teaspoon ground nutmeg |
| 1 tablespoon butter, melted | 1¾ cups milk |
| ½ teaspoon salt | 2 slightly beaten eggs |
| ½ teaspoon ground cinnamon | 1 unbaked 9-inch pastry shell with edges crimped high |

Combine squash, sugar, butter, salt, and spices. Stir in milk and eggs. Pour mixture into pastry shell. Bake at 400° till knife inserted off-center comes out clean, about 50 minutes. (Filling may seem soft.) Cool.

## Boston Cream Pie

| | |
|---|---|
| 1 egg white | 3 tablespoons cooking oil |
| ¾ cup sugar | 1 egg yolk |
| 1 cup all-purpose flour | 1 teaspoon vanilla |
| 1½ teaspoons baking powder | Vanilla Cream Filling |
| ½ cup milk | Chocolate Glaze |

Beat egg white to soft peaks. Gradually add ¼ *cup* sugar; beat till very stiff and glossy. Set aside. In small bowl stir together flour, remaining sugar, baking powder, and ½ teaspoon salt. Blend in ¼ *cup* milk, oil, egg yolk, and vanilla. Beat 1 minute at medium speed of electric mixer; scrape bowl. Add remaining milk; beat 1 minute. Fold in egg white. Grease one 9x1½-inch round baking pan; line with waxed paper and grease again. Turn batter into pan. Bake at 350° for 25 to 30 minutes. Cool 10 minutes; remove from pan. When cool, split cake into 2 layers. Fill with Vanilla Cream Filling. Spread Chocolate Glaze over cake; allow to flow down sides.

*Vanilla Cream Filling:* In saucepan combine ⅓ cup sugar, 2 tablespoons all-purpose flour, 1 tablespoon cornstarch, and ¼ teaspoon salt. Blend in 1⅓ cups milk. Cook and stir till thickened and bubbly. Beat 2 eggs slightly. Stir moderate amount of hot mixture into eggs; return to saucepan. Cook and stir till thick, 1 to 2 minutes more. Remove from heat; stir in 1 teaspoon vanilla. Cover surface with waxed paper; cool without stirring.

*Chocolate Glaze:* Melt one 1-ounce square unsweetened chocolate and 1 tablespoon butter over low heat; stir often. Remove from heat. Stir in ¾ cup sifted powdered sugar and ½ teaspoon vanilla till crumbly. Blend in 2 teaspoons very hot water. Beat in 3 to 4 teaspoons additional hot water, 1 teaspoon at a time, to make glaze of pouring consistency.

*A pie that's not a pie but a cake! This old-time favorite once was made with sour milk or buttermilk and soda and had numerous variations, such as Washington Pie, Parker House Chocolate Pie, and Martha Washington Pie—all cakes, of course!*

## Oysters Elegante

| | |
|---|---|
| 18 oysters in shells | ⅓ cup dry white wine |
| Rock salt | 1 3-ounce can sliced mushrooms |
| ½ cup chopped green onion | 2 tablespoons snipped parsley |
| 1 clove garlic, minced | Dash bottled hot pepper |
| 2 tablespoons butter | sauce |
| 2 tablespoons all-purpose | ½ cup soft bread crumbs |
| flour | 2 tablespoons grated |
| ⅔ cup chicken broth | Parmesan cheese |
| 1 egg yolk | 1½ teaspoons butter, melted |

Remove oysters from shells; wash shells. Place each oyster in deep half of shell. Arrange shells on bed of rock salt in shallow pan; set aside.

Cook onion and garlic in 2 tablespoons butter till onion is tender. Blend in flour and ¼ teaspoon salt. Add chicken broth. Cook and stir till thickened and bubbly. Combine egg yolk and wine. Add moderate amount hot mixture to egg and wine; return to hot mixture. Drain mushrooms; stir into hot mixture with parsley and hot pepper sauce. Cook and stir till sauce almost boils. Toss crumbs and cheese with melted butter. Bake oysters at 400° for 5 minutes; top each with 1 tablespoon sauce mixture and 1 teaspoon crumb mixture. Bake till heated through, 10 to 12 minutes. Serves 6.

*For the early settlers of New England, oysters were an important food source. Whether raw on the half-shell, baked, broiled, fried, in stew, or as a delicate canapé such as Oysters Elegante, oysters turn any meal into "something special," particularly suitable for a Christmas Day feast.*

## Standing Rib Roast with Stuffed Mushroom Crowns

| | |
|---|---|
| **1 6- to 8-pound beef**<br>**standing rib roast**<br>**(3 or 4 ribs)**<br>**12 large whole fresh mushrooms**<br>**¼ cup sliced green onion** | **3 tablespoons butter**<br>**⅓ cup fine dry bread crumbs**<br>**½ teaspoon dried dillweed**<br>**¼ teaspoon salt**<br>**Dash Worcestershire sauce** |

Place roast, fat side up, in shallow roasting pan. Sprinkle with salt and pepper. Insert meat thermometer, avoiding bone. Roast at 325° till thermometer registers 150° for medium rare, 2½ to 3½ hours. Meanwhile, remove stems from mushrooms. Chop stems; cook with onion in butter till tender. Stir in remaining ingredients; use to fill mushroom crowns. Bake on baking sheet at 325° for 15 minutes. Serve with roast. Serves 12.

*Pictured opposite:* The *Standing Rib Roast* is always thought of as an appropriate meat for an elegant meal. Delight your guests and family and add even more elegance by surrounding the roast with *Stuffed Mushroom Crowns.*

## Casserole Potato-Sausage Dressing

| | |
|---|---|
| **1 pound bulk pork sausage**<br>**1 cup chopped onion**<br>**¾ cup finely chopped celery**<br>**1 teaspoon poultry seasoning** | **Packaged instant mashed**<br>**potatoes, enough**<br>**for 8 servings )**<br>**2 eggs** |

Cook sausage, onion, and celery till meat is browned; drain. Stir in poultry seasoning and ¼ teaspoon pepper. Prepare potatoes following package directions, *except* reduce salt to ½ teaspoon. Beat in eggs. Stir in meat mixture. Bake, covered, in 2-quart casserole at 325° for 30 minutes. Makes 6 cups.

*The hearty eating, early New Englanders liked solid, "stick-to-the-ribs" food because it was good insulation against the biting winter cold. This dressing, a good example of this substantial fare, is delicious as an accompaniment for the holiday turkey.*

## Oven-Cooked Cranberries

In 13x9x2-inch baking pan stir together one 16-ounce package cranberries (4 cups), 2 cups sugar, and ¼ cup water. Cover pan with foil. Bake at 350°, stirring occasionally, till cranberries pop, 50 to 60 minutes. Makes 4 cups.

## Swiss Potatoes au Gratin

| | |
|---|---|
| **5 tablespoons butter**<br>**2 tablespoons all-purpose**<br>**flour**<br>**½ teaspoon dry mustard**<br>**½ teaspoon Worcestershire**<br>**sauce**<br>**3 cups milk** | **1 cup shredded Swiss cheese**<br>**6 medium potatoes, peeled and**<br>**thinly sliced (6 cups)**<br>**1 4-ounce jar sliced pimiento,**<br>**chopped**<br>**¼ cup finely chopped onion**<br>**1½ cups soft bread crumbs** |

Melt *3 tablespoons* butter; blend in flour, mustard, Worcestershire, 1½ teaspoons salt, and ⅛ teaspoon pepper. Add milk; cook and stir till thickened and bubbly. Remove from heat. Add cheese; stir to melt. Stir in potatoes, pimiento, and onion. Bake, covered, in 2½-quart casserole at 350° for 45 minutes. Melt remaining butter; toss with bread crumbs. Sprinkle crumbs atop potatoes; bake, uncovered, 30 minutes more. Serves 6.

## Creamed Onions

*American Indians used a strongly flavored wild onion in their stews, and the sturdy onion ever since has been a staple in New England cooking. This particular dish is a favorite holiday accompaniment to the traditional Christmas turkey or roast beef.*

3 medium onions
3 tablespoons butter
2 tablespoons all-purpose flour

Dash white pepper
1⅓ cups milk
1 cup shredded Muenster cheese
Parsley sprigs

Cut onions in small wedges; cook in boiling salted water till nearly tender, 8 to 10 minutes. Drain. In saucepan melt butter; blend in flour, pepper, and ¼ teaspoon salt. Add milk; cook and stir till mixture is thickened and bubbly. Add cheese; stir to melt. Stir in drained onions; heat through. Place in serving bowl. Garnish with parsley. Makes 6 to 8 servings.

## Holiday Fruit Salad

Drain one 13¼-ounce can pineapple chunks; reserve ½ cup syrup. Set pineapple aside. Combine ¼ cup sugar and 4 teaspoons cornstarch; stir in reserved syrup. Cook and stir till thick and bubbly; cook 1 minute more. Remove from heat; stir in 2 tablespoons lemon juice. Chill dressing. Slice 4 peeled medium oranges; halve slices. Combine with 1 cup red grapes, halved and seeded; ¾ cup sliced celery; ½ cup broken walnuts; and pineapple. Toss with dressing. Serve on lettuce-lined plates. Makes 8 servings.

## Fluffy Graham Muffins

1¼ cups all-purpose flour
½ cup whole wheat flour
¼ cup sugar
2½ teaspoons baking powder

¾ teaspoon salt
1 beaten egg
¾ cup buttermilk
⅓ cup cooking oil

Stir together flours, sugar, baking powder, and salt; make well in center. Mix egg, buttermilk, and oil; add to dry ingredients. Stir to moisten. Fill greased muffin pans ⅔ full. Bake at 400° for 20 to 25 minutes. Makes 12.

## Molasses Taffy

*Taffy pulls are an age-old winter entertainment on cold evenings in New England, and once were especially popular with young people. Of all the taffy variations, molasses has been the special favorite — particularly so before granulated sugar became readily available.*

2 cups sugar
1 cup light molasses
2 teaspoons vinegar

2 tablespoons butter *or* margarine
½ teaspoon baking soda

In buttered 2-quart saucepan combine sugar, molasses, and ¼ cup water. Cook slowly and stir till sugar dissolves. Bring to boiling; add vinegar and cook to soft-crack stage (270° on candy thermometer). Remove from heat. Add butter and sift in soda; stir to mix. Turn out (don't scrape pan) onto buttered platter or large shallow pan. Use spatula to turn edges to center. Butter hands so candy won't stick. Using fingertips, pull when cool enough to handle. When candy is light tan color and hard to pull, quarter and pull each piece into ½-inch-thick strand. With buttered scissors, snip into bite-size pieces. Wrap in clear plastic wrap. Makes 1½ pounds.

# Christmas in the Deep South

Christmas in the Deep South—what image does this conjure up? Yule logs and old plantations, kisses exchanged under the mistletoe, and newly fallen leaves covering the ground? A true image, but only part of the colorful, eclectic, and exciting kaleidoscope that is a southern Christmas.

Among the new colonies, Christmas was first celebrated in the South. Louisiana, Alabama, and Arkansas were the first states to recognize Christmas as a legal holiday. But even before, and ever since, everywhere throughout the South, Christmas has been masses of greens scattered throughout the house, often in gleaming bowls, great cedar trees decorated with glistening tinsel ropes and fragile glass ornaments, and lavish arrangements that include camellias, roses, hibiscus, poinsettias, and magnolia blossoms.

Southern people are known for their warmth and hospitality. Christmas is a time for a steady stream of this hospitality accented with eggnog and for open houses for kin and neighbors. This friendly, personal holiday greeting is worth much more to the Southern host and hostess than the most elaborate printed card fetched from the mailbox.

This is the season of good will and even better eating, when sweets dominate and a table isn't fully dressed unless it wears at least two or three special festive cakes, arrangements of tarts and petits fours, and bowls of tempting divinity, pralines, peanut brittle, toffee, fudge, and other holiday dainties to be savored, enjoyed, and praised.

Many homemakers begin planning during the summer for their Christmas gifts. They make jams, jellies, and preserves from fruits—plums, peaches, figs, and grapes such as muscadines and scuppernongs. And they use tomatoes, cucumbers, watermelon rind, and peaches to make pickles. These homemade treats are kept on hand just to give "something" to *all* the friends who are neighborly enough to drop in for a holiday visit.

And then there's the big dinner for Christmas Day. The large turkey or country-style ham is picked out right after Thanksgiving. And to make the meat especially tasty, it's served with mildly seasoned cornbread dressing. Southern giblet gravy with giblets and hard-cooked eggs is poured over turkey, dressing, and fluffy rice. A green vegetable is "fancied up" and candied sweet potatoes (or yams) are never forgotten. And the Southern Christmas meal would surely be incomplete without the delicious ambrosia—a natural combination of oranges and grated fresh coconut delicately sweetened and mellowed—the perfect light accompaniment for the always heavy feast.

## Menu
(see photo, pages 8-9)

*Roast Turkey*
*(see chart, page 91)*
*with*
*Cornbread Dressing*
*Southern Giblet Gravy*
*Seasoned Rice*
*Scalloped Oysters*
*Asparagus au Gratin*
*Pecandied Yams*
*Ambrosia*
*Beverage*

## Ambrosia (see photo, pages 8-9)

1 13¼-ounce can pineapple chunks
3 medium oranges, sectioned
½ cup maraschino cherries, halved and drained
½ cup shredded coconut

Drain pineapple chunks, reserving ¼ cup of the syrup. Combine pineapple chunks, the ¼ cup reserved pineapple syrup, orange sections, and maraschino cherries. Cover; chill. Just before serving, fold in coconut. Garnish with fresh mint leaves, if desired. Makes 6 servings.

*Any Southern recipe that calls for coconut traditionally refers to fresh coconut. Buy one fresh coconut, grate it, and then use it for several delicious recipes.*

## Cornbread Dressing (see photo, pages 8-9)

*Cornbread Dressing long has been a popular accompaniment for any bird, but especially for the holiday turkey. Throughout the South, this mealy stuffing is made by using the typically unsweet Southern Cornbread. Usually not used as a stuffing, it is baked outside the bird and ranges in moistness from very wet to slightly dry. When the turkey giblets are not used in the gravy, they are included in the dressing.*

Southern Cornbread
1 cup chopped celery with leaves
1 cup chopped onion

2 cups chicken broth
2 beaten eggs
1 teaspoon poultry seasoning

Prepare Southern Cornbread; cool. Crumble enough cornbread for 6 cups. In saucepan cook celery and onion in broth till tender, about 5 minutes; cool slightly. Thoroughly mix eggs, poultry seasoning, vegetables with broth, cornbread, and ¼ teaspoon salt. Use to stuff 8-pound turkey or bake in 1½-quart casserole at 325° for 30 to 35 minutes. Makes 6 cups.

*Southern Cornbread:* Combine 1½ cups yellow cornmeal, ½ cup all-purpose flour, 1 teaspoon baking soda, and ½ teaspoon salt. Add 1½ cups buttermilk, 2 tablespoons melted shortening, and 1 beaten egg; stir to blend. Pour into greased 9x9x2-inch baking pan. Bake at 400° for 20 minutes.

## Pecandied Yams (see photo, pages 8-9)

⅓ cup packed brown sugar
4 teaspoons cornstarch
¼ teaspoon salt
¾ cup orange juice
¾ cup orange marmalade
2 tablespoons butter *or* margarine

2½ pounds yams *or* sweet potatoes, cooked, peeled, and cut crosswise in thick pieces
• • •
⅓ cup pecan halves

In saucepan combine brown sugar, cornstarch, and salt. Stir in orange juice and marmalade. Cook and stir till thickened and bubbly. Remove from heat. Stir in butter. Arrange yams in 12-inch skillet. Pour orange sauce over, coating all sides of yams. Sprinkle with pecans. Cover and simmer till yams are glazed and heated through, basting often. Makes 12 servings.

## Asparagus au Gratin

2 10-ounce packages frozen asparagus spears *or* frozen cut asparagus
2 tablespoons butter *or* margarine
2 tablespoons all-purpose flour
½ teaspoon salt

1 cup milk
1 cup shredded sharp American cheese
• • •
½ cup soft bread crumbs
1 tablespoon butter *or* margarine, melted

Cook asparagus following package directions. Melt 2 tablespoons butter in a saucepan. Blend in flour and salt. Add milk all at once. Cook and stir till thickened and bubbly. Stir in cheese. Cook and stir till cheese is melted. Arrange asparagus in a 10x6x2-inch baking dish; pour cheese mixture over. Toss crumbs with melted butter. Sprinkle atop sauce. Bake at 350° till heated through, 15 to 20 minutes. Makes 6 to 8 servings.

## Scalloped Oysters

Cook ¼ cup chopped celery and 2 tablespoons sliced green onion in ¼ cup butter *or* margarine till tender but not brown. Blend in ¼ cup all-purpose flour, ¼ teaspoon salt, ¼ teaspoon paprika, and dash pepper. Cook and stir 3 minutes. Stir in 1 pint undrained shucked oysters, 1 teaspoon lemon juice, and ½ teaspoon Worcestershire sauce. Pour into 1-quart casserole. Combine ½ cup soft bread crumbs and 1 tablespoon melted butter *or* margarine. Sprinkle atop oyster mixture. Bake at 400° for 30 minutes. Serves 8 to 10.

*Oysters are bountiful in most Southern states because of the nearby waters—Gulf of Mexico and Atlantic Ocean. They are especially plentiful during the winter months, and are small and sweet at this time making them very good to use in holiday menus.*

## Southern Giblet Gravy (see photo, pages 8-9)

| | |
|---|---|
| ½ pound turkey *or* chicken giblets and neck | Few celery leaves |
| 1 small onion, sliced | ½ cup all-purpose flour |
| 1 teaspoon salt | 2 hard-cooked eggs, chopped |
| | Seasoned Rice |

Remove liver from giblets and set aside. In saucepan combine neck and remaining giblets, onion, salt, celery leaves, and 3 cups water. Cover; simmer 1½ hours. Add the liver; simmer 20 to 30 minutes. Cool giblets in broth; remove from broth and chop. Add enough broth to turkey roasting drippings to make 3 cups. (If making gravy when not roasting a turkey, use only giblet broth.) In screw-top jar combine flour, *1 cup* broth mixture, and dash pepper; shake well. In saucepan combine the flour mixture and remaining broth. Cook and stir till thickened and bubbly. Stir in giblets and eggs. Heat through. Serve with Seasoned Rice and/or dressing. Makes 6 servings.

*Seasoned Rice:* Cook 1 cup long grain rice following package directions *except* add 2 tablespoons chopped green onion and ½ teaspoon poultry seasoning in addition to the water and salt.

## Lane Cake

| | |
|---|---|
| 2¼ cups sugar | 1½ cups milk |
| 1¼ cups butter *or* margarine | 8 stiffly beaten egg whites |
| 2 teaspoons vanilla | Lane Cake Filling |
| 3⅓ cups sifted cake flour | Fluffy White Frosting |
| 4½ teaspoons baking powder | (see recipe, page 18) |

Cream sugar and butter till light. Add vanilla; mix well. Sift together flour, baking powder, and 1½ teaspoons salt; add to creamed mixture alternately with milk, beating after each addition. Fold in egg whites. Bake in 3 greased and lightly floured 9x1½-inch round baking pans at 375° for 18 to 20 minutes. Cool 10 minutes; remove from pans. Cool well. Spread Lane Cake Filling between cake layers. Frost with Fluffy White Frosting.

*Lane Cake Filling:* Melt 6 tablespoons butter; add ¾ cup sugar, 3 tablespoons bourbon, and 2 tablespoons water. Bring just to boiling; stir to dissolve sugar. Stir moderate amount hot mixture into 6 slightly beaten egg yolks; return to saucepan. Cook and stir till thickened, about 3 minutes more; remove from heat. Stir in ¾ cup finely chopped raisins, ½ cup chopped pecans, ⅓ cup flaked coconut, and ½ teaspoon vanilla. Chill.

*Lane Cake, a southern favorite, is a light cake baked in three layers. The layers are held together with a heavy fruit-liquor filling and then swathed with a rich frosting.*

## Coconut Cake

*To prepare a fresh coconut,
pierce the three eyes of
the coconut with a sharp
instrument such as an ice
pick and drain the milk.
Then tap all over with a
hammer until the shell
cracks and falls off or
can be pulled off. Use a
vegetable parer or a sharp
knife to remove the brown
skin covering.*

*Then, cut the peeled
meat into small cubes
and grate using an electric
blender, a shredder
attachment of an electric
mixer, or a hand shredder.*

⅔ cup shortening
1 tablespoon grated orange
   peel
1½ teaspoons grated lemon peel
1½ cups sugar
3 eggs
2½ cups sifted cake flour

2½ teaspoons baking powder
¾ cup milk
2 tablespoons lemon juice
Lemon Filling
Fluffy White Frosting
1 cup grated fresh coconut
   *or* shredded coconut

In mixing bowl combine shortening, orange peel, and lemon peel. Gradually add sugar; cream till light and fluffy. Add the eggs, one at a time, beating well after each. Sift together the flour, baking powder, and ¾ teaspoon salt. Combine milk and lemon juice. Add dry ingredients to creamed mixture alternately with the milk-lemon juice mixture; beat smooth after each addition. Bake in 2 greased and lightly floured 9x1½-inch round baking pans at 375° for 22 to 25 minutes. Cool 10 minutes; remove from pans. Cool. Split cake into 4 layers. Spread Lemon Filling between layers of cake. Frost the top and sides with Fluffy White Frosting. Sprinkle frosted cake with coconut.

*Lemon Filling:* Combine ¾ cup sugar, 2 tablespoons cornstarch, and dash salt; gradually stir in ¾ cup cold water. Add 2 beaten egg yolks, 1 teaspoon grated lemon peel, and 3 tablespoons lemon juice. Cook and stir till thickened and bubbly. Cook 1 minute; remove from heat. Stir in 1 tablespoon butter *or* margarine. Cover surface with waxed paper; cool without stirring.

*Fluffy White Frosting:* In saucepan combine 1 cup sugar, ⅓ cup water, ¼ teaspoon cream of tartar, and dash salt. Bring to boiling, stirring till sugar dissolves. Very slowly add sugar syrup to 2 egg whites in mixing bowl, beating constantly with electric mixer till stiff peaks form, about 7 minutes. Beat in 1 teaspoon vanilla.

## Chocolate Charlotte Russe

*Charlotte Russe's origins
are obscure, though it is
believed to be a French
creation of the early
nineteenth century. Records
indicate it was served in
the White House as early
as the 1830's, but its
peak of popularity — in the
South and elsewhere — was
the opulent 1880's.
Its specialness as a holiday
dessert makes it timeless.*

1 envelope unflavored gelatin
3 1-ounce squares semisweet
   chocolate
4 egg yolks
¾ cup sugar
2 tablespoons rum

4 egg whites
½ teaspoon cream of tartar
1 cup whipping cream
24 whole ladyfingers, split
   lengthwise
Slivered almonds, toasted

Soften gelatin in ¼ cup cold water. Melt chocolate in ½ cup water, over low heat, stirring constantly. Stir in gelatin till dissolved. Remove from heat. Beat egg yolks till thick and lemon-colored; gradually beat in ½ *cup* sugar. Add rum and dash salt. Gradually stir in chocolate mixture. Chill till partially set, stirring often. Beat egg whites and cream of tartar to soft peaks. Gradually add remaining ¼ cup sugar, beating till stiff peaks form. Whip chocolate mixture till smooth. Fold in egg whites. Whip cream; fold into chocolate mixture. Line bottom and sides of 9-inch springform pan with *32 ladyfinger halves* (cut ½ inch off those that stand around sides). Fill with *half* the chocolate mixture. Add another layer ladyfingers. Add remaining chocolate mixture. Chill overnight. Remove sides of pan. Before serving, sprinkle with almonds. Makes 12 to 16 servings.

# A Southwestern Christmas

Christmas in the Southwest is a spicy brew of Mexican and Spanish customs with a touch of Indian, giving a vibrant zing to the traditional holiday.

Vibrant is almost an understatement for the gay carryings-on. Celebrations among Mexican-Americans begin nine days before Christmas with joyful *posadas,* pageants relating to the search of Mary and Joseph for lodging. As groups move from house to house the request for lodging is sung. Initially, the ''innkeeper'' or host refuses admittance, but finally relents and invites the group for Christmas prayer beside the *nacimiento* (crèche), and an evening of singing, dancing, snacking, and pinata-breaking.

Pinatas are clay or paper mâché pots filled with candies, nuts, fruits, and small gifts. The pots are concealed in decorative crepe paper exteriors of different shapes and suspended on a movable wire in the garden. Each child is blindfolded and allowed three whacks with a strong stick at the pinata. When finally broken, goodies descend for all to enjoy. At midnight Christmas Eve, towns vibrate with the noise of bells and fireworks welcoming the birth of the Christ child. After midnight mass, feasting begins in earnest and partying continues till dawn, time for the *missa del gallo* (mass of the cock). Special foods including tamales, posole, *empanaditas,* and memorable spiced coffee play an important role.

In certain parts of New Mexico, young boys wander through town singing *los pastores* through the night, in exchange for small gifts, coins, or hospitality. In parts of Texas, *los pastores* (''the shepherds'') take the form of improvised nativity plays performed on Christmas Eve.

A magical touch of a Southwest Christmas is the custom of *luminarias*—paper bags in which large candles have been anchored in sand. The bags are placed a few feet apart along walks, rooftops, and lawns. The candles are lighted at dusk to guide visitors from house to house.

Fire is an ancient Southwestern harbinger of Christmas for the Indians. In Albuquerque where Christmas is known as Night Fire, fires blaze in the plaza and churchyards. At certain Christian Indian churches, Pueblo Indians perform ritual dances before midnight mass. After mass they go home and, like other gregarious Southwesterners, enjoy celebrating with family and neighbors. The hospitality is casual, spontaneous, and warm-hearted, and the conversation and laughter continue till the cock crows.

*Menu*
(see photo, page 21)

*Tamales*
*Posole*
*Red Chili Sauce*
*Green Salad*
*with*
*Guacamole Dressing*
*Pastelitos   Biscochitos*
*Empanaditas*
*Sweet Red Wine*

## Green Salad with Guacamole Dressing (see photo, page 21)

¼ cup dairy sour cream
1 tablespoon thinly sliced
   green onion
1 tablespoon lime juice
½ teaspoon salt
¼ teaspoon taco sauce

2 large ripe avocados, peeled,
   seeded, and sliced
8 cups torn mixed greens,
   chilled
2 tomatoes, sliced

In blender container combine sour cream, onion, lime juice, salt, taco sauce, and ¼ cup water; add avocados. Cover and blend till smooth. Chill. Place greens in bowl; top with tomatoes and dressing. Toss lightly. Makes 8 servings.

*Guacamole, a piquant avocado sauce, makes a delicious dressing for salad greens or dip for chips and crackers. Spaniards discovered the avocado in Mexico and brought the treasure to plant north of the border.*

# Red Chili Sauce

¼ cup shortening
¼ cup all-purpose flour
½ cup chili powder

2 cups water
1 16-ounce can tomato sauce
1 teaspoon garlic salt

Melt shortening in skillet. Stir in flour. Add chili powder, stirring till completely moistened. Gradually stir in water; stir till chili powder is dissolved, making sure no lumps form. Stir in tomato sauce, garlic salt, and 1 teaspoon salt. Cover; simmer 15 minutes. Makes about 4 cups.

# Tamales

2 pounds boneless beef *or*
 pork, cubed
3 tablespoons cooking oil
¼ cup all-purpose flour
1 cup Red Chili Sauce
6 tablespoons finely chopped
 green chili peppers

2 cloves garlic, minced
1½ teaspoons salt
¼ teaspoon dried oregano,
 crushed
Cornhusks, parchment, *or*
 foil
Tamale Dough

In saucepan combine beef or pork cubes and enough water to cover; simmer till meat is well done, about 1½ hours. Drain meat, reserving 1½ cups stock. Shred meat; brown in cooking oil. Stir in flour; cook till flour is browned, stirring constantly. Stir in Red Chili Sauce, green chili peppers, garlic, salt, oregano, and reserved stock. Simmer, covered, about 30 minutes.

For tamale wrappers, cut cornhusks, parchment, or foil into 8x8-inch squares. Measure ½ *cup* Tamale Dough into center of each wrapper. Spread dough to 6x5-inch rectangle; spoon ⅓ *cup* meat mixture down center of each dough rectangle. Fold two opposite sides of wrapper toward center. Gently peel edges of dough from wrapper; seal dough edges to enclose filling. Fold wrapper edges together several times to seal. Tuck ends under or tie. Place tamales on rack in large steamer or electric skillet. Add water to just below rack. Cover and steam 1½ hours, adding water when necessary. Makes 12.

*Tamale Dough:* With electric mixer cream 1½ cups lard and 1½ teaspoons salt. Mix 4½ cups masa harina and 2⅔ cups warm water; beat into lard.

# Posole (puh soul′ ee)

1½ pounds boneless pork, diced
2 14½-ounce cans golden hominy
¼ cup chopped onion
1 clove garlic, minced

½ teaspoon ground cumin
¼ teaspoon dried oregano,
 crushed
Red Chili Sauce

Trim fat from pork; cook trimmings in a heavy 4-quart Dutch oven till 2 tablespoons drippings accumulate. Remove trimmings; brown diced pork in hot drippings. Stir in 2 cups water and 1 teaspoon salt. Cover; reduce heat and simmer till meat is very tender, 1½ to 2 hours. Add the undrained hominy, onion, garlic, cumin, oregano, and ¼ teaspoon salt. Cover and simmer 15 minutes. Serve with the Red Chili Sauce. Makes 6 servings.

*Pictured opposite:* Clockwise around the *Tamales* are *Empanaditas, Pastelitos, Biscochitos* (see recipes, page 22), *Green Salad with Guacamole Dressing* (see recipe, page 19), *Posole,* and *Red Chili Sauce.*

*Tamales, typically Mexican in origin, are a perfect make-ahead dish. Since they take a relatively long time to cook, prepare and wrap the tamales, then refrigerate overnight. Steam the next day. By doing this, you'll save time for the holiday extras that always seem to pop up at the last minute.*

*In the Southwest, posole is both the name of this dish and the type of hominy used to make it. Our version of this stew uses canned hominy so that everyone can make and enjoy this tasty regional specialty.*

## Empanaditas (em pan uh dee' tas) (see photo, page 21)

(see photo, page 21)

*Sometimes nicknamed a "South American sandwich," an Empanadita is a little pie filled with sweet meats, fruits, or meat. When baked golden brown, Empanaditas are delicious served warm with dark red wine, or strong coffee.*

| | |
|---|---|
| 1 package active dry yeast | ½ teaspoon salt |
| ½ cup warm water (110°) | 1 cup shortening |
| 3 cups all-purpose flour | 1 egg |
| 1 tablespoon sugar | Empanadita Filling |

Soften yeast in water; set aside. Stir together flour, sugar, and salt. Cut in shortening till crumbly. Combine egg and yeast mixture; add to flour mixture. Mix well. Turn out on lightly floured surface. Knead gently 8 to 10 times. Quarter; roll one part at a time to ⅛-inch thickness. Cut with a 3-inch biscuit cutter. Place scant teaspoon Empanadita Filling off-center of each pastry circle. Moisten one half of the edge of the circle; fold over filling. Tightly seal pastry using tines of fork. Bake on ungreased baking sheet at 450° till golden, 9 to 10 minutes. Makes about 6 dozen.

*Empanadita Filling:* In covered saucepan simmer ¼ pound beef stew meat in water till very tender, about 2 hours. Drain and cool. Put meat and 2 medium apples, peeled, cored, and cut up, through food grinder, using coarse blade. Combine meat-apple mixture with ¼ cup raisins, 2 tablespoons sugar, 2 tablespoons dark corn syrup, ¼ teaspoon ground cinnamon, ¼ teaspoon salt, and ⅛ teaspoon ground cloves. Heat through. Stir in 1 tablespoon sherry. Cool thoroughly. Stir in ¼ cup pine nuts.

## Biscochitos (bisco cheet' os) (see photo, page 21)

*Anise-flavored Biscochitos are customarily holiday cookies. Traditionally cut freehand into a fleur-de-lis pattern, they make a decorative addition to a Christmas cookie platter.*

Cream 1 cup butter with ¾ cup sugar and 1 teaspoon aniseed; beat in 1 egg. Stir together 3 cups all-purpose flour, 1½ teaspoons baking powder, and ½ teaspoon salt; stir into creamed mixture alternately with ¼ cup brandy, beating after each addition. Turn out on floured surface; knead several times. Roll to ⅛-inch thickness. Cut into fancy shapes. Dust tops of cookies with mixture of ¼ cup sugar and 1 tablespoon ground cinnamon. Bake on ungreased baking sheet at 350° for 8 to 10 minutes. Makes 66 to 72.

## Pastelitos (pas tuh lee' tos) (see photo, page 21)

*Pastelitos, a Spanish word, means little pies. These sweet "pies" are a Christmas favorite among southwesterners— whether Mexican, Spanish, Indian, or Anglo descent.*

| | |
|---|---|
| 1 cup dried apricots | ½ teaspoon baking powder |
| ½ cup sugar | ⅔ cup lard |
| ½ teaspoon vanilla | 4 to 6 tablespoons ice water |
| 2 cups all-purpose flour | Confectioners' Glaze (see |
| ¾ teaspoon salt | recipe, page 112) |

Cook apricots, covered, in 1 cup water for 20 minutes. Transfer to blender container; cover and blend till smooth. Combine blended apricots and sugar; cook till thick, 5 minutes. Cool slightly; stir in vanilla. Stir together flour, salt, and baking powder. Cut in lard till crumbly. Add ice water, one tablespoon at a time, tossing with fork till dough holds together. Divide in half; roll each half to 14x10-inch rectangle. Line 13x9x2-inch baking pan with *half* the dough. Spread apricot mixture evenly over dough. Place remaining dough atop; seal edges. Prick top crust. Bake at 400° for 30 minutes. Frost with Confectioners' Glaze. Cool; cut in squares. Makes 24.

# Christmas on the Plains

If there is any "typical" American Christmas it is perhaps celebrated in the heartland of our country—the Midwest. Here customs of other lands and cultures are woven into a big, joyful tapestry entitled "Christmas." The festivities of a midwestern Christmas are echoed elsewhere, but it is in the breadbasket of the nation that the bounteous harvest of the holiday season is epitomized in sumptuous good food and celebration.

German, Norwegian, Swedish, Polish, Czech, Irish, Russian, and other heritages have blended together into a totally American experience—Christmas trees, pine wreaths, midnight or early morning church services, gift-giving, and a lavish Christmas Day feast for relatives and friends.

A midwestern house at Christmas, whether a clapboard farm in the Grant Wood fields of Iowa, a 1920s stucco bungalow in Milwaukee, or a stately Victorian duplex in Minneapolis, is filled with greenery—there's a huge decorated tree and very likely a wreath on the front door.

Christmas Day usually begins with church, whether at midnight or early morning. The fir-scented warmth inside the church contrasts sharply with the brisk outside—most likely snow-covered.

The German *St. Nicholas,* mischievous Scandinavian sprites, *julenissen,* and Dutch *Sante Klaas* have melted together into the kind, jolly American Santa Claus, symbol of giving. Gifts are a big part of the holiday, but gift-opening time is optional, depending on family tradition. In some homes presents are inspected Christmas Eve or after midnight mass. Others rise just after dawn, the children with unsuppressible excitement about what Santa has brought, and open gifts before breakfast.

Midafternoon Christmas Day, relatives arrive to visit and enjoy the bounty. Some of the finest foreign cooking is found throughout the Midwest, but Christmas dinner has become a truly American meal with a huge turkey, cranberry relish, Waldorf salad, and mince or pumpkin pie.

After dinner, all help clear the table, wash up, and put away the good silver and fancy plates. Children retreat to quiet nooks to try new games or begin reading new Christmas books. Grandpa dozes in front of the TV.

Later, there is usually a gathering in the kitchen for a late snack of turkey sandwiches and maybe one more piece of pie. "I'll get back on my diet tomorrow," somebody murmurs. Everyone declares definitively that "this is the best Christmas ever"—and it usually is.

### Menu

(see photo, page 24)

*Roast Turkey*
*(see chart, page 91)*
*with*
*Giblet Stuffing*
*Mashed Potatoes   Gravy*
*Mallowed Sweet Potatoes*
*Buttered Green Beans*
*Waldorf Salad*
*Spiced Peaches*
*Batter Rolls   Butter*
*Mince-Apple Pie*
*Coffee*

## Waldorf Salad

| | |
|---|---|
| 3 cups diced apples | ½ cup mayonnaise *or* |
| ½ cup chopped celery | salad dressing |
| ½ cup red grapes, halved | 1 tablespoon sugar |
| and seeded | ½ teaspoon lemon juice |
| ½ cup chopped walnuts | ½ cup whipping cream |

Combine apples, celery, grapes, and walnuts. Combine mayonnaise, sugar, and lemon juice. Whip cream till soft peaks form; fold into mayonnaise mixture. Fold all into fruit mixture. Chill. Makes 6 servings.

*Apples and nuts are age-old symbols of prosperity and fertility, long associated with gift-giving at Christmas-time. It is no wonder, then, that Waldorf Salad has become so much a part of a Midwestern Christmas feast.*

## Giblet Stuffing

| | |
|---|---|
| Giblets from 10- to 14-<br>    pound turkey | ⅓ cup chopped onion |
| 1 cup shredded carrot | ½ cup butter *or* margarine |
| 1 cup chopped celery | 7 cups dry bread cubes |
| | 2 teaspoons ground sage |

Cook giblets in salted water to cover till tender, about 1 hour; drain, reserving ½ cup liquid. Chop giblets. Cook vegetables in butter till tender. Combine with the bread cubes, sage, ½ teaspoon salt, ¼ teaspoon pepper, and giblets. Toss with reserved liquid. Use to stuff turkey *or* bake, covered, in 2-quart casserole at 375° for 30 to 35 minutes. Makes about 5 cups.

*Pictured opposite:* Before the big Christmas feast, whet your guests' appetites with *Double Cheese Balls* and *Zippy Tomato Appetizer* (left rear). These foods are fitting preludes to the golden turkey, which is filled with *Giblet Stuffing* and served with green beans and spiced peaches.

## Zippy Tomato Appetizer

| | |
|---|---|
| 1 10½-ounce can condensed<br>    beef broth | 1 46-ounce can vegetable<br>    juice cocktail, chilled |
| ½ teaspoon dried marjoram,<br>    crushed | 2 tablespoons lemon juice |
| | Dash garlic powder |

Simmer beef broth and marjoram together 5 minutes; cool. Combine with vegetable juice, lemon juice, and garlic powder. Chill. Serve in punch bowl; float lemon slices atop, if desired. Makes 12 (5-ounce) servings.

## Double Cheese Balls

| | |
|---|---|
| 1 cup packaged biscuit mix | ¼ cup milk |
| ¼ cup shredded sharp<br>    American cheese | 2 tablespoons mayonnaise<br>    *or* salad dressing |
| ¼ cup crumbled blue cheese | |

Thoroughly blend together the biscuit mix, American cheese, blue cheese, milk, and mayonnaise with fork. Shape into ½-inch balls. Bake on greased baking sheet at 450° for 6 to 8 minutes. Makes about 30.

*Midwestern states, especially Minnesota and Wisconsin, are major cheese producers. No wonder an appetizer with both American cheese and blue cheese is a typical holiday food for people from this area.*

## Mince-Apple Pie

| | |
|---|---|
| 1 9-ounce package instant<br>    condensed mincemeat | 1 teaspoon rum flavoring |
| ¼ cup sugar | Pastry for 2-crust 9-inch<br>    pie (see recipe, page 124) |
| 2 cups thinly sliced apples | Fluffy Hard Sauce (see<br>    recipe, page 120) |
| ¼ teaspoon grated lemon peel | |
| 1 tablespoon lemon juice | |

Prepare mincemeat following package directions *except* use ¼ cup sugar. Combine mincemeat with apples, lemon peel, lemon juice, and rum flavoring. Line 9-inch pie plate with pastry; pour in mincemeat mixture. Adjust top crust and crimp edges. Cut slits in top for escape of steam. Bake at 400° for 40 to 45 minutes. Serve warm with Fluffy Hard Sauce.

*When the first colonists landed in America, they discovered that the Indians used a strange, round, orange gourd almost as much as they used corn. Boiled, baked, and dried in meal, pumpkin was an all-purpose vegetable. It soon became so also for the settlers west of the Mississippi River.*

*In the Midwest, pumpkins are planted in large numbers almost anywhere —such as between rows of corn. They add to a bounteous fall harvest of fruits and vegetables. It's no wonder that Pumpkin Pie is a holiday favorite on the plains.*

## Pumpkin Pie

Combine 1½ cups canned pumpkin, ¾ cup sugar, 1 to 1¼ teaspoons ground cinnamon, ½ to 1 teaspoon ground ginger, ½ teaspoon salt, ¼ to ½ teaspoon ground nutmeg, and ¼ to ½ teaspoon ground cloves. Blend in 3 eggs, 1¼ cups milk, and one 5⅓-ounce can evaporated milk. Pour into an unbaked 9-inch pastry shell (have edges crimped high). Bake at 400° till knife inserted just off-center comes out clean, about 50 minutes. Cool.

## Mallowed Sweet Potatoes

| | |
|---|---|
| **6 medium sweet potatoes, cooked and peeled** | **1 teaspoon salt** |
| **¾ cup packed brown sugar** | **¼ cup butter *or* margarine** |
| | **½ cup tiny marshmallows** |

Cut sweet potatoes in ½-inch slices; place in buttered 1½-quart casserole. Sprinkle with sugar and salt; dot with butter. Bake, uncovered, at 375° till glazed, about 25 minutes. Top with marshmallows; bake till marshmallows are lightly browned, about 5 minutes more. Makes 6 servings.

## Batter Rolls

| | |
|---|---|
| **3¼ cups all-purpose flour** | **¼ cup sugar** |
| **1 package active dry yeast** | **1 egg** |
| **1¼ cups milk** | **Milk** |
| **½ cup shortening** | **1 tablespoon poppy seed** |

In large mixing bowl combine *2 cups* of the flour and yeast. Heat 1¼ cups milk, shortening, sugar, and 1 teaspoon salt just till warm (115-120°); stir constantly. Add to dry mixture in mixing bowl; add egg. Beat at low speed of electric mixer for ½ minute, scraping bowl. Beat 3 minutes at high speed. At low speed beat in remaining flour till batter is smooth, about 2 minutes. (Use rubber spatula to push batter away from beaters.)

Cover; let rise till double (about 1 hour). Stir down; beat well. Let rest 5 minutes. Drop into greased 2¾-inch muffin pans, filling half full. Cover; let rise till double (about 30 minutes). Brush tops with milk; sprinkle with poppy seed. Bake at 400° till done, 12 to 15 minutes. Makes 20.

## Cranberry Relish

| | |
|---|---|
| **½ cup raisins** | **1½ cups sugar** |
| **1 16-ounce package cranberries** | **2 oranges** |
| | **1 grapefruit** |

In saucepan cover raisins with water; bring to boil. Remove from heat; let stand 5 minutes. Drain. Put cranberries through food grinder using coarse blade; stir in sugar. Peel, section, and dice oranges and grapefruit. Stir oranges, grapefruit, and raisins into cranberries. Chill overnight; stir occasionally till sugar dissolves. Makes 3 cups.

# Hawaiian Christmas

In Hawaii, where pastel fir trees are adorned with tinsel and tiny Chinese lanterns, Santa Claus arrives by outrigger. Usually, the Christmas celebrants settle down under a tropical sun to a feast of barbecued pig. It is a congenial mix of peoples—Polynesian, Caucasians, Chinese, Filipinos, and Japanese—and climate that makes a Hawaiian Christmas unique.

It all began in 1786 with a Christmas Eve party offshore in the harbor of Waimea Bay. That night a British sea captain, Portlock, spent his Christmas Eve doling out trinkets and trifles to Hawaiian children on shore. The following day, his seamen celebrated the birth of Christ with a succulent feast of roast pig and coconut punch. This mixture of the European and Asian customs has continued ever since.

Nowadays, the Christmas dinner often is a family affair with twelve to twenty relatives enjoying a luau. This feast of feasts is an indigenous Polynesian custom in Hawaii that once was religious in nature but now is held to honor a number of events. Among the many dishes are roasted pig *(kailua)*, sweet potato pudding *(koele paloa)*, and Portuguese sweet bread *(pao doce)*.

Each nationality adds special details to the Christmas dinner and celebration. Japanese-Americans like their chicken or turkey *teriyaki* and numerous pickled dishes. They trim their trees with many Japanese folk toys, symbols of long life and happy times. Mostly Catholic, Filipinos celebrate by attending midnight mass or *missa del gallo* (mass of the cock) at dawn. All Hawaiian-Americans enjoy the colorful aspects of Christmas and celebrate with their usual island warmth and good humor.

## Portuguese Sweet Bread

| | |
|---|---|
| 1 cup diced, peeled potato | 6 tablespoons butter *or* |
| 7¼ to 7½ cups all-purpose flour | margarine |
| 2 packages active dry yeast | 2 teaspoons salt |
| 2 teaspoons grated lemon peel | 4 eggs |
| 1 cup sugar | 1½ cups raisins |
| | 1 beaten egg |

Cook potato, covered, in 2 cups boiling water till tender, about 20 minutes. Drain and reserve 1⅔ cups liquid. Mash potato. In large mixing bowl combine *2½ cups flour,* yeast, and lemon peel. Heat and stir sugar, butter, salt, and reserved liquid just till warm (115-120°). Add to yeast mixture with 4 eggs and mashed potato. Beat at low speed of electric mixer for ½ minute, scraping sides of bowl. Beat 3 minutes at high speed. By hand, stir in raisins and enough remaining flour to make moderately stiff dough.

Turn out onto lightly floured surface; knead till smooth and elastic (8 to 10 minutes). Shape into ball. Place in lightly greased bowl; turn once. Cover; let rise till double (1 to 1¼ hours). Punch down. Turn out; divide into thirds. Cover; let rest 10 minutes. Shape into 3 round loaves; place on greased baking sheets. Cover; let rise till almost double (about 45 minutes). Brush tops lightly with beaten egg. Bake at 375° for 35 to 40 minutes. Cover with foil after 20 minutes to prevent overbrowning. Makes 3 loaves.

*The Portuguese were among the first European settlers on the Hawaiian Islands and they have contributed much to the verve and spontaneity of island life. This popular, fine-textured bread, called* pao doce, *was traditionally served Christmas morning, along with highly spiced pork cubes, green olives, and a favorite Portuguese wine. It makes a delicious and festive holiday bread with or without the traditional accouterments.*

## Turkey Teriyaki

*Pictured opposite:* Boneless turkey roast and pineapple brushed with a marinade of soy sauce, sherry, and ginger are grilled over medium coals to make *Turkey Teriyaki*. This delightful blend of flavors is a special Hawaiian Christmas treat.

| | |
|---|---|
| 1 28-ounce frozen white meat turkey roast | 2 tablespoons cooking oil |
| ½ cup packed brown sugar | 2 teaspoons vinegar |
| ½ cup soy sauce | 1 teaspoon ground ginger |
| ¼ cup dry sherry | 1 clove garlic, minced |
| | 1 fresh pineapple |

Partially thaw turkey roast; cut into twelve slices. Arrange in shallow dish. Mix brown sugar, soy sauce, dry sherry, cooking oil, vinegar, ginger, garlic, and ½ cup water for marinade; pour over turkey slices. Cover and chill 1 hour; drain, reserving marinade. Grill over *medium* coals till done, about 25 minutes; turn and baste often with reserved marinade.

Meanwhile, remove crown from pineapple; peel and remove eyes. Wash, quarter lengthwise, and remove core. Cut fruit lengthwise into spears. Grill pineapple spears till golden, about 10 minutes; turn and baste often with marinade. Serve pineapple spears with turkey slices. Makes 6 servings.

## Coconut Milk Punch

*If you enjoy the flavor of coconut, you'll want to try more recipes developed especially for fresh coconut. Make candied Coconut Chips (see recipe, page 190) before the brown skin has been peeled away from the white meat. Then use the remaining white coconut meat chips for Coconut Milk Punch and Christmas Coconut Pie.*

| | |
|---|---|
| 1 fresh coconut | 2 jiggers brandy (3 ounces) |
| Milk | 1 jigger maraschino cherry |
| 2 cups crushed ice | juice (1½ ounces) |
| 3 jiggers light rum (4½ ounces) | 2 tablespoons powdered sugar |
| | Maraschino cherries |

Pierce coconut eyes; drain and reserve liquid. Remove shell; peel off brown skin. Coarsely chop the coconut. Add milk to reserved liquid to make 2 cups; heat till hot but not boiling. Place chopped coconut and hot liquid in blender container; cover and blend 1 minute. Chill well. In shaker combine blended mixture, ice, rum, brandy, cherry juice, and sugar; shake well. Strain into glasses; garnish with cherries. Makes 6 (4-ounce) servings.

## Christmas Coconut Pie

| | |
|---|---|
| 1 envelope unflavored gelatin | 4 egg whites |
| ⅓ cup sugar | ½ cup sugar |
| 4 beaten egg yolks | ½ cup whipping cream |
| ¾ cup unsweetened pineapple juice | 1 cup shredded fresh coconut *or* flaked coconut |
| 1 teaspoon vanilla | 1 *baked* 9-inch pastry shell |

Combine gelatin, ⅓ cup sugar, and ¼ teaspoon salt. Stir together egg yolks and pineapple juice; add to gelatin mixture. Cook and stir over medium heat just till mixture thickens. Remove from heat; stir in vanilla. Chill, stirring occasionally, till mixture mounds. Beat egg whites till soft peaks form; gradually add ½ cup sugar, beating till stiff peaks form. Fold into gelatin mixture. Whip cream; fold into gelatin mixture with coconut. Pile into pastry shell. Chill in the refrigerator till firm. Garnish the pie with additional whipped cream, toasted coconut, and maraschino cherries, if desired.

# Canadian Christmas

There are two main Christmases in Canada—French and English. Each group celebrates the season in its own way.

For the French-Canadians, the big day is Christmas Eve. It is mainly a family day. Most of French-Canada is Catholic, so the overtones reflect both the religion and the nationality. Midnight mass, or *messe de minuet*, is followed by *reveillon de noel*, a night-long celebration of food, fun, and frivolity punctuated about four or five in the morning by an exchange of gifts. Essential to the feasting is the regional favorite tourtiere, a delicious well-seasoned pork pie, as well as meatballs, ragout, roast pork, and sometimes even turkey. There are numerous accouterments as well, pâtés, special homemade pickles, and for dessert, a Christmas cake and the fabulous *buche de Noel*, a Christmas specialty shaped like a yule log and covered with "bark" made of rich chocolate frosting. (See recipe, page 120.)

On the other hand, Christmas Day is preferred by the English. This is a happy family time, with a large fir tree covered with tinsel, brightly colored ornaments, and twinkling lights. Gifts are exchanged Christmas morning, and the day is marked by an enormous feast of turkey, fall vegetables, side dishes, and the inevitable English plum pudding.

Canada is not as large a melting pot of diverse nationalities as the United States, but the Canadian pot does offer certain ethnic seasonings. The Ukrainians of Winnipeg and Edmonton, for instance, are famous for a delicious braided Christmas bread. And in Toronto, where a large Italian population congregates, Christmas assumes a decidedly Italian flavor.

There are other variations that punctuate the traditional celebrations. In remote regions, Eskimos celebrate by visiting. The people of one village descend *en masse* on another village where they're feasted, doted upon, and regaled with song and dance. They turn about the next year.

In the Cape Breton area of Nova Scotia, where Scottish highlanders settled, houses seem almost to vibrate with robust song during the Christmas holidays. Carols and old Scottish favorites are belted out with gusto. And in Newfoundland, certain villages on the water have the custom of "fishing for the church" during Christmas week. Proceeds of all the fish caught and sold during the week go to support the local church.

With snow caps on all the bushes and trees, Christmas in Canada is usually a wonderland of whiteness, just as St. Nicholas likes to see it.

## Sugar Tartlets

*Traditional Canadian sugar pie is a relative of the maple sugar pie Vermonters enjoy. People in cold climates seem to rely on such quick-energy-producing sweets. In this miniature form, the syrupy sweet pie is a pleasure to eat.*

**Pastry for 2-crust 8-inch
   pie (see recipe,
   page 124)**

¾ cup packed brown sugar
⅓ cup whipping cream
¼ cup chopped walnuts

Roll pastry to ⅛-inch thickness. Cut sixteen 4-inch pastry circles. Fit into 2-inch muffin pans. In saucepan mix brown sugar and whipping cream. Bring to boiling; stir in walnuts. Spoon *1 tablespoon* filling into each pastry-lined muffin cup *(do not fill any fuller)*. Bake at 375° for 15 to 18 minutes. Cool 10 minutes. Carefully remove from pans. Makes 16.

## Tourtière (tor' tee air)

| | |
|---|---|
| 1 pound lean ground pork | Dash ground nutmeg |
| 1 cup water | Pastry for 2-crust 9-inch |
| ½ cup finely chopped onion | pie (see recipe, |
| ½ cup fine dry bread crumbs | page 124) |
| Dash ground sage | |

Brown pork in skillet; drain off fat. Stir in water, onion, bread crumbs, sage, nutmeg, ¾ teaspoon salt, and dash pepper. Simmer, covered, 30 minutes; stir often. Line 9-inch pie plate with pastry; fill with meat mixture. Adjust top crust; seal. Cut slits in top to permit escape of steam. Bake at 400° till golden brown, about 35 minutes. Makes 6 servings.

*The pig has long been associated in rural cultures with Christmas and the symbolism of a good harvest. Pork pie, a favorite of French-Canadians, is served after midnight mass*

## Sugar-Glazed Ham

| | |
|---|---|
| 1 8-pound boneless fully cooked ham | ½ teaspoon ground cloves |
| | Apple juice |
| 1 cup packed brown sugar | 1 cup raisins |
| 2 tablespoons apple juice | ¼ cup cold water |
| 1 teaspoon dry mustard | 2 tablespoons cornstarch |

Place ham on rack in shallow baking pan; insert meat thermometer. Bake at 325° till meat thermometer registers 130°, about 2 hours. Combine sugar, the 2 tablespoons apple juice, mustard, and cloves; spread over ham. Return to oven and bake 15 minutes longer. Remove ham to platter; keep warm. Add enough apple juice (about 2 cups) to pan juices to measure 2½ cups; stir in raisins. Heat to boiling. Blend cold water slowly into cornstarch; stir into raisin mixture. Cook, stirring constantly, till mixture is thickened and bubbly. Pass the raisin sauce with ham. Makes 12 to 16 servings.

## Stuffed Cabbage Rolls

| | |
|---|---|
| 1 cup long grain rice | 1 24-ounce can vegetable juice cocktail |
| ½ cup chopped onion | 1 tablespoon sugar |
| 2 tablespoons butter *or* margarine | Dairy sour cream |
| ¼ cup snipped parsley | Snipped parsley *or* 3 slices bacon, crisp-cooked and crumbled |
| 12 large cabbage leaves | |
| Salt | |

Cook rice according to package directions. Meanwhile, cook onion in butter till tender but not brown. Combine cooked rice, onion, and ¼ cup parsley. Cut about 2 inches of heavy center vein out of cabbage leaves. Immerse leaves in boiling water just till limp, about 3 minutes; drain. Sprinkle leaves generously with salt. Place about ¼ cup rice mixture in center of each leaf; fold in sides and roll ends over rice. Place, seam side down, in 12x7½x2-inch baking dish. Combine vegetable juice cocktail and sugar; pour over cabbage rolls. Bake, covered, at 350° for 1 hour. Before serving, garnish with sour cream and sprinkle with parsley or crumbled bacon. Serves 6.

*An old Slavic legend tells of a peasant who stole a cabbage on Christmas Eve. The Christ Child rode by on a white horse, saw him and said, "Because thou hast stolen on the Holy Night, thou shalt immediately sit in the moon with the basket of cabbage." And that is the story of the Man in the Moon. Despite the moral of the story, meatless stuffed cabbage rolls are a Christmas Eve favorite of the Ukrainians who settled in Canada.*

# Christmas in Williamsburg

*Pictured opposite:* Try serving these festive dishes to celebrate Christmas in the style of old Williamsburg.

## Menu

*Turkey*
*(see chart, page 91)*
*with*
*Mincemeat Stuffing*
*Sweet Potato-Date Puffs*
*Buttered Broccoli*
*Mashed Potatoes*
*Cranberry Chutney*
*Regal Plum Pudding*
*Fluffy Hard Sauce*
*Hot Lemon Punch*

"You can't go home again," Southern novelist Thomas Wolfe once wrote. Obviously, he hadn't been to colonial Williamsburg. For it is possible to see what Christmas in the grand homes of eighteenth-century Virginia was like in the re-creation of it at twentieth-century Williamsburg today.

The English love of Christmas did not suffer a sea change when the colonists reached Virginia. If anything, absence made the settlers' hearts grow fonder of their old-fashioned home-style Christmas celebrations, and English traditions were carried on to a fare-thee-well.

Christmas followed a treasured English pattern of hearty and prolonged eating and exuberant drinking that began a week ahead of the holiday and reached a crescendo on the Twelfth Night, January 6th. Williamsburg ladies did their share of baking, too—pies, plum puddings, and all the sweets and candies needed for the many guests who descended during the holidays.

Christmas Day itself was a holy day, with church services, prayers, and carols. Later in the day was the massive feast. The burnished wooden table must have moaned under the weight of the many dishes served—oysters, ham, roast beef, wild turkey, venison, hot breads and rolls, vegetables such as garden peas and squash, parsnips, sweet potatoes, accompanied by numerous sauces and relishes, which were called "corner dishes" because of their placement at the corners of the table. These many splendors were followed by plum puddings, cream pies, fruitcakes, mincemeat pies, nuts, and candies, as well as wine, dark beer, mulled cider, and punch.

Then, as now, all the windows in Williamsburg houses have lighted candles on each of the seven evenings before Christmas. This "Grand Illumination" casts a unique magical spell on the lovely restored old town. Nowadays there are Christmas trees in Williamsburg, unknown to the town until 1842. A huge outdoor tree on Market Square is lighted Christmas Eve in a special ceremony, signaling the beginning of all the games, musical events, and other gaieties to come during the holiday season.

Although the setting at Williamsburg is of the colonial period, many of the Christmas foods seem contemporary because the recipes for them have been handed down and enjoyed by English families wherever they settled throughout the new world. And the plum puddings, fruitcakes, rum pies, and brandy snaps do nicely in modern kitchens with the cooks using store-bought ingredients. (Even better are the molded wine mixtures with commercial gelatin replacing the calves' foot jelly.)

## Hot Lemon Punch

*Punch was a stand-by at all the Christmas balls of colonial Williamsburg. At each ball, there were several types, some of which were served warm to take the chill off the cool large ballrooms.*

**5 cups water**
**1 cup sugar**
**1 cup lemon juice**

**1 cup gin (optional)**
**Lemon slices**

In a large saucepan, combine water, sugar, and lemon juice. Cook and stir till sugar is dissolved and mixture just begins to boil. Add gin, if desired; heat mixture through. Carefully pour into a punch bowl. Float lemon slices on top to serve. Makes about 15 (4-ounce) servings.

## Regal Plum Pudding (see photo, page 33)

*Plum pudding evolved from a watery wheat porridge called frumenty to a mixture of meat broth, cows' tongues, wine, spices, and raisins to what is known today as a rich, sweet dessert. The word plum referred to the way the raisins "plumped" up in the cooking. The English called it simply "Christmas pudding" and couldn't imagine the holiday without it. Earlier recipes call for more suet and sugar, which may have provided inner fuel in colonial times, but are much less needed today.*

4 slices bread, torn in pieces
1 cup milk
• • •
6 ounces beef suet, ground
1 cup packed brown sugar
2 slightly beaten eggs
¼ cup orange juice
1 teaspoon vanilla
2 cups raisins
1 cup snipped pitted
 dates

½ cup diced mixed candied
 fruits and peels
½ cup chopped walnuts
1 cup all-purpose flour
2 teaspoons ground cinnamon
1 teaspoon ground cloves
1 teaspoon ground mace
1 teaspoon baking soda
½ teaspoon salt
Fluffy Hard Sauce
 (see recipe, page 120)

Soak bread in milk and beat to break up. Stir in ground suet, brown sugar, eggs, orange juice, and vanilla. In bowl combine raisins, dates, candied fruits and peels, and nuts. Stir together flour, cinnamon, cloves, mace, soda, and salt; add to the mixed fruits and mix well. Stir in bread-suet mixture. Pour into well-greased 2-quart mold (do not use ring mold or tube pan). Cover with foil and tie foil on tightly with string.

Place the mold on rack in deep kettle; add boiling water to the kettle 1 inch deep. Cover and steam the pudding 3½ hours; add more boiling water if needed. Cool the pudding about 10 minutes before removing from the mold. Serve the pudding with Fluffy Hard Sauce. Makes 16 servings.

## Mincemeat Stuffing (see photo, page 33)

In saucepan combine one 9-ounce package instant condensed mincemeat and 1¾ cups water. Bring to boiling; reduce heat and simmer till mixture thickens slightly, 1 to 2 minutes. In large skillet cook 1 cup chopped onion in ½ cup butter *or* margarine till tender but not brown. Add 12 cups dry bread cubes (about 18 slices bread), 1 tablespoon poultry seasoning, 1 teaspoon salt, and the prepared mincemeat mixture. Toss lightly. Use to stuff one 9- to 10-pound turkey *or* bake, covered, in 2-quart casserole at 375° for 30 to 35 minutes. Makes 8 cups.

## Sweet Potato-Date Puffs (see photo, page 33)

1 17-ounce can sweet potatoes,
 drained
¾ cup snipped pitted
 dates

6 slices canned pineapple
¼ cup butter *or* margarine
¼ cup packed brown sugar
2 tablespoons honey

Mash sweet potatoes; stir in ¼ *cup* of the dates. Shape into six balls. Drain the pineapple, reserving 2 tablespoons syrup. In medium skillet melt butter or margarine; stir in brown sugar, honey, reserved pineapple syrup, and the remaining dates. Heat and stir till sugar dissolves. Place the 6 slices pineapple into syrup in skillet; top each with a potato ball. Cover; simmer over low heat for 10 to 12 minutes, spooning the syrup over the sweet potato balls several times during cooking. Makes 6 servings.

## Cranberry Chutney (see photo, page 33)

1 16-ounce package cranberries
2¼ cups packed brown sugar
1 cup light raisins
1 cup water
½ cup coarsely chopped
   macadamia nuts *or*
   toasted almonds

¼ cup snipped candied
   ginger
¼ cup lemon juice
2 teaspoons salt
1 teaspoon grated onion
¼ teaspoon ground cloves

*One of the early colonists'
favorite discoveries was
the cranberry, and up and
down the coast they quickly
learned to use it in various
ways, as in this spicy
companion to the holiday
bird or boar.*

In large saucepan combine all ingredients; stir together. Bring mixture to boiling, stirring constantly. Simmer, uncovered, over low heat for 15 minutes; stir occasionally. Ladle chutney into hot sterilized jars, leaving ½-inch headspace. Adjust lids. Process in boiling water bath 15 minutes. (Or, refrigerate for up to 2 weeks.) Makes about 5 half-pints.

## Burgundy Cran-Apple Salad

1 6-ounce *or* two 3-ounce
   packages strawberry-
   flavored gelatin
1 16-ounce can whole
   cranberry sauce

1 cup apple cider *or*
   apple juice
½ cup Burgundy
2 cups chopped apples

Dissolve gelatin in 1½ cups boiling water. Beat in cranberry sauce. Stir in apple cider and Burgundy. Chill till partially set; fold in apples. Pour into 6½-cup mold; chill till firm. Makes 10 to 12 servings.

## Yorkshire Christmas Meat Pie

1 1½- to 2-pound ready-to-
   cook rabbit
½ cup finely chopped celery
¼ cup finely chopped onion
¼ cup snipped parsley
3 tablespoons butter *or*
   margarine
3 tablespoons all-purpose
   flour
1 teaspoon salt

½ teaspoon ground savory
¼ teaspoon ground nutmeg
¼ teaspoon pepper
¼ teaspoon ground thyme
⅛ teaspoon ground cloves
1½ cups chicken *or* turkey broth
2 cups diced cooked chicken
   *or* turkey
Pastry for 2-crust 9-inch
   pie (see recipe, page 124)

*One Olde English recipe
for Christmas pie called
for "four geese, two turkeys,
four wild ducks, two rabbits,
two curlews, seven
blackbirds, six pigeons,
four partridges, six snipe,
two woodcocks, two neats'
tongues, two bushels of
flour, and twenty pounds
butter." Because of the
English people in
Williamsburg, pie-making
was a standard part of
Christmas there. This
version is not so flamboyant
as the one mentioned
above, but it is just as tasty.*

Simmer rabbit in salted water till tender, about 1 hour. Set aside to cool. Remove cooled meat from bones; dice. In saucepan cook celery, onion, and parsley in butter till tender. Stir together flour, salt, savory, nutmeg, pepper, thyme, and cloves. Blend into celery mixture; stir in broth. Cook and stir over medium heat till mixture is thickened and bubbly. Combine mixture with cooked rabbit and chicken or turkey. Line 9-inch pie plate with pastry; spoon in meat mixture. Adjust top crust; seal. Cut slits for steam to escape. Bake at 375° till golden brown, about 40 minutes. Cover the edges of the pastry with foil if necessary to prevent overbrowning.

## Brandy Snaps

*The southern sweet tooth is prevalent in Williamsburg, too, and easily is satisfied with Brandy Snaps. Originally made as a small wafer on a hot griddle by English immigrants, it has evolved to an oven-baked cookie. Allow yourself plenty of time to practice—the amount of batter is ample to let you experiment. This fancy rolled wafer has a beautiful lacy and crisp texture— not exactly a cookie, not exactly a candy. A rich filling of whipped cream flavored with candied ginger and brandy graces this holiday delight.*

½ cup packed brown sugar
6 tablespoons butter *or*
   margarine, melted
¼ cup molasses
1 tablespoon brandy
¾ cup all-purpose flour
½ teaspoon ground ginger

½ teaspoon ground nutmeg
⅛ teaspoon salt
   Whipped cream *or* frozen
    whipped dessert topping,
    thawed
   Candied ginger, chopped
   Brandy

In bowl combine brown sugar, melted butter, molasses, and 1 tablespoon brandy; mix well. Stir together flour, ginger, nutmeg, and salt. Stir into butter mixture. Drop level teaspoonful 4 inches apart onto ungreased cookie sheet. Bake at 350° for 5 to 6 minutes. *(Bake only 3 at a time.)* Let cool *2 minutes* on cookie sheet; remove with wide spatula. *Immediately* roll each cookie to form a cone. (Reheat in oven for about 30 seconds if cookies harden before they are rolled.) Cool completely; store in airtight container. Just before serving, combine whipped cream and chopped candied ginger; flavor to taste with brandy. Use to fill cookies. Makes about 60.

## Rum Cream Pie

In saucepan combine ¾ cup sugar, 3 tablespoons cornstarch, and ¼ teaspoon salt; gradually stir in 1¾ cups milk. Cook and stir over medium heat till mixture is thickened and bubbly. Cook and stir 2 minutes more. Remove from heat. Stir a moderate amount of hot mixture into 3 beaten egg yolks; immediately return to hot mixture and cook 2 minutes more, stirring constantly. Remove from heat. Stir in ¼ cup rum, 2 tablespoons butter *or* margarine, and ½ teaspoon vanilla. Pour into one *baked* 8-inch pastry shell, cooled. (To prevent skin from forming on surface of filling put waxed paper directly on top of hot filling.) Chill thoroughly. Just before serving garnish with whipped cream and grated semisweet chocolate.

## Gingerbread

*A colonial favorite, ginger was used in Williamsburg in all sorts of cookies and especially in gingerbread. In Williamsburg today you still can smell the spicy fresh gingery scent familiar to our forefathers.*

½ cup shortening
½ cup packed brown sugar
½ cup molasses
1 egg
1½ cups all-purpose flour
¾ teaspoon ground ginger

¾ teaspoon ground cinnamon
½ teaspoon salt
½ teaspoon baking powder
½ teaspoon baking soda
½ cup boiling water
   Lemon Sauce

Cream shortening and brown sugar till light. Add molasses and egg; beat well. Stir together flour, ginger, cinnamon, salt, baking powder, and soda. Add to creamed mixture alternately with boiling water, beating after each addition. Pour into a greased and floured 9x1½-inch round baking pan. Bake at 350° for 35 to 40 minutes. Serve warm with Lemon Sauce. Makes 8 servings.

*Lemon Sauce:* Mix ½ cup granulated sugar, 1 tablespoon cornstarch, and ⅛ teaspoon *each* salt and ground nutmeg. Add 1 cup boiling water. Cook and stir till thickened. Blend in 2 tablespoons *each* butter and lemon juice.

# Christmas in New Orleans

If America has produced one single great cuisine, it is indisputably Creole—especially the cooking of New Orleans. Here, the Creole spirit of *joie d'vivre* sparkles at Christmas-time with the flavorful blend of French and Spanish culinary habits as well as those of African slaves from the West Indies.

In the past, this spirit of *joie d'vivre* was seen also in the spontaneous and sometimes raucous cheerfulness of the people of New Orleans. To celebrate the birth of Christ, for example, high-spirited settlers would discharge their guns in the air, following an old French custom. Much of this tradition is carried over into today's festivities.

Today in each house, the family crèche, with all the *santons,* is artfully arranged with fresh greenery or holly as background for the *Petit Jesu* and has a tiny star of Bethlehem suspended over it. These crèche figures, the petite clay *santons,* are derived from the French Christmas markets, where Nativity figures are sold in stalls. Families enjoy adding to their elaborate Bethlehem scenes, forming entire miniature villages.

The entire house is swathed in greenery and flowers. The yule log, transformed today into the *buche de Noel*—a chocolate-covered cake in the shape of a yule log (see recipe, page 120)—was once an important part of a New Orleans Christmas. It was believed by Creoles that the yule log prevented chilblains and cured cattle diseases. As long as the log burned during the holiday season, the family slaves were released from work.

Traditionally, New Orleans' great Christmas dining comes late Christmas Eve, after midnight mass. The feast is called *le reveillon* ("toward dawn") and often lasts until the wee hours of the morning. *Reveillon* symbolized the Three Kings' wanderings, but now it is a way to welcome in Christmas. Dinner after midnight mass signals the appearance of rich, succulent game. Goose was once the bird supreme in France, where it was believed that geese welcomed the Three Kings to the stable at Bethlehem. In recent times, chicken and turkey have become favorites as well.

The Christmas table is at its most festive on this gala evening. On it there is usually champagne punch and candy dishes piled with pralines. This is a time for carol singing, story telling, happy family reminiscing, and finally, cups of strong New Orleans chicory coffee served as *café au lait.* Christmas Day is a family day, restful and recuperative, as well it might be, after such a long night of feasting and merrymaking.

### Café au Lait (ka′ fay oh lay′) (see photo, page 39)

| | |
|---|---|
| **3 cups cold water** | **3 cups light cream** |
| **¾ cup chicory-blend coffee** | ***or* milk** |

Measure cold water into percolator. Measure the chicory-blend coffee into basket. Cover; place over heat. Bring to boiling; reduce heat and perk gently 6 to 8 minutes. Remove basket; keep coffee hot over very low heat till ready to serve. Meanwhile, heat cream or milk over low heat. Beat with rotary beater till foamy. Transfer to warmed container. Pour hot coffee and hot cream in equal amounts into serving cups. Makes 10 servings.

Café au Lait, *or coffee with milk, is a New Orleans institution. The milk mellows the strong chicory flavor. Chicory was introduced during the Civil War when regular coffee was hard to get. Now it is a local favorite.*

## Cauliflower with Dilly Shrimp Sauce

*Pictured opposite:* Merry Christmas celebrated New Orleans style! At no time is Creole cooking so rich, varied, luxurious, or triumphant as during the Christmas season. *Turtle Soup, Café au Lait* (see recipe, page 37), and *Chicken Jambalaya* (see recipe, page 40) help make it so.

1 medium head cauliflower
2 tablespoons butter
2 tablespoons all-purpose flour

½ teaspoon dried dillweed
1½ cups milk
1 cup fresh *or* frozen shelled shrimp, cooked and drained

Cook whole cauliflower, covered, in boiling salted water till tender, 20 to 25 minutes; drain. Meanwhile, melt butter; blend in flour, dillweed, ¼ teaspoon salt, and dash pepper. Add milk; cook and stir till thickened. Cut up shrimp; stir into sauce. Heat through. Drizzle some sauce over hot cauliflower. Pass remaining sauce. Makes 4 to 6 servings.

## Turtle Soup

*It has been said that the entire magic of the Creole kitchen is contained in a spoonful of good Turtle Soup. Served with thin mushroom slices floating atop, this soup is a meal in itself. Crusty French bread and red wine are the only accompaniments needed. Hearty and savory, it is a holiday season favorite.*

1 pound boned turtle meat, cut in ½-inch cubes
Cooking oil
6 cups water
2 cups chopped cabbage
2 stalks celery with leaves, cut up
2 medium carrots, cut up
1 medium onion, cut in wedges

6 whole peppercorns
3 sprigs parsley
2 cloves garlic
2 bay leaves
1½ teaspoons salt
1 cup thinly sliced fresh mushrooms
½ cup dry sherry
¼ teaspoon Kitchen Bouquet

Brown turtle meat in small amount of hot oil. Stir in *1 cup* water; bring to boiling. Reduce heat; simmer, covered, till tender, 1½ hours. Meanwhile, in large saucepan combine cabbage, celery, carrots, onion, peppercorns, parsley, garlic, bay leaves, salt, and remaining water. Bring to boiling; simmer, covered, 1 hour. Strain broth from vegetables; discard vegetables and spices. Return broth to saucepan; stir in undrained turtle meat, mushrooms, and sherry. Heat through. Stir in Kitchen Bouquet. Makes 4 to 6 servings.

## New Orleans Dirty Rice

*A Louisianian eats five times as much rice as any other American. A popular way to prepare it is as Dirty Rice, a rather unpalatable name for a delicious dish. The "dirty" look comes from the chicken livers. Defying all the rules about rice preparation—rice should be white, fluffy, and dry—Dirty Rice is murky, wet, and soft as Louisiana swamp air. It is also a unique Creole food.*

1 14-ounce can beef broth
¾ cup long grain rice
3 tablespoons butter
3 tablespoons all-purpose flour
1 cup finely chopped onion
½ cup finely chopped celery

½ cup finely chopped green pepper
½ teaspoon garlic powder
⅛ teaspoon cayenne
1 pound chicken livers
1 3-ounce can sliced mushrooms

In saucepan combine beef broth and rice; bring to boiling. Cover and cook according to rice package directions. In saucepan melt butter; stir in flour. Cook and stir till golden brown. Stir in onion, celery, green pepper, garlic powder, cayenne, and ½ teaspoon salt. Cook till onion is tender. Coarsely chop chicken livers. Stir livers and undrained mushrooms into onion mixture. Cover; cook over low heat till livers are tender, 6 to 8 minutes, stirring often. Fold liver mixture into cooked rice. Makes 6 servings.

## Creole Gumbo

3 tablespoons butter *or*
  margarine
3 tablespoons all-purpose
  flour
½ cup chopped onion
1 clove garlic, minced
1 16-ounce can tomatoes,
  cut up
1½ cups water
½ cup chopped green pepper
2 bay leaves
1 teaspoon dried oregano,
  crushed

1 teaspoon dried thyme,
  crushed
½ teaspoon salt
¼ teaspoon bottled hot pepper
  sauce
1 10-ounce package frozen
  cut okra, thawed
2 4½-ounce cans shrimp,
  drained and cut up
1 7½-ounce can crab meat,
  drained and cartilage
  removed
Hot cooked rice

In large saucepan melt butter or margarine; blend in flour. Cook, stirring constantly, till mixture is golden brown. Stir in onion and garlic; cook till onion is tender but not brown. Stir in undrained tomatoes, water, green pepper, bay leaves, oregano, thyme, salt, and hot pepper sauce. Bring to boiling; reduce heat and simmer, covered, about 20 minutes.

Remove the bay leaves. Stir in the okra. Bring mixture to boiling, then stir in shrimp and crab; heat mixture through. Serve the gumbo over hot cooked rice in soup plates. (Traditionally, rice is mounded in a heated soup plate and the gumbo spooned around it.) Makes 6 servings.

*In the mid-nineteenth century a Swedish connoisseur visiting New Orleans declared that "gumbo is the crown of all the savory and remarkable soups in the world—a regular elixir of life." Gumbo has been called the evolution of bouillabaisse into something tastier. It does show what French culinary skills accomplished with Choctaw Indian herbs and vegetables. Old Creole cooks reputedly did not write down their recipes. Nor did they tell them. They whispered them to their descendants. This recipe picks up the whispers.*

## Chicken Jambalaya (see photo, page 39)

2 cups cubed fully cooked ham
¾ cup chopped onion
1 clove garlic, minced
2 tablespoons butter *or*
  margarine
1 28-ounce can tomatoes,
  cut up
1 13¾-ounce can chicken broth
1½ cups water
1¼ cups long grain rice
2 bay leaves, crushed
1 teaspoon sugar
1 teaspoon dried thyme,
  crushed
½ teaspoon salt

¼ teaspoon chili powder
¼ teaspoon bottled hot
  pepper sauce
2 cups cubed cooked chicken
  *or* turkey
5 ounces fresh *or* frozen
  shelled shrimp, cooked,
  drained, and halved, *or*
1 4½-ounce can shrimp,
  drained
½ cup coarsely chopped
  green pepper
¼ cup sliced pitted ripe
  olives
Sliced pitted ripe olives

In large saucepan cook the ham, onion, and garlic in butter till onion is tender. Stir in undrained tomatoes, chicken broth, water, rice, bay leaves, sugar, thyme, salt, chili powder, and hot pepper sauce. Bring mixture to boiling; reduce heat. Cover and simmer till rice is tender, about 20 minutes. Stir in chicken, shrimp, green pepper, and ¼ cup olives. Simmer, uncovered, till of desired consistency, about 5 minutes. Garnish with sliced pitted ripe olives, if desired. Makes 6 to 8 servings.

*A local tale in New Orleans tells of the Creole who entered Heaven and asked the first angel he met, "Where's the nearest pot of jambalaya?" When he learned that there was no jambalaya on the premises, he quickly leaped from Paradise, thereby proving that "a Louisianian will gladly go to Hell for a dish of jambalaya."*

*Whether the above is true or not, the Creole name, jambalaya, derives from the French for ham (jambon). Often a good excuse to use up leftovers, it is rarely the same twice. This Chicken Jambalaya is a festive dish in and of itself.*

## Pecan Pie

1½ cups light corn syrup
½ cup sugar
¼ cup butter *or* margarine
• • •
1 cup coarsely chopped pecans

1 unbaked 9-inch pastry shell
3 eggs
1 teaspoon vanilla
Dash salt

In saucepan combine corn syrup, sugar, and butter or margarine; bring to boiling. Boil gently, uncovered, 5 minutes, stirring occasionally. Cool syrup mixture slightly. Place the pecans in bottom of pastry shell. Combine eggs, vanilla, and salt. Pour cooled syrup mixture into egg mixture; beat well. Pour over nuts (pecans will rise to top). Bake at 375° till knife inserted off-center comes out clean, 30 to 35 minutes.

*Whether in pie, cake, tarts, or sweet potato dishes, the fat, meaty pecans of Louisiana play an important role in indigenous New Orleans cooking. Pecan Pie has long been associated in northern eyes as the pièce de résistance of New Orleans cooking. This recipe illustrates why.*

## Sausage Dressing

½ pound turkey *or* chicken
   giblets and neck
Salt
½ pound bulk pork sausage
10 cups soft bread
   cubes (13 slices)
2 cups diced peeled apple

1 cup chopped onion
½ cup raisins
1 teaspoon salt
1 teaspoon ground sage
¼ teaspoon pepper
3 beaten eggs

Remove liver from giblets; set aside. Place giblets and neck in saucepan; add water just to cover and salt lightly. Add a few celery leaves and onion slices to water, if desired. Cover; simmer for 1 to 2 hours for chicken (2 hours for turkey). Add the liver and continue to simmer for 5 to 10 minutes for chicken liver (20 to 30 minutes for turkey liver). Cool giblets and neck in broth; remove and chop, reserving broth. Meanwhile, cook pork sausage till lightly browned; drain. Combine sausage with bread cubes, apple, onion, raisins, 1 teaspoon salt, ground sage, pepper, and chopped giblets. Stir in beaten eggs and enough of the reserved broth to make desired moistness (½ to 1 cup broth). Use to stuff 9-pound turkey *or* bake, covered, in a 2-quart casserole at 375° about 45 minutes. Makes 7 cups.

## New Orleans Pralines

2 cups sugar
¾ teaspoon baking soda
1 cup light cream

1½ tablespoons butter *or*
   margarine
2 cups pecan halves

In 3-quart saucepan combine sugar and soda; mix well. Stir in cream. Bring to boiling over medium heat, stirring constantly. Cook and stir to soft-ball stage (234° on candy thermometer). (Mixture caramelizes slightly as it cooks.) Remove from heat; add butter. Stir in pecans. Beat the candy till thick enough to drop from spoon (2 to 3 minutes). Drop tablespoonsful onto waxed paper. If the candy becomes too stiff to drop, add a little hot water to make the right consistency. Makes 24.

*Pralines were named for the French Marshal Duc de Choiseul Praslin, whose recipe led to the divine pralines of New Orleans. Praslin believed that nuts coated with sugar were more digestible. Unquestionably, these mouth-watering candies are a delicious use for pecans.*

# A Sacramento Christmas

Steamboats churning up and down the harbor bringing friends and relatives for a holiday visit, greenhorn miners coming to town just to celebrate and Pony Express riders bringing in Christmas mail and packages from the folks back East were all a part of Christmas in historic Sacramento. Now this rugged gold rush town has become a bright, modern city and Christmas customs have changed right along with it.

Because the people of this area have no long-standing traditions to follow, they have created new customs of their own. Perhaps the most distinctive feature of this area is the open house. For weeks before Christmas and especially on Christmas Eve, friends and family gather for informal buffets. Often held inside because it is the rainy season, these cheery repasts include appetizers, dips, finger sandwiches, plenty of salads, and desserts such as Grapefruit Chiffon Cake that use fresh fruit.

Whole neighborhoods plan group activities such as door decorating contests and progressive holiday dinners. At these dinners each participant prepares a favorite Christmas dish, and the party moves from house to house. If many of the group have differing ethnic backgrounds, the dinner may take on a cosmopolitan flavor and is often truly international.

*Pictured opposite:* For a festive Christmas open house serve: (clockwise from center) *Apple-Date Sandwiches* (see recipe, page 44), *Deviled Party Sandwiches* (see recipe, page 44), *Blue Cheese Pâté, Cottage Bacon Dip,* and *Coffee Nog* (see recipe, page 44).

## Cottage-Bacon Dip

   **2 slices bacon**
   **2 tablespoons milk**
   **2 teaspoons lemon juice**
**1½ cups cream-style cottage
     cheese**
  **¼ cup mayonnaise**

**½ small avocado, peeled
   and pitted**
**¼ teaspoon garlic salt**
**¼ teaspoon onion powder**
  **Vegetable dippers**

In a skillet cook bacon till crisp; drain and crumble. Set aside. In blender container combine milk, lemon juice, cottage cheese, mayonnaise, avocado, garlic salt, and onion powder. Cover and blend till smooth, stopping to scrape down sides as necessary. Remove from blender container. Stir in bacon pieces. Cover and chill thoroughly. Garnish with celery leaves, if desired. Serve with assorted vegetable dippers. Makes about 2 cups.

## Blue Cheese Pâté

In a small mixing bowl beat together one 8-ounce package cream cheese, softened; one 4¾-ounce can liver spread; ½ cup crumbled blue cheese; and 2 tablespoons dry sherry till fluffy. Stir in ½ of an 8-ounce can water chestnuts, drained and chopped; 2 slices bacon, crisp-cooked, drained, and crumbled; 2 tablespoons finely chopped onion; and 2 tablespoons chopped pimiento-stuffed green olives. Press into small bowl lined with clear plastic wrap. Cover; chill. To serve, invert bowl onto plate. Remove bowl and plastic wrap. Garnish with sliced pimiento-stuffed green olives, if desired. Serve with assorted crackers. Makes about 2⅔ cups.

## Menu

*Deviled Party Sandwiches*
*Apple-Date Sandwiches*
*Cottage-Bacon Dip*
*Vegetable Dippers*
*Blue Cheese Pâté*
*Assorted Crackers*
*Coffee Nog*

## Apple-Date Sandwiches (see photo, page 42)

1 8-ounce package cream
   cheese, softened
½ cup applesauce
½ cup snipped pitted dates

½ cup finely chopped celery
1 to 2 teaspoons lemon juice
16 slices firm-textured raisin
   bread

Beat together cream cheese and applesauce. Stir in dates, celery, and lemon juice. Spread mixture on *8* bread slices; top with remaining bread. Trim off crusts; cut in quarters diagonally. Wrap. Chill. Makes 32.

## Deviled Party Sandwiches (see photo, page 42)

Blend two 4½-ounce cans deviled ham and 1 tablespoon prepared mustard. Spread *about 1½ tablespoons* ham mixture on *each* of 12 thin whole wheat bread slices. Carefully spread two softened 3-ounce packages cream cheese with chives on both sides of 6 thin white bread slices. Place white bread slices atop *half* the whole wheat bread slices. Top with remaining whole wheat slices, ham side down. Trim crusts. Cut each sandwich in half; cut each half lengthwise to form fingers. Makes 24 sandwiches.

## Grapefruit Chiffon Cake

*Californians put their tangy grapefruit to good use in Grapefruit Chiffon Cake. This Sacramento Christmas favorite is so light and airy, it makes an ideal headliner for a holiday gathering in any part of the country.*

2¼ cups sifted cake flour
1½ cups sugar
  3 teaspoons baking powder
½ teaspoon salt
     • • •
½ cup cooking oil
5 egg yolks

1 tablespoon grated grapefruit
   peel
⅔ cup grapefruit juice
8 egg whites
½ teaspoon cream of tartar
Cream Cheese Frosting

Sift together flour, sugar, baking powder, and salt. Make a well in the center; add in order oil, egg yolks, grapefruit peel, and grapefruit juice. Beat till smooth. Beat egg whites with cream of tartar till very stiff peaks form. Pour flour mixture in a thin stream over surface of egg whites; fold in gently. Bake in ungreased 10-inch tube pan at 350° till done, 50 to 60 minutes. Invert; cool thoroughly. Remove cake from pan. Spread Cream Cheese Frosting over top of cake allowing some to drip down sides.

*Cream Cheese Frosting:* Cream together one 3-ounce package cream cheese, softened, and 1 cup sifted powdered sugar till light and fluffy. Beat in 1 tablespoon grated grapefruit peel and ½ teaspoon vanilla. Add enough grapefruit juice (1 to 2 teaspoons) to make of spreading consistency.

## Coffee Nog (see photo, page 42)

Mix 4 cups canned *or* dairy eggnog and 1½ cups milk. Dissolve 4 teaspoons instant coffee crystals in 2 tablespoons boiling water. Blend into milk mixture. Stir in ½ cup brandy, if desired. Chill well. Pour into mugs; top with a dollop of whipped dessert topping. Makes 8 (6-ounce) servings.

# Italian-American Christmas

An Italian-American Christmas or *Natale* is a joyous confection of religious and secular delights. Much of the holiday centers around food—and rightly so in a culture where creativity in the kitchen is as prized as it is expected. For days before Christmas, the fragrance of baking wafts through the house. The air vibrates with the scent of currants, citron, and other familiar holiday favorites. *Panettone,* the popular Christmas bread which used to take twenty-four hours to make, now is made much faster (see recipe, page 116). Other holiday favorites include *crostoli,* the popular fig cookies, *cucidata,* and all the candies the children love so much—the *frutta candita* (crystallized figs, oranges, and tangerines), and the *amaretti* (macaroons).

In the past, Christmas Eve was a fast day, so traditionally the evening meal is meatless. This does not mean it is sparse. On the contrary, a classic Christmas Eve supper might include as many as twenty-five different dishes, many of them seafood. It is a meal that Italian-Americans look forward to for weeks and savor all night long.

Accompanying the fish are fried or braised vegetables, hot or cold vegetable salads, and homemade pasta in abundance with a rich home-cooked tomato sauce. Then, of course, there are the ubiquitous sweets, always star performers during the Christmas holidays. As most Italian-Americans are from southern Italy or Sicily, the ever popular Sicilian *cannoli* are almost always on the Christmas Eve table. And so is *pignolata,* a rich dough that is cut into bits and fried. The small balls then are mixed together with nuts and honey and formed into a pyramid. Colored sugar candies are sprinkled over it to make an inviting (and edible) centerpiece—the object of continuous nibbling by all the youngsters in the family.

Gift giving formerly was associated with Epiphany or the Feast of the Three Kings, eight days after Christmas. The gifts were brought by *Befana,* an old woman who, according to legend, was visited by the Three Kings on their way to Bethlehem. She wanted to accompany them, but was delayed. When she followed later, she was too late to see the Christ Child, so she was doomed to roam the earth in search of Him. Gifts nowadays are usually exchanged Christmas day when relatives and friends visit.

Though the big holiday event is Christmas Eve supper, there is also a generous feast, this time with meat dishes, on Christmas day. Christmas is a family time, a time of eating, singing, and visiting.

*Menu*

(see photo, page 47)

*Ravioli*
*Spaghetti*
*with*
*Anchovy-Tomato Sauce*
*Oven Chicken Romano*
*Artichokes Parmesan*
*Hot Bean and Onion Salad*
*Cannoli Cake*
*Italian Fig Cookies*
*Chianti          Coffee*

## Oven Chicken Romano (see photo, page 47)

| | |
|---|---|
| 2 2½- to 3-pound ready-to-cook broiler-fryer chickens, cut up | 1⅓ cups seasoned fine dry bread crumbs |
| 1 cup butter, melted | ⅔ cup grated Romano cheese |
| | ½ cup snipped parsley |

Dip chicken into butter; roll in a mixture of bread crumbs, cheese, and parsley. Place pieces, skin side up, not touching in *two* greased large shallow baking pans. Top with remaining butter and crumb mixture. Bake at 375° till done, about 1 hour. Garnish with parsley, if desired. Makes 8 servings.

*For many Italians, chicken was long considered a delicacy reserved for special occasions such as Christmas. Although now served year-round on Italian-American tables, it is still a Christmas favorite.*

## Spaghetti with Anchovy-Tomato Sauce

*Pictured opposite:* This sumptuous Italian-American Christmas dinner includes everything from *Ravioli* to *Cannoli Cake* (for complete menu, see page 45).

¾ cup chopped onion
1 clove garlic, minced
2 tablespoons cooking oil
2 tablespoons anchovy paste
2 16-ounce cans tomatoes,
   mashed
2 6-ounce cans tomato paste
1 cup water
1 bay leaf

1 teaspoon sugar
1 teaspoon dried basil,
   crushed
½ teaspoon salt
¼ teaspoon pepper

• • •

Fine dry bread crumbs
Hot cooked spaghetti

In saucepan cook onion and garlic in oil till onion is tender. Blend in anchovy paste. Stir in tomatoes, tomato paste, water, bay leaf, sugar, basil, salt, and pepper. Simmer, uncovered, for 30 to 40 minutes. Meanwhile, carefully brown fine dry bread crumbs in a skillet without butter or shortening. Remove bay leaf from tomato mixture. Serve over cooked spaghetti. Pass bread crumbs to sprinkle atop. Makes 8 servings.

## Ravioli

Basic Pasta
2 tablespoons chopped onion
1 tablespoon olive oil
1 10-ounce package frozen
   chopped spinach
1 egg

½ cup ricotta cheese
¼ cup grated Parmesan cheese
1 cup finely diced cooked
   chicken
Spicy Tomato Sauce

*It is difficult to contemplate how the Neapolitan cuisine survived before the introduction to Italy in 1554 of the* pomodoro — *apple of gold — better known as the tomato. The first tomatoes brought from Mexico to Europe by Cortes were yellow. Today's tomatoes are red and are used in many Italian-American recipes such as Ravioli. Reportedly developed on shipboard by Genoese seamen as a way to use leftovers (*rabiole — "*things of little value"), Ravioli can be served as a main dish or side dish.*

On floured surface roll Basic Pasta as thin as possible; cover and let rest a few minutes. Repeat rolling and resting till dough measures 20x18-inches. Let rest 20 minutes. Cut into ten 18x2-inch strips.

Cook onion in oil till tender. Cook spinach according to package directions. Drain, pressing out excess liquid. Measure ½ cup of spinach (use remaining elsewhere). Combine egg, ricotta, and Parmesan. Add the ½ cup spinach, onion, and chicken; mix well. On one dough strip place 1 teaspoon of spinach mixture at 2-inch intervals beginning 1 inch from end of strip. Top with second strip of dough. Cut dough at 2-inch intervals making squares. Moisten edges with water; seal edges well with tines of fork. Repeat with remaining filling and pasta strips. Dry for 1 hour, turning once.

Cook ravioli in kettle of rapidly boiling salted water till tender, 8 to 10 minutes. Rinse ravioli in cold water; drain thoroughly. Place on a warm platter or serving dish. Pour Spicy Tomato Sauce over. Pass additional grated Parmesan, if desired. Makes 6 to 8 servings.

*Basic Pasta:* In bowl stir together 3 cups all-purpose flour and ¼ teaspoon salt. Make a well in center and add 2 eggs. Beat well. Stir in just enough of ⅓ cup water to form a very stiff dough. Turn out onto lightly floured surface. Knead till dough is smooth and elastic, about 10 minutes.

*Spicy Tomato Sauce:* Combine one 15-ounce can tomato sauce; one 8-ounce can tomatoes, cut up; 1 cup water; ¼ cup finely chopped onion; 2 tablespoons snipped parsley; 2 teaspoons sugar; 1 teaspoon salt; and 1 teaspoon dried oregano, crushed. Simmer 30 to 40 minutes, stirring often.

## Hot Bean and Onion Salad (see photo, page 47)

2 9-ounce packages frozen
    Italian green beans
1 small onion, sliced into
    rings
3 tablespoons olive oil

3 tablespoons red wine vinegar
½ teaspoon dried oregano,
    crushed
¼ teaspoon salt
Dash pepper

Cook green beans according to package directions. Drain. Mix hot beans with onion rings. In screw-top jar combine oil, vinegar, oregano, salt, and pepper; shake well. Pour over bean mixture. Toss lightly to coat. Serves 8.

*Natives of Tuscany are called "magiafagioli" — bean-eaters — because they are so fond of beans. Often, they serve them hot with a dressing as in Hot Bean and Onion Salad.*

## Artichokes Parmesan (see photo, page 47)

Wash 8 small artichokes. Cut off 1 inch of the top, the stem, and tips of leaves. Remove choke and any loose outer leaves. Brush cut edges with lemon juice. Cook 1 tablespoon sliced green onion and 1 clove garlic, minced, in 3 tablespoons butter *or* margarine till tender. Mix together 1½ cups soft bread crumbs, ¼ cup grated Parmesan cheese, and 2 tablespoons snipped parsley. Add onion mixture; mix lightly. Spoon into artichokes. Place in large saucepan, making sure artichokes won't tip over. Add water to saucepan to a depth of 1 inch. Bring to boil; reduce heat. Cover tightly; simmer for about 30 minutes. Add a little additional water during cooking if necessary. Makes 8 servings.

*Originally a wild thistle from Abyssinia, the artichoke is an abundant vegetable in Italy. Also grown in our country, it is a favorite among Italian-Americans, especially when stuffed and steamed as in this recipe.*

## Italian Fig Cookies (see photo, page 47)

8 ounces dried figs (1½ cups)
4 ounces light raisins (¾ cup)
¼ cup slivered almonds
¼ cup sugar
¼ cup hot water
¼ teaspoon ground cinnamon
    Dash pepper
2½ cups all-purpose flour
⅓ cup sugar

¼ teaspoon baking powder
½ cup shortening
2 tablespoons butter *or*
    margarine
½ cup milk
1 beaten egg
    Confectioners' Glaze
    (see recipe, page 112)

Put figs, raisins, and almonds through food grinder. In mixing bowl combine the ¼ cup sugar, hot water, cinnamon, and pepper; stir into fruit mixture. Set aside. Combine flour, ⅓ cup sugar, and baking powder. Cut in shortening and butter or margarine till mixture resembles the size of small peas. Stir in milk and egg till all dry mixture is moistened. Divide dough in half. On lightly floured surface roll each half to an 18x16-inch rectangle. Cut each rectangle into four strips 18x4-inches. Spread *about ⅓ cup* of the fig mixture over each strip dough. Roll dough up jelly-roll fashion, starting at long side. Cut each filled strip into six 3-inch lengths. Place cookies, seam side down, on un-greased cookie sheets. Curve each cookie slightly. Snip outer edge of curve 3 times. Bake at 350° till lightly browned, 20 to 25 minutes. Remove from cookie sheets and cool on rack. Frost with Confectioners' Glaze. At once, sprinkle with small multicolored decorative candies, if desired. Makes 24.

*An ancient Italian proverb tells you to "peel a fig for your friend, a peach for your enemy." Certainly figs are a way of life throughout Italy, where they grow in great profusion. The best figs are reputed to be the luscious purple figs of Sicily. So naturally these cookies, called cucidata, are Christmas favorites with many Italian-American families.*

## Cannoli Cake (kuh no′ lee)

3 eggs
1½ cups granulated sugar
1½ cups all-purpose flour
1½ teaspoons baking powder
¼ teaspoon salt
¾ cup milk
1 tablespoon butter *or*
    margarine
¾ cup granulated sugar
3 tablespoons cornstarch
¾ cup milk
1 pound ricotta cheese

1½ teaspoons vanilla
½ cup semisweet chocolate
    pieces, coarsely chopped
2 tablespoons candied citron,
    finely chopped
2 tablespoons pistachio nuts,
    ground
    Green food coloring
¾ cup shortening
1 teaspoon vanilla
3 cups sifted powdered sugar
    Milk

To prepare the cake, beat eggs till thick and lemon-colored. With electric mixer gradually beat in 1½ cups granulated sugar; beat 4 minutes. Stir together flour, baking powder, and salt. Add to egg mixture; stir just till blended. Heat ¾ cup milk and butter or margarine just till butter melts; stir into batter. Pour into 2 foil-lined 9x1½-inch round baking pans. Bake at 350° for 25 to 30 minutes. Cool completely; remove from pan. Split layers in half horizontally for a total of 4 cake layers.

For the filling, combine ¾ cup granulated sugar and cornstarch in a saucepan slowly stir in ¾ cup milk. Cook and stir till mixture is thickened and bubbly. Cover surface with wax paper; cool without stirring. With electric mixer beat ricotta till creamy; blend in cornstarch mixture and 1½ teaspoons vanilla. Stir in chopped chocolate pieces and chopped citron. Spread filling on *three* of the cake layers; stack. Top with remaining cake.

Tint pistachio nuts with a few drops green food coloring; set aside. With electric mixer cream shortening and 1 teaspoon vanilla thoroughly. Beat in sifted powdered sugar just till mixed. Stir in 2 tablespoons milk. Thin with more milk, if necessary, to make frosting of spreading consistency. Frost top and sides of cake. Sprinkle tinted pistachio nuts around cake edge. Chill before serving. Makes 16 servings.

*Cannoli were originally called* cappello di turco *(turkish hats), after the Saracens who first introduced sweets to Sicily in the ninth century. Cannoli are "big reeds" stuffed with a rich cream filling as tempting as the pipes of Pan to anyone, Sicilian or not. They are perennial Italian-American Christmas favorites. Our recipe, Cannoli Cake, is somewhat easier to make and is traditionally served at Sicilian weddings. It combines the rich* cannoli *filling with sponge cake and a creamy frosting.*

## Crostoli (cross toe′ lee)

2 tablespoons butter *or*
    margarine
1½ cups all-purpose flour
3 eggs
2 tablespoons granulated sugar

½ teaspoon almond extract
½ teaspoon orange extract
⅛ teaspoon salt
    Fat for frying
    Sifted powdered sugar

In a small mixing bowl cut butter into flour till it resembles the size of small peas. Combine eggs, granulated sugar, almond extract, orange extract, and salt. Stir into flour mixture. Turn out onto a lightly floured surface; knead till smooth. Cover and let rest for about 30 minutes. Divide dough into 2 equal pieces. Roll each half to a 12x6-inch rectangle. Cut each rectangle into sixteen 6x¾-inch strips. Carefully tie dough strips into knots. Fry a few at a time in deep hot fat (375°) till golden, about 3 minutes, turning once. Drain well. Cool and sprinkle with powdered sugar. Makes 32.

# German-American Christmas

Wreaths, fir trees, and the aroma of ginger and nutmeg wafting through the house, all evoke the spirit of Christmas in German-American households.

In fact, German-Americans have contributed much to what we now think of as a traditional "American" Christmas. Take, for example, our Christmas tree. The first Christmas tree in America seems to have made its appearance early in the nineteenth century in German areas of Pennsylvania. Another favorite German-American custom is the Advent wreath, which gave impetus to the wreath so many Americans now hang on their front doors. Also we owe a debt to German-Americans for our Christmas cards. It was Louis Prang, a German immigrant who began selling cards at Christmas.

Trimming the tree is part of the German-American festive fun. Many of the ornaments are edible and are joyfully made by children—popcorn balls, cranberry necklaces, and cookies shaped like bells, stars, and angels.

Marzipan (see recipe, page 186) is also very much a part of a German-American Christmas. Often it is purchased, but in some families it is still homemade. Part of the youngsters' fun is to shape the rich almond paste into miniature fruits and hang them on the tree or serve them to visitors.

Baking is as much a part of German-American Christmas as marzipan. Alternating with the scent of almond is the delicious aroma of *springerle,* *lebkuchen,* and cinnamon stars a'baking. Special holiday breads are baked ahead such as fruit-filled *hutzelbrot* and *stollen,* the famous Christmas yeast loaf shaped like a manger. (see recipe, page 112).

Customs vary from region to region. For Berliners, the Christmas Eve supper, served early in the evening, is relatively simple. The meal is followed with a *bunte teller* (a "colored plate"), a special cardboard plate with gay Christmas scenes. Each family member is served a *bunte teller* filled with candies, nuts, marzipan, cookies, and tangerines.

Bavarian Catholics wait until after midnight mass for a vast feast of sausages, numerous cold foods such as sauerkraut salad, a warm, spicy punch, and the ubiquitous cookies. Christmas carols are sung with spirit all evening long. Gifts are usually exchanged Christmas Eve—after dinner.

A substantial, hearty dinner for family and friends is the order of the day for Christmas Day. The main course in most German homes is roast goose. Accompanying the gleaming bird are assorted side dishes such as *spaetzle,* red cabbage and other vegetables, salads, and of course rich desserts.

## Sauerkraut Salad

*A popular German dish, Sauerkraut Salad is sometimes garnished with hard-cooked eggs or tiny beets. The sweet-sour technique is especially popular among German-Americans in Pennsylvania and the Milwaukee area.*

1 16-ounce can sauerkraut
¼ cup finely chopped celery
¼ cup chopped onion
¼ cup shredded carrot
¾ cup sugar
¼ cup vinegar

Drain and snip sauerkraut, reserving liquid. Rinse sauerkraut under cold running water. Mix drained sauerkraut, celery, onion, and carrot. In a saucepan combine reserved liquid, sugar, and vinegar; bring to boiling, stirring constantly. Remove from heat; pour over vegetable mixture. Toss to coat evenly. Chill salad several hours or overnight. Makes 6 servings.

## German Potato Salad

| | |
|---|---|
| 10 to 12 slices bacon (½ pound) | 1 teaspoon celery seed |
| ½ cup chopped onion | ½ cup vinegar |
| 2 tablespoons all-purpose flour | 6 cups sliced, cooked potatoes |
| 2 tablespoons sugar | 2 hard-cooked eggs, sliced |

Cook bacon till crisp; drain and crumble, reserving ¼ cup drippings. Cook onion in reserved drippings till tender. Blend in flour, sugar, celery seed, 1½ teaspoons salt, and dash pepper. Add vinegar and 1 cup water. Cook and stir till thickened. Add bacon, potatoes, and eggs. Heat well, tossing lightly. Garnish with parsley, if desired. Serves 8 to 10.

*Served warm, this version of potato salad is a far cry from the salad Americans eat at summer picnics. The contrasting sugar and vinegar dressing on the potatoes and bacon makes this a hearty, zesty complement to roast goose or other fowl.*

## Spaetzle (spet′zel)

| | |
|---|---|
| 2 cups all-purpose flour | ¾ cup milk |
| 1 teaspoon salt | ½ cup fine dry bread crumbs |
| 2 eggs | ¼ cup butter, melted |

Stir together flour and salt. Combine eggs and milk; stir into flour mixture. Place in coarse-sieved (¼-inch holes) colander. Hold over kettle of boiling salted water. Press batter through colander for spaetzle. Cook and stir 5 minutes; drain. Combine crumbs and butter; sprinkle over spaetzle. Makes 4 cups.

*Spaetzle, Swabian egg dumplings, are sometimes called noodles. They are best cooked al dente—not overcooked. A traditional accompaniment to sauerbraten and other roasts in southern Germany, Spaetzle are usually sprinkled with buttered bread crumbs. Spaetzle is to southern Germans what potatoes are to northerners. German-Americans enjoy the best of both crops and eat both Spaetzle and potatoes—though not at the same meal.*

## Firetong Punch

Heat one ⅘-quart bottle dry red wine with ½ cup sugar, 6 whole cloves, one 3x½-inch strip orange peel, ½ cup orange juice, one 2x½-inch strip lemon peel, and ¼ cup lemon juice. *Do not boil.* Pour hot mixture into a flame-proof punch bowl. Soak 8 sugar cubes in ¼ cup *heated* rum; place cubes in a strainer over punch. Ignite sugar cubes; as they flame gradually spoon more heated rum from a ladle over cubes. When sugar has melted, add a few orange slices. Serve hot. Makes about 10 (4-ounce) servings.

## Roast Goose with Apple-Raisin Stuffing

| | |
|---|---|
| 1 10- to 12-pound ready-to-cook goose | 1 cup raisins |
| 2 tablespoons butter | ½ cup chopped almonds |
| 1½ cups chopped apple | ½ cup chicken broth |
| ¾ cup chopped onion | ¼ cup snipped parsley |
| 4 cups soft bread cubes | 1 teaspoon dried marjoram, crushed |

Finely chop goose liver; cook in butter till done. Cover apple and onion with water; simmer till tender. Drain. Mix onion mixture, liver, remaining ingredients, 1 teaspoon salt, and ⅛ teaspoon pepper. Toss to combine. Use stuffing to fill goose cavity; roast according to chart on page 91. (Or bake stuffing in 1½-quart covered casserole at 325° for 45 minutes.) Serves 10 to 12.

*Roast goose stuffed with apples illustrates a basic of German cooking—combining fruits with meat or game. Apfel, Nuss, and Mandelkern—apple, nut, and almond—symbolize the foods of Christmas according to an old German rhyme. No wonder they are combined with the Christmas goose.*

## Springerle (spring′ er lee)

| | |
|---|---|
| 4 eggs | 1 teaspoon baking soda |
| 2 cups sifted powdered sugar | ¼ teaspoon salt |
| Few drops anise oil | ¼ cup butter, melted |
| 3½ cups all-purpose flour | Aniseed |

Beat eggs till light. On high speed of electric mixer gradually add sugar, beating till like a soft meringue. Add anise oil. Stir together flour, soda, and salt; stir in butter. Blend into egg mixture, using low speed. Cover tightly and refrigerate for 3 to 4 hours. Divide dough in fourths. On floured surface roll each fourth to an 8-inch square. Let stand 1 minute. Dust springerle rolling pin or mold with flour; roll or press dough hard enough to make a clear design. Cut cookies apart. Place on floured surface; cover and *let stand overnight.* Grease cookie sheets and sprinkle each with 1½ to 2 teaspoons aniseed. Brush excess flour from cookies; rub underside of each cookie lightly with cold water. Place on cookie sheets. Bake at 300° till light straw color, 15 to 20 minutes. Makes 2 dozen cookies.

## Cinnamon Stars

Using fine blade of food grinder slowly add 2 cups blanched almonds to grinder. Mix ground almonds and 1 teaspoon ground cinnamon. Beat 3 egg whites to soft peaks. Slowly add 2 cups sifted powdered sugar and ½ teaspoon grated lemon peel, beating with electric mixer till well blended, about 5 minutes. Set aside ¾ cup egg white mixture; fold almond mixture into remaining egg white mixture. On floured surface, pat or roll dough to ⅛-inch thickness. (If dough is too soft, let stand at room temperature till stiffened.) Cut in star shapes with cookie cutter. Place on well-greased and floured cookie sheet. Place about 1 teaspoon reserved egg white mixture on each star; spread to points. Bake at 375° for 10 to 12 minutes. Makes 36.

## Dark Pfeffernuesse (fef′ fer noos)

| | |
|---|---|
| ⅓ cup packed brown sugar | ¼ teaspoon baking powder |
| ⅓ cup dark corn syrup | ¼ teaspoon vanilla |
| 2 tablespoons milk | ⅛ teaspoon ground cloves |
| 2 tablespoons shortening | ⅛ teaspoon ground cardamom |
| 1 egg | 2½ cups all-purpose flour |
| ½ teaspoon anise extract | Sifted powdered sugar |

Mix brown sugar, syrup, milk, and shortening; heat to boiling. Cool; beat in egg. Add anise extract, baking powder, vanilla, cloves, cardamom, ⅛ teaspoon salt, and dash pepper; mix well. Mix in enough of the flour to make a very stiff dough, kneading in last addition. On a board dusted with powdered sugar shape into rolls ⅜ *or* ¾ inch thick. Cut each roll in pieces ⅜ *or* ¾ inch long. Bake on ungreased cookie sheet at 375° till brown, 8 to 12 minutes. Cool 1 to 2 minutes; remove from sheet. (Cookies harden on standing.) For soft cookies, store in airtight container with apple slice. Makes 32 dozen small (⅜-inch) or 8 dozen large (¾-inch).

## Lebkuchen (laib′ koo kuhn)

1 egg
¾ cup packed brown
   sugar
½ cup honey
½ cup dark molasses
3 tablespoons brandy
½ teaspoon grated lemon
   peel
1 teaspoon lemon juice
4 cups all-purpose flour

1 teaspoon ground cinnamon
½ teaspoon baking soda
½ teaspoon ground cloves
½ teaspoon ground ginger
¼ teaspoon ground cardamom
½ cup chopped almonds
½ cup finely chopped mixed
   candied fruits and peels

• • •

Lemon Glaze

In a mixing bowl beat egg; add brown sugar. Beat till light and fluffy. Stir in honey, dark molasses, brandy, grated lemon peel, and lemon juice. Mix thoroughly. Stir together flour, cinnamon, baking soda, cloves, ginger, and cardamom. Blend into molasses mixture. Stir in almonds and candied fruits and peels. Chill dough several hours. Divide dough in half. On a lightly floured surface, roll each half to a 14x9-inch rectangle; cut into 3x2-inch cookies. Bake on a lightly greased cookie sheet at 350° about 12 minutes. Cool slightly; remove from cookie sheet and cool on rack. While cookies are still warm brush with Lemon Glaze. Makes 3½ dozen cookies.

*Lemon Glaze:* Combine 1 beaten egg white, 1 tablespoon lemon juice, and dash salt. Stir in 1½ cups sifted powdered sugar.

*Ginger and Christmas go hand in hand in German baking. Lebkuchen, or ginger cookies, are traditional favorites in southern Germany and among midwestern German-Americans. Actually, the flavoring in Lebkuchen is more delicate than in gingerbread. Use the lemon glaze on other cookies as well as on a Christmas coffee cake.*

## German Fruit Bread

1 cup chopped dried pears
1 cup chopped pitted dried
   prunes
4 cups water
2 tablespoons shortening
1 tablespoon sugar
1½ teaspoons salt

2 packages active dry yeast
5½ to 5¾ cups all-purpose flour
½ teaspoon ground cinnamon
¼ teaspoon ground cloves

• • •

½ cup raisins
½ cup chopped walnuts

In a medium saucepan cook dried pears and prunes in the water according to package directions; drain well, reserving 2 cups liquid. Set fruit aside. Stir shortening, sugar, and salt into reserved liquid. Cool to lukewarm. In a large mixing bowl combine yeast, *2 cups* of the flour, cinnamon, and cloves. Add reserved liquid mixture and beat at low speed of electric mixer for ½ minute, scraping sides of bowl constantly. Beat 3 minutes more at high speed. By hand, stir in drained pears and prunes, raisins, walnuts, and enough of the remaining flour to make a moderately stiff dough. Turn out onto a lightly floured surface. Knead till smooth and elastic (about 8 minutes). Place in a greased bowl, turning once to grease surface. Let rise in warm place till double (about 1 hour). Punch dough down; divide in half. Cover and let rest 10 minutes. Shape into 2 loaves. Place in two greased 8½x4½x2½-inch loaf pans. Let rise in a warm place till almost double (about 30 minutes). Bake at 375° till golden brown, 35 to 40 minutes. Cover loosely with foil during the last 15 minutes of baking time to prevent overbrowning. Remove from baking pans. Cool on rack. Makes 2 loaves.

*This delicious fruit bread is a relative of hutzelbrot, a fruit bread popular in southern Germany. Full of fruits, nuts, and spices, its fragrance while baking spells magic in the house at the holiday season. Freshly baked, sweet nut and fruit breads combined with fresh hot coffee are the makings of a kaffeeklatsch, a happy German-American custom!*

# Polish-American Christmas

Christmas Eve, called the Festival of the Star in memory of the star over Bethlehem the night Christ was born, is a quietly joyful time with many religious memories and much symbolism for Polish-Americans.

Preparation for this festival is begun early in the day. In traditional homes, a sheaf of wheat is placed in a corner of each room, as a remembrance of the stable in Bethlehem. The wheat also is a token to ensure a fine Christmas feast and symbolizes hope for the next year's harvest. The table is set with straw on or under the white tablecloth. Often, butter is molded in the shape of a reclining lamb and attached to a straw mat as a table centerpiece. An extra place is set for the Unknown Traveler or, according to an old Polish belief, the Christ Child.

In some homes twelve courses are served at the Christmas Eve meal with one dish symbolizing each of the Apostles. Other Polish-Americans serve nine courses to represent the nine months of Mary's pregnancy before Christ's birth. Since this supper is traditionally one of fasting, the dishes are meatless. Sometimes the dishes are selected to represent natural forces— one course from the woods (probably mushrooms), one from the fields (a wheat dish such as the traditional *kutia*), fish from the water (usually carp), and fruit from the orchard (most likely the popular *kompot z suszu*).

As soon as the first evening star is sighted on Christmas Eve, the celebration begins. The first and most important ritual in the Polish-American Christmas Eve supper, after father says grace, is the breaking of *oplatki,* thin wafers about 6x4 inches stamped with Nativity scenes and blessed by the priest. First, the oldest family member breaks a piece with the next oldest. They exchange kisses and good wishes for the new year. Then, the next oldest turns to the next in progression and on down to the youngest child.

In communities where many Polish-American families live, certain traditions remain strong. The star man, often a priest or family elder, still visits after supper to ask the children in the family to recite their catechism or school lessons, to be sure they have been good all year. Then, the family joins together to sing carols, in both Polish and English, until it is time for midnight mass, *pasterka.*

Christmas Eve is still a marvelous night for Polish-Americans. It is indeed *wesolych swigt—*a happy holiday!

## Kutia (koo' tee ah)

*Wheat plays a dual role in a Polish-American Christmas. First, as part of the decor to suggest the manger, and second, on the table as Kutia, a ritual dish always served Christmas Eve. Symbolically, Kutia represents a good harvest.*

| | |
|---|---|
| ⅔ cup cracked wheat cereal | ½ cup honey |
| ⅓ cup poppy seed | ¼ cup slivered almonds |
| ⅔ cup raisins | 1 teaspoon vanilla |
| ½ cup chopped walnuts | ¼ cup whipping cream |

Cook wheat in 3 cups water till tender, about 1 hour. Drain. Place cooked wheat, half at a time, in a blender container; cover and blend into a paste. Cook poppy seeds in 1 cup boiling water till soft, about 10 minutes. Drain. Mix together wheat paste, poppy seed, raisins, walnuts, honey, almonds, and vanilla. Chill. Stir in the unwhipped cream. Makes 4 cups.

## Polish Apple Squares

*Apples, a winter fruit and a symbol of a good harvest, make an especially appropriate Christmas dessert for the Polish-American holiday table. This elegant apple dessert is particularly rich and suited to the occasion.*

1¾ cups all-purpose flour
½ cup sugar
2 teaspoons baking powder
½ cup butter *or* margarine
2 eggs

1 cup dairy sour cream
1 teaspoon vanilla
Apple Filling
Powdered sugar

Stir together flour, sugar, and baking powder. Cut in butter till pieces resemble small peas. Combine eggs, sour cream, and vanilla; add to flour mixture. Stir till well mixed. Spread *half* of the batter into greased 9x9x2-inch baking pan. Bake at 350° for 15 minutes. Spread Apple Filling over layer in pan. Carefully spoon remaining batter atop. Bake at 350° for 35 minutes. Sprinkle with powdered sugar. Cut into squares. Makes 16.

*Apple Filling:* Peel, core, and finely chop 1½ pounds cooking apples. In a bowl combine the finely chopped apples, ½ cup raisins, ¼ cup sugar, 1 teaspoon ground cinnamon, and 1 teaspoon vanilla.

## Kompot Z Suszu

Cut up large pieces of one 8-ounce package mixed dried fruits. Mix fruits and 2½ cups water. Cover; bring to boiling. Reduce heat; simmer for 30 to 35 minutes. Stir in ½ cup sugar, 1 teaspoon grated lemon peel, 1 tablespoon lemon juice, and 2 inches stick cinnamon. Return to boiling; reduce heat. Simmer 10 minutes more. Chill. Remove cinnamon. Serves 4 to 6.

## Gingerbread Layer Dessert (see photo, page 55)

*This American version of the Polish gingerbread layer cake is a rich and sumptuous dessert cake. And, of course, it's especially fitting for the all-important Christmas Eve supper celebrated by Polish-Americans. It's said to have been Abraham Lincoln's favorite Christmas dessert, too.*

1 cup honey
1 teaspoon ground ginger
1 teaspoon ground cinnamon
½ teaspoon ground cloves
2¼ cups all-purpose flour
1 teaspoon baking powder
1 teaspoon baking soda
½ cup packed brown sugar
½ cup butter *or* margarine

1 egg
½ teaspoon grated lemon peel
1¼ cups buttermilk
1½ cups whipping cream
1 tablespoon granulated sugar
2 teaspoons shredded orange peel
1 1-ounce square semisweet chocolate, grated

In saucepan combine honey, ginger, cinnamon, and cloves. Stir together flour, baking powder, soda, and ½ teaspoon salt. In large mixing bowl cream brown sugar and butter till light and fluffy. Gradually beat in honey mixture using high speed of electric mixer. Add egg and lemon peel; mix well. Add flour mixture and buttermilk alternately; stirring well after each addition. Pour into 2 greased and lightly floured 8x1½-inch round baking pans. Bake at 350° for 30 to 35 minutes. Cool in pans 10 minutes. Turn out onto rack; cool completely. Whip cream with granulated sugar till soft peaks form. Spread one layer with *half* of the whipped cream. Sprinkle with *half* of the orange peel and *half* the grated chocolate. Top with second layer. Frost with remaining whipped cream; sprinkle with remaining orange peel and chocolate. Chill at least 1 hour in the refrigerator.

## Pierogi (pie' row ghee)

| | |
|---|---|
| 1 beaten egg | 1 tablespoon butter *or* |
| 1 cup water | margarine, softened |
| ½ teaspoon salt | 1½ teaspoons sugar |
| 3 cups all-purpose flour | ¼ teaspoon salt |
| 1½ cups cream-style cottage | 1 cup chopped onion |
| cheese, drained | 6 tablespoons butter *or* |
| 1 beaten egg yolk | margarine |

Combine egg, water, and salt. Stir in flour to make a stiff dough. Knead till smooth. On lightly floured surface roll till less than ⅛ inch thick. Cut into 3-inch circles. Combine cottage cheese, egg yolk, 1 tablespoon butter, sugar, and salt. To make pierogi, place *1 teaspoon* filling on each dough circle. Fold over pressing edges together tightly with fork; set aside. Cook onion in the 6 tablespoons butter till lightly browned, about 20 minutes. Keep warm. Meanwhile, in large kettle bring 12 cups salted water to boiling. Add 10 to 12 pierogi; cook for 8 to 10 minutes. Drain on paper toweling. Transfer to serving dish and keep warm. Repeat till all are cooked. Serve topped with fried onions and butter. Makes 8 servings.

*The blintz-like Pierogi is a year-round favorite in Polish-American households and lends itself to various treatments, either stuffed with cottage- or pot-cheese and egg or with sauerkraut, potatoes, mushrooms, or fruit. Tender morsels, Pierogi are a standard accompaniment to the Christmas Eve feast.*

## Poppy Seed Loaf (see photo, page 55)

| | |
|---|---|
| 2 packages active dry yeast | 1 cup boiling water |
| 5¼ to 5¾ cups all-purpose flour | ¾ cup poppy seed |
| 1½ cups milk | • • • |
| ⅓ cup sugar | ½ cup chopped nuts |
| ⅓ cup shortening | ⅓ cup honey |
| 1 teaspoon salt | 1 teaspoon grated lemon peel |
| 3 eggs | 1 stiffly beaten egg white |

In large mixing bowl combine yeast with *2 cups* of the flour. In saucepan heat together milk, sugar, shortening, and salt just till warm (115-120°), stirring constantly. Add to dry ingredients. Add eggs. Beat at low speed of electric mixer ½ minute, scraping bowl constantly. Beat 3 minutes at high speed. By hand, stir in enough of the remaining flour to make a moderately stiff dough. Turn out onto lightly floured surface; knead till smooth and satiny (5 to 10 minutes). Shape into ball. Place in a lightly greased bowl, turn once to grease surface. Cover and let the dough rise in warm place till double (about 1 hour).

Meanwhile, pour boiling water over poppy seed; let stand 30 minutes. Drain thoroughly. Place poppy seed in blender container; cover and blend till ground. (Or put through the finest blade of food grinder.) Stir in chopped nuts, honey, and grated lemon peel. Fold in the stiffly beaten egg white. Punch bread dough down. Divide dough into 2 parts. Cover and let rest 10 minutes. On lightly floured surface roll one part of the dough to a 24x8-inch rectangle; spread with *half* the poppy seed mixture. Roll up jelly-roll style, starting with the 8-inch side; seal. Place, seam side down, in greased 8½x4½x2½-inch loaf pan. Repeat with remaining dough and filling. Cover; let rise till double (30 to 45 minutes). Bake at 350° for 35 to 40 minutes. Remove from pans; cool on rack. Makes 2 loaves.

*In Polish lore, poppy seeds are symbols of good luck and are abundantly used at all festive occasions. A poppy seed and honey paste is a popular filling for this Christmas loaf bread and for cakes and cookies favored by Polish-Americans year-round.*

# Scandinavian-American Christmas

If Christmas didn't exist, Scandinavians would have had to invent it. They take to Christmas as if it were their own creation. Much of what Americans love about the holiday actually is Scandinavian—the barrage of baking weeks before, teasing elves, reindeer, hauling the fir tree through the snow, and festive gatherings for the whole family.

Not all Scandinavians celebrate Christmas the same way. For Swedes, the season begins on December 13, St. Lucia's Day, when the eldest daughter, who wears a Lucia crown of pine boughs or bilberry twigs (with seven lighted candles in the crown), takes her parents a tray of "wake up" steaming hot coffee and Lucia "cats," special saffron buns. She is dressed in a white dress with a red sash and is accompanied by her brothers and sisters, also dressed in white and with tinsel in their hair.

By Christmas Eve most Scandinavian households are a Christmas wonderland of heavenly cinnamon-and-cardamom scents, *julenissen* (elves) cut out of folded colored paper or thin painted wood, and candlesticks "planted" everywhere—on mantels, windowsills, and tables. Sometimes the candlesticks even have prongs to hold fresh shiny apples.

The magnet of much of the baking and decorating is the Christmas tree. Part of the pre-Christmas fun is for the youngsters to join in the cookie cutting and tree decorating. This takes place on Christmas Eve morning when the family joins together to decorate the tree, happily nibbling cookies and sipping coffee or glögg as they work.

Cookies and homemade caramels wrapped in silver or gold paper along with angels, reindeer, and yarn ornaments are hung on the traditional Swedish tree. Danes decorate their trees with garlands of bright red-and-white Danish paper flags, gilded apples and walnuts, hearts woven of shiny paper, heart-shaped baskets or cups filled with tiny marzipan sculptures, sugary morsels, and gingerbread cutouts.

Scandinavian hospitality outdoes itself at Christmas-time. According to Danish tradition, it is considered unlucky if a visitor during the holidays—even a stranger—leaves the house without having sampled several of the holiday cookies and baked goods. Among Norwegians, December 26 is the day on which families visit one another and "harvest the tree" of the tiny baskets that are filled with delicious Christmas tidbits.

The elaborate Christmas Eve dinner begins with a smorgasbord of hot and cold treats such as fruit soup, pickled herring with fresh dill, meatballs, headcheese, pâtés, sausage, and numerous cheeses. The main course might be ham or some pork dish; for Danes it is a roast goose. Swedes, Norwegians, and Finns all enjoy lutefisk, a large, codlike fish soaked in a lye solution weeks ahead, washed thoroughly, then poached and served with boiled potatoes and melted butter. Norwegians enjoy lefse, a rolled pancake made from mashed potatoes and eaten with lingonberries. Essential to the meal is the legendary rice pudding with a lucky almond inside.

The main meal on Christmas Day in Scandinavian-American homes is likely to be another elaborate smorgasbord, cold this time. It is no wonder they say *"god jul"* or *"glaedelig jul"* with such genuine happiness.

## Goose with Prunes and Apples

| | |
|---|---|
| 1 cup pitted dried prunes | Pepper |
| Boiling water | 3 large apples, peeled |
| 1 10- to 12-pound ready- | and quartered |
| to-cook goose | 1 medium onion, quartered |
| Salt | Poached Apples |

Cover the prunes with boiling water; let stand 2 minutes, then drain. Rinse the goose and remove excess fat from the body cavity. Pat goose dry with paper toweling. Sprinkle the goose cavity with salt and pepper. Combine drained prunes, quartered apples, and the onion. Spoon the prune mixture into the cavity of goose. Tuck the legs under band of skin or tie legs to the tail; tuck wings behind the shoulders.

Place the goose, breast side up, on rack in shallow roasting pan. Roast, uncovered, at 325° till done, 2½ to 3 hours. Remove the fat from pan several times during roasting. Remove and discard prune mixture. Serve goose with Poached Apples on warm serving platter. Makes 8 servings.

*Poached Apples:* Halve and core 4 large cooking apples. In 2-quart saucepan combine 3 cups water and ¾ cup sugar. Bring to boiling; boil 3 minutes. Add the apple halves; cover and simmer till just tender, about 8 minutes. Remove apples with slotted spoon; keep warm. To serve, fill centers of apples with currant jelly. Arrange apples around goose.

*Roast goose Christmas Eve is a Danish expectation — long anticipated. Like other northern Europeans, the Danes and Danish-Americans enjoy the contrast of cooking fruit with meat or fowl. For the tenderest goose, choose a young one, no more than twelve pounds.*

## Sweet-Sour Red Cabbage

| | |
|---|---|
| 6 cups shredded red cabbage | 2 tablespoons vinegar |
| ¼ cup currant jelly | ¾ teaspoon caraway seed |
| 2 tablespoons butter *or* | ½ teaspoon salt |
| margarine | |

In large saucepan cook shredded cabbage in boiling salted water till just tender, 10 to 12 minutes; drain well. In same saucepan combine the currant jelly, butter or margarine, vinegar, caraway seed, and salt. Heat and stir till butter is melted. Return drained cabbage to pan; toss and stir till the cabbage is heated through. Makes 4 or 5 servings.

*This so-called Christmas vegetable among Scandinavian-Americans not only makes a superb accompaniment with ham, pork or goose, but also adds a colorful touch to the holiday table.*

## Herring Salad

| | |
|---|---|
| 1 cup cubed pickled herring | 1 cup mayonnaise *or* salad |
| 1 cup cubed cooked potatoes | dressing |
| 1 cup cubed cooked beets | 2 tablespoons sugar |
| ½ cup chopped peeled apple | 2 tablespoons vinegar |
| ¼ cup chopped onion | 2 tablespoons dry sherry |
| ¼ cup chopped green pepper | |

In mixing bowl combine pickled herring, cubed potatoes, beets, chopped apple, onion, and green pepper. Stir together mayonnaise or salad dressing, sugar, vinegar, and dry sherry. Toss mayonnaise mixture with herring mixture. Chill the salad thoroughly. Makes 6 to 8 servings.

*Herring Salad in Scandinavian countries consists of many variations. Sometimes whipped cream or sour cream is substituted for the mayonnaise. Whatever the preference, most Scandinavians would agree, it wouldn't be a Christmas without Herring Salad.*

## Cardamom Braid

In mixing bowl combine ¾ cup all-purpose flour, 1 package active dry yeast, and 1 teaspoon ground cardamom. Heat together ¾ cup milk, ⅓ cup sugar, ¼ cup butter *or* margarine, and ½ teaspoon salt just till warm (115-120°), stirring constantly. Add to dry mixture in mixing bowl; add 1 egg. Beat at low speed with electric mixer for ½ minute, scraping sides of bowl constantly. Beat 3 minutes at high speed. By hand, stir in enough of 2 cups all-purpose flour to make a moderately soft dough. Knead on lightly floured surface till dough is smooth and elastic (5 to 8 minutes).

Place in greased bowl; turn once. Cover; let rise till double (about 1¼ hours). Punch down. Turn out onto lightly floured surface and divide dough in thirds; form into 3 balls. Let dough rest 10 minutes. Roll each ball to a 16-inch long rope. Line up the 3 ropes, 1 inch apart, on greased baking sheet. Braid loosely beginning in middle and working toward ends. Pinch ends together and tuck under. Cover; let dough rise till almost double (about 40 minutes). Brush the surface with a little milk. Sprinkle 1 tablespoon sugar atop. Bake at 375° for 18 to 20 minutes. Makes 1 loaf.

## Fattigmann (fah′ tee mahn)

| | |
|---|---|
| **6 egg yolks** | **2 cups all-purpose flour** |
| **¼ cup sugar** | **1 teaspoon ground cardamom** |
| **1 tablespoon butter, melted** | **Fat for frying** |
| **⅓ cup whipping cream** | **Powdered sugar** |

Beat egg yolks till thick and lemon-colored; gradually beat in sugar. Gently stir in butter. Whip cream till soft peaks form. Fold into egg yolk mixture. Stir together flour, cardamom, and ½ teaspoon salt; fold into egg yolk mixture. Chill. Divide dough in half. Roll one half thinly on lightly floured surface. Cut in 2-inch wide strips, then cut diagonally at 3-inch intervals to make diamonds. Cut 1-inch slits lengthwise in center of each diamond; pull one end through. Repeat with remaining dough. Fry a few at a time in deep hot fat (375°) till very light golden, 1 to 1½ minutes. Drain cookies on paper toweling. While warm, dust with powdered sugar. Makes 5 dozen cookies.

## Glögg

| | |
|---|---|
| **3 ⅘-quart bottles dry red wine** | **2 to 3 tablespoons broken stick cinnamon** |
| **1 cup raisins** | **½ teaspoon whole cloves** |
| **¼ cup sweet vermouth** | **Peel from 1 orange** |
| **6 whole cardamom pods, crushed slightly** | **1 cup sugar** |
| | **1 cup whole blanched almonds** |

In saucepan mix *1 bottle* of wine, raisins, and vermouth. Place cardamom, cinnamon, and cloves in cheesecloth bag; add to wine mixture. Simmer, covered, 15 minutes. Add peel; simmer 5 minutes. Remove spices and peel. Stir in remaining wine and sugar; heat through. Add almonds. Serve hot with spoons to scoop up raisins and almonds. Makes 24 (4-ounce) servings.

## Stags' Antlers (see photo, page 61)

(see photo, page 61)

*Norwegian-Americans call them hojotetakk, or Stag's Antlers. Light, delicate, and crisp, like most Norwegian cookies, these are a holiday favorite in the old—and new—country.*

¾ cup sugar
½ cup butter *or* margarine
2 egg yolks
1 egg
¼ cup milk
½ teaspoon ground cardamom
2¼ cups all-purpose flour
½ cup cornstarch
1 teaspoon baking soda
Sugar

In mixing bowl cream together ¾ cup sugar and butter till light and fluffy. Beat in egg yolks and whole egg. Add milk and cardamom; mix well. Thoroughly stir together flour, cornstarch, baking soda, and ½ teaspoon salt. Add to egg mixture; blend thoroughly. Chill. On lightly floured surface roll *half* of the dough to a 12x6-inch rectangle. Cut into thirty-six 2x1-inch strips. Place on ungreased cookie sheets. Cut 2 slits in each strip, ¾-inch from each end and cutting across a little more than half the width of the strip. Curve to open slits. Sprinkle with additional sugar. Bake at 350° till cookies are golden, 12 to 15 minutes. Cool on racks. Repeat with the remaining dough. Store the cookies in airtight container. Makes 72 cookies.

## Currant-Almond Bars

1 cup butter *or* margarine
¾ cup sugar
4 egg yolks
1 teaspoon grated lemon peel
3 tablespoons lemon juice
3 tablespoons water
2 cups all-purpose flour
1 teaspoon baking powder
½ teaspoon salt
4 stiffly beaten egg whites
¾ cup currants
1 tablespoon sugar
½ cup chopped almonds, toasted

In mixing bowl cream butter and ¾ cup sugar till light and fluffy. Add egg yolks, one at a time, beating well after each. Stir in lemon peel, lemon juice, and water. Stir together flour, baking powder, and salt; stir into creamed mixture. Fold in egg whites. Pour into well-greased and floured 15½x10½x1-inch baking pan. Toss currants with 1 tablespoon sugar to coat. Sprinkle currants and almonds evenly over batter. Bake at 350° for 20 to 25 minutes. Let cool 10 minutes before removing from pan; cool on rack. When thoroughly cool, cut into diamond-shaped pieces. Makes 48.

## Rice Porridge

*Risengrod or risgrynsgrot is equally popular with all Scandinavians, but only Danes serve this porridge at the beginning of the meal. A single almond is hidden in the pudding. The one who finds it in his portion receives a prize.*

3 cups milk
½ cup long grain rice
⅓ cup raisins
¼ teaspoon salt
1 whole blanched almond
Butter *or* margarine
¼ cup sugar
¼ teaspoon ground cinnamon

In heavy, medium saucepan bring milk to boiling; gradually stir in rice, raisins, and salt. Cover and cook over low heat, stirring occasionally, till most of milk is absorbed and rice is creamy, 30 to 45 minutes. Stir in almond; spoon into dessert dishes. Serve warm with pats of butter or margarine; sprinkle with a mixture of the sugar and cinnamon. Makes 6 servings.

## Lucia Buns

| | |
|---|---|
| 2 tablespoons boiling water | 1¼ cups milk |
| ¼ teaspoon powdered saffron | ½ cup butter *or* margarine |
| 3½ to 4 cups all-purpose flour | ⅓ cup sugar |
| | 1 teaspoon salt |
| 1 package active dry yeast | 1 egg |

Pour boiling water over saffron and let stand. In large mixing bowl combine *2 cups* of the flour and the yeast. In saucepan heat together milk, butter, sugar, and salt just till warm (115-120°), stirring constantly. Add to dry mixture in mixing bowl; add egg and saffron mixture. Beat at low speed with electric mixer for ½ minute, scraping sides of bowl constantly. Beat 3 minutes at high speed. By hand, stir in enough of the remaining flour to make a soft dough. Knead on lightly floured surface for 8 to 10 minutes. Place dough in a greased bowl, turning once to grease surface. Cover; let the dough rise in warm place till double (about 1½ hours).

Punch dough down. Turn out on lightly floured surface. Divide dough in quarters. Cut each quarter into 12 equal pieces. Roll each piece of dough into a 12-inch long rope. On lightly greased baking sheet, form rope into an S-shape, coiling the ends in snail fashion. Repeat with remaining ropes. (For double buns, place two of the S-shaped pieces together to form a cross.) Cover and let dough rise till nearly double (about 40 minutes). Bake at 375° for 12 to 15 minutes. Makes 48 single or 24 double buns.

*These saffron-colored Lucia Buns or Lucia cats are absolutely essential to a Swedish-American Christmas. Associated with St. Lucia's Day, December 13th, they are enjoyed throughout the holiday season. Often the buns are baked ahead and frozen, then used as the holiday progresses. Youngsters in the family enjoy shaping the dough into fancy forms. Most popular is an S-shape, but a Swedish-American mother usually has a wide repertoire of designs at her quick fingertips.*

## Finnish Viipuri Twist (vie′ puh ree)

| | |
|---|---|
| 5½ to 5¾ cups all-purpose flour | ¾ cup sugar |
| | ¼ cup butter *or* margarine |
| 2 packages active dry yeast | 1 teaspoon salt |
| ½ teaspoon ground cardamom | 2 eggs |
| ½ teaspoon ground nutmeg | 1 tablespoon water |
| 2 cups milk | |

In large mixing bowl combine *2½ cups* of the flour, yeast, cardamom, and nutmeg. Heat together milk, sugar, butter, and salt just till warm (115-120°), stirring constantly. Add to dry mixture in mixing bowl; add *1 egg*. Beat at low speed with electric mixer for ½ minute, scraping bowl constantly. Beat 3 minutes at high speed. By hand, beat in enough of the remaining flour to make a moderately stiff dough. Knead on lightly floured surface till smooth and elastic (3 to 5 minutes). Place in greased bowl; turn once to grease surface. Cover and let rise in warm place till double (1 to 1½ hours).

Punch down. Divide into thirds; let rest 10 minutes. On lightly floured surface, shape ⅓ of dough into a rope at least 36 inches long. Form dough rope into circle leaving each end extended 6 inches at bottom. Holding ends of dough rope toward center of circle, twist together twice. Press ends together and tuck under center of top of circle, forming a pretzel-shaped roll. Place on greased baking sheet. Repeat with the remaining dough to make a total of 3 twists. Let rise till almost double (30 to 45 minutes). Bake twists at 375° till done, about 20 minutes. Beat remaining egg slightly with fork; stir in water. Brush egg mixture on hot breads. Makes 3 loaves.

*Finnish Christmas customs are much like other Scandinavians', but this special holiday bread owes its origins to ancient days, dating as far back as the fifteenth century. Light to the touch and taste, it makes a delicious accompaniment to strong Finnish coffee.*

# Greek-American Christmas

The Greeks have a word for it—*Christouyena*. Translated, that means Christmas, but to Greek-Americans, the word needs little translation. They have easily bridged the gap of the sea voyage to America and enjoy the *kalanda* and *vasilopita* of their old homeland, as well as the Christmas trees, mistletoe, and Santa Claus of their new adopted land.

The gregarious Greeks have a way of savoring life to the fullest, and this is obvious during Christmas which is strung like a twinkling row of tree lights from St. Nicholas Day, December 6th, to Epiphany, January 6th.

After fasting, Christmas is anticipated in the Greek community as a time of feasting and celebrating the birth of Christ. Feasting begins Christmas Eve as a family affair. Traditionally meatless, the menu consists of favorite fish and seafood dishes, numerous appetizers and sweet desserts.

Christmas Eve is *kalanda* or caroling time. Neighbors give carolers nuts and fruit, all of which are called the "luck of Christ."

Christmas Day is also a family event, with an extensive midafternoon meal, featuring roast lamb or perhaps turkey or ham. The meal formally begins with the breaking of the *Christopsomo*, a honey-glazed Christmas bread. Always there are the delectable side dishes, such as stuffed grape leaves, artichokes with a dill or lemon sauce, and a generous Greek green salad with anchovies, olives, and feta cheese, followed by a variety of sweet pastries like *baklava* and the cookies *kourabiedes*. Much toasting with the Greek wine *retsina* accompanies the meal.

New Year's or St. Basil's Day is as important to Greek-Americans as to Greeks. On this day, the ultra-special *vasilopita* is eaten. This round bread, with a coin baked inside, is broken in a special ritual, with the first piece offered to St. Basil, the second to the poor, the third to the eldest family member present, and so on according to age. Each piece of bread is dipped in wine, with words such as "This is for Father, St. Basil" spoken. The remains are left on the table for St. Basil. In some Greek-American homes individual miniature loaves are baked, each with a coin inside, for each family member.

## Grecian Stuffed Lamb

*Grecian Stuffed Lamb blends two basics of Grecian cuisine—lamb and herbs. This elegant roast leg of lamb flavored with thyme will provide a hearty change of pace for meals any time during the holiday season.*

1 6- to 7-pound lamb leg, boned but not tied
½ teaspoon dried thyme, crushed

• • •

1 egg
¼ cup milk
1 clove garlic, crushed

¼ teaspoon salt
Dash pepper
½ pound ground fully cooked ham
½ cup snipped parsley
¼ cup finely chopped pine nuts *or* almonds
¼ cup soft rye bread crumbs

With a sharp knife, enlarge cavity of lamb leg. Rub lamb inside and out with thyme. Combine egg, milk, garlic, salt, and pepper. Add ground ham, parsley, pine nuts, and rye bread crumbs. Mix well. Fill cavity. Tie lamb and place on a rack in a shallow roasting pan. Bake at 325° till desired doneness; allow 2¼ to 2½ hours for medium. Makes 8 to 12 servings.

## Honey-Glazed Christmas Bread

| | |
|---|---|
| 2½ to 3 cups all-purpose flour | 1 egg |
| 1 package active dry yeast | ½ teaspoon grated lemon peel |
| ¾ cup milk | ½ cup light raisins |
| ¼ cup sugar | ½ cup chopped dried figs |
| ¼ cup butter *or* margarine | ½ cup chopped walnuts |
| ½ teaspoon salt | 2 tablespoons honey |

In a large mixing bowl combine *1 cup* flour and the yeast. In a saucepan heat together milk, sugar, butter, and salt just till warm (115-120°), stirring constantly. Add to dry mixture in mixing bowl. Add egg and lemon peel. Beat at low speed of electric mixer for ½ minute, scraping sides of bowl constantly; beat 3 minutes more at high speed. By hand, stir in enough remaining flour to make moderately stiff dough.

Turn dough out onto a lightly floured surface. Knead till smooth and elastic, 5 to 10 minutes; shape into a ball. Place in a lightly greased bowl, turning once to grease surface. Cover and let rise till nearly double (1 to 1½ hours). Knead in raisins, figs, and walnuts. Let rest 10 minutes, covered. Shape into an 8-inch round loaf. Place in a greased 9x1½-inch round baking pan. Let rise till nearly double (about 45 minutes). Bake at 375° about 30 minutes. Cover with foil during the last 15 minutes to prevent overbrowning. While still hot, remove from pan and brush with honey. Makes 1 loaf.

*This special Christmas bread Christopsomo sometimes is baked with a coin or almond inside, bestowing good fortune on the recipient. The bread is baked during Advent and saved for the big Christmas feast. Sometimes the top is frosted with designs representing the occupation of the householder. Thus a farmer's loaf would be adorned with a plow, and a shepherd's with a sheep. In some regions of Greece, the bread is shaped like a harness and nailed to the wall, to remain uneaten the entire next year.*

## Kourabiedes (koor' ah bee ay des)

| | |
|---|---|
| 1 cup butter *or* margarine | ¼ cup finely chopped almonds |
| ½ cup sifted powdered sugar | 2 cups all-purpose flour |
| 1 egg yolk | ½ teaspoon baking powder |
| ½ teaspoon vanilla | Whole cloves |
| ¼ teaspoon ground aniseed | Powdered sugar |

Cream together butter and ½ cup powdered sugar. Add egg yolk, vanilla, and aniseed; mix well. Stir in almonds. Stir together flour and baking powder. Blend into sugar mixture. Wrap and chill dough for 30 minutes. Form dough into 1-inch balls; stud each with a single whole clove. Arrange on an ungreased baking sheet. Bake at 325° till a pale sand color, about 20 minutes. Cool. Sprinkle with more powdered sugar. Makes 4 dozen.

*Usually round in shape, these ultra-rich butter cookies are essential tidbits at a Greek-American Christmas celebration. When they are soaked in honey, they are served as a tasty sweet called* melomacaroma.

## Fritters with Honey Syrup

Stir together 2¼ cups all-purpose flour, 1 package active dry yeast, and ½ teaspoon salt. Heat 1 cup water, ¼ cup milk, and 2 tablespoons cooking oil just till warm (115-120°). Add to flour mixture along with 1 egg; blend till smooth. Cover; let stand till batter almost doubles (about 45 minutes). Drop by tablespoons into deep hot fat (375°); fry till golden, 2 to 3 minutes. Turn once if necessary. Drain. Serve with Honey Syrup. Makes 24.

*Honey Syrup:* In saucepan combine 1 cup sugar, ½ cup honey, ½ cup water, and 2 tablespoons lemon juice. Cook and stir till sugar dissolves. Boil, uncovered, till syrup reaches 220° on candy thermometer. Set aside to cool.

*Fried golden brown, these feathery balls of dough are usually sweetened with a honey syrup. Sometimes ground cinnamon and chopped nuts are sprinkled on top as well.*

## Baklava (bah' kluh vah)

This classic Greek pastry is a favorite throughout the Middle East. Greeks generally end their meals with fruit and reserve sweets such as Baklava for between-meal snacks, served with hot foamy coffee. Christmas is an exception. During this season the festive table is laden with Baklava and other sweet desserts.

1 pound frozen fillo dough (21 16x12-inch leaves)
1 cup butter, melted
1 cup walnuts, finely chopped *or* ground
½ cup blanched almonds, finely chopped *or* ground

2 tablespoons sugar
1 teaspoon ground cinnamon
½ teaspoon ground nutmeg
⅛ teaspoon ground cloves

• • •

Lemon-Honey Syrup

Thaw fillo dough at room temperature for 2 hours. Cut sheets of fillo in half crosswise. Cover with slightly damp towel. Lightly butter the bottom of 14x10x2-inch baking pan. Lay *10 of the half sheets* of fillo in pan, *brushing each sheet* with some of the melted butter. Mix walnuts, almonds, sugar, cinnamon, nutmeg, and cloves. Sprinkle *half* of the nut mixture over fillo in pan. Drizzle with some of the melted butter. Top with *another 20 of the half sheets* of fillo, *brushing each* with more of the melted butter. Repeat with another layer of the nut mixture, remaining butter, and remaining fillo. Cut *without cutting through bottom layer,* into diamond-shaped pieces or squares. Bake at 350° for 50 to 55 minutes. Finish cutting; cool thoroughly. Pour warm Lemon-Honey Syrup over. Makes about 2 dozen diamonds.

*Lemon-Honey Syrup:* In a saucepan combine 1 cup sugar, 1 cup water, and ½ lemon, sliced. Boil gently for 15 minutes. Remove lemon slices. Add 2 tablespoons honey. Stir till blended. Keep the syrup warm.

## St. Basil's Bread

This special New Year's bread is baked in honor of St. Basil, the patron saint of Greece. Sometimes the bread is baked with a cross on top. Traditionally a gold or silver coin is baked inside, and the lucky one who receives it will have a year of good fortune.

4 to 4¼ cups all-purpose flour
1 package active dry yeast
1 teaspoon grated lemon peel
½ teaspoon aniseed, crushed
1 cup milk
¼ cup butter *or* margarine

¼ cup sugar
¾ teaspoon salt
2 eggs
1 beaten egg yolk
Sesame seed

In large mixing bowl combine *2 cups* flour, yeast, lemon peel, and aniseed. Heat together milk, butter, sugar, and salt just till warm (115-120°), stirring constantly. Add to dry mixture; add 2 eggs. Beat at low speed of electric mixer for ½ minute, scraping sides of bowl constantly. Beat 3 minutes at high speed. By hand, stir in enough of the remaining flour to make a moderately stiff dough. Turn out on lightly floured surface; knead till smooth and satiny (6 to 8 minutes). Shape into ball; place in lightly greased bowl, turning once to grease surface. Cover; let rise till double (1 to 1¼ hours). Punch down. Divide dough into thirds. Cover; let rest 10 minutes. Shape one-third of dough into flat, 8-inch round loaf. Place in greased 8x1½-inch round baking pan. Repeat with second third; place in another 8x1½-inch round baking pan. Divide remaining dough in half. Shape *each half* into a strand 18 inches long. Twist each strand like rope and seal ends to form a 7-inch circle. Place one circle atop each loaf. Combine egg yolk with 1 tablespoon water; brush on loaves. Sprinkle with sesame seed. Let rise in warm place till double (30 to 45 minutes). Bake at 375° till done, 20 to 25 minutes. Remove from pans. Cool thoroughly on rack. Makes 2 round loaves.

# A Contemporary Christmas

Staying home for Christmas? Not everyone travels over the holidays—time off is limited, children are in pageants, or grandparents live too far away. In fact, many people simply prefer to enjoy the fun of decorating and entertaining at home. It's a time to mix and match traditional and modern recipes with party ideas to suit personal plans.

If many of the same friends will be attending several holiday parties, no doubt you are looking for recipes that will make your party something special. Instead of the usual roast turkey and cranberry sauce, plan an informal buffet dinner around Orange-Sauced Ham with Brandied Cranberries. Or, serve a fondue Christmas meal featuring one or more fondues such as Creamy Cheese Fondue or Eggnog Fondue.

An appetizer buffet is a tasty prelude (or finale) to a Christmas concert or an evening out. Try one of the menus in this section or plan your own menu by checking the index to take advantage of the wide variety of party-special appetizers throughout the book.

*Menu*

(see photo, page 68)

*Orange-Sauced Ham*
*with*
*Brandied Cranberries*
*Candied Banana Squash*
*Broccoli Bake*
*Frozen Pineapple Salads*
*Hot Rolls      Butter*
*Spice Cake*
*Beverage*

## Frozen Pineapple Salads (see photo, page 68)

1 8-ounce package cream
   cheese, softened
¼ cup granulated sugar
¼ cup packed brown sugar
1 15¼-ounce can crushed
   pineapple (juice pack)

2 cups pineapple yogurt
• • •
2 tablespoons chopped pecans
2 tablespoons chopped red and
   green candied cherries

In a small mixing bowl beat together cream cheese, granulated sugar, and brown sugar thoroughly. Drain crushed pineapple well. Stir drained pineapple and pineapple yogurt into sugar mixture. Spoon into 10 paper bake cups in muffin pans. Combine pecans and cherries; spoon some of the nut mixture atop each cup. Cover; freeze till firm. Let cups stand at room temperature 10 minutes before serving. Makes 10 servings.

## Candied Banana Squash (see photo, page 68)

1 banana squash (2¼ to 2½
   pounds)
¼ cup granulated sugar
¼ cup packed brown sugar

¼ cup butter *or* margarine
½ teaspoon salt
   Dash pepper

Scrub banana squash; cut in serving-size pieces, removing seeds and membrane. In medium saucepan mix together granulated sugar, brown sugar, butter or margarine, salt, and pepper. Cook and stir till sugars dissolve. Arrange squash pieces, skin side down, in large shallow baking pan. Spoon sugar mixture into squash cavities. Cover with foil. Bake at 350° till squash pieces are tender, 50 to 60 minutes, spooning sauce over once or twice. Garnish with celery leaves, if desired. Makes 10 servings.

*Candied Banana Squash features a banana-shaped vegetable that is grown on the West Coast. It varies from a light greenish-gray color to light pink and has a light orange, fine-grained flesh.*

## Broccoli Bake

| | |
|---|---|
| 3 10-ounce packages frozen cut broccoli | 1 cup shredded sharp American cheese (4 ounces) |
| • • • | ½ cup mayonnaise *or* salad dressing |
| 1 10¾-ounce can condensed cream of mushroom soup | • • • |
| 1 10½-ounce can condensed cream of chicken soup | 2 tablespoons butter *or* margarine |
| | 1½ cups soft bread crumbs |

In a large saucepan cook the frozen broccoli according to the package directions, *except* omit the salt; drain the cooked broccoli thoroughly. In a large bowl blend together the cream of mushroom soup, cream of chicken soup, shredded sharp American cheese, and the mayonnaise or salad dressing. Add the drained, cooked broccoli to the soup mixture and stir together carefully. Turn the mixture into a 2-quart casserole.

In a small saucepan melt the butter or margarine. Add the bread crumbs to the melted butter and toss lightly. Sprinkle the buttered crumbs atop the broccoli mixture. Bake, uncovered, at 375° till the mixture is heated through and crumbs are lightly browned, about 45 minutes. Makes 12 servings.

*Pictured opposite:* Give Christmas dinner a contemporary look by serving (from upper left) *Broccoli Bake, Candied Banana Squash* (see recipe, page 67) *Orange-Sauced Ham with Brandied Cranberries,* and *Frozen Pineapple Salads* (see recipe, page 67).

## Orange-Sauced Ham with Brandied Cranberries

| | |
|---|---|
| 1 16-ounce package cranberries (4 cups) | 3 medium oranges |
| 2 cups sugar | • • • |
| ⅓ cup brandy | ⅔ cup light corn syrup |
| • • • | 1 tablespoon cornstarch |
| 1 5-pound boneless fully cooked ham | ¾ teaspoon ground nutmeg |
| | Parsley sprigs |

Place the cranberries in a 13x9x2-inch baking pan. Sprinkle sugar evenly over the cranberries. Cover and bake at 300° for 1 hour. Stir occasionally during baking time. Remove from oven. Stir in the brandy. Store the brandied cranberries in a covered container in the refrigerator.

Place the ham on a rack in shallow roasting pan; score top in diamond pattern. Insert meat thermometer, avoiding any fat; bake at 325° till meat thermometer registers 140°, for 2 to 2¼ hours.

Meanwhile, halve the oranges, using a sawtooth pattern. Scoop out the pulp from *one* orange; reserve pulp and shell. Squeeze juice from remaining orange halves; reserve shells. Measure juice; add enough water to measure 1½ cups liquid. Remove the membrane from orange shells; set the shells aside. Mix reserved orange pulp, orange juice-water mixture, light corn syrup, cornstarch, and ground nutmeg. Cook, stirring constantly, till the sauce is thickened and bubbly; set the sauce aside.

Baste ham with orange sauce during last 20 minutes of baking. Remove ham to platter. Spoon excess fat off pan drippings. Heat and pass drippings with ham. Fill reserved orange shells with brandied cranberries and arrange around ham. Garnish with parsley sprigs. Makes 10 to 12 servings.

*Orange halves cut in a sawtooth pattern are attractive serving containers for relishes, cranberry sauce, or sweet potatoes. To make the zigzag pattern, insert a small, sharp knife in center of orange at an angle. Pull knife out and make next cut at a reverse angle. Repeat around orange. Carefully pull halves apart. Remove fruit from each half.*

*Get those fondue pots and chafing dishes ready for a holiday fondue party featuring an assortment of delicious fondues and hot dips. Be sure to include an assortment of dippers such as chips, bite-size pieces of bread, cakes, and fresh or canned fruit.*

## Creamy Cheese Fondue

Coat 4 cups shredded American cheese with 1 tablespoon all-purpose flour; set aside. In saucepan cook 2 tablespoons finely chopped green pepper in 1 tablespoon butter till tender but not brown. Stir in 1 cup dry white wine; heat slowly till just bubbling. Gradually add shredded cheese, stirring constantly till smooth and bubbly. Stir in two 3-ounce packages cream cheese with chives and 1 teaspoon prepared mustard; cook and stir over low heat till smooth. Transfer to fondue pot; place over fondue burner. Dip small breadsticks or melba toast rounds in fondue. Makes 3½ cups.

## Chili-Bean Dip

| | |
|---|---|
| 1 16-ounce can refried beans | 3 tablespoons finely chopped |
| 1 11-ounce can condensed | canned green chili |
| Cheddar cheese soup | peppers |
| ¼ cup milk | Tortilla chips |

In saucepan combine beans, soup, milk, and chili peppers. Heat slowly, stirring constantly, till smooth and bubbly. Transfer to fondue pot; place over fondue burner. Dip tortilla chips in fondue. Makes 3 cups.

## Creamy Apricot Fondue

| | |
|---|---|
| 1 21-ounce can apricot pie filling | 1 4-ounce container whipped cream cheese, softened |
| ⅓ cup milk | 2 tablespoons butter *or* |
| ¼ cup brandy | margarine |
| ¼ cup sugar | Ladyfingers, split lengthwise |
| 1 tablespoon cornstarch | and cut in half |

In blender container combine pie filling, milk, brandy, sugar, and cornstarch. Cover; blend till smooth. Pour into saucepan. Cook and stir till thickened. Stir in cream cheese and butter; cook and stir till smooth. Transfer to fondue pot; place over fondue burner. Dip ladyfingers in fondue. Makes 3 cups.

## Eggnog Fondue

| | |
|---|---|
| 1 3- *or* 3¼-ounce package *regular* vanilla pudding mix | Angel cake *or* pound cake, cut in bite-size pieces |
| 1½ cups dairy *or* canned eggnog | Bananas, cut in bite-size pieces |
| 2 tablespoons light rum | |

In medium saucepan combine vanilla pudding mix and eggnog. Cook, stirring constantly, till mixture thickens and bubbles. Stir in rum. Transfer pudding mixture to fondue pot. Place over fondue burner. Spear cake or banana pieces with fondue fork; dip in fondue, swirling to coat. (If mixture becomes too thick, stir in a little additional eggnog.) Makes 4 servings.

## Hot Coffee Eggnog

| | |
|---|---|
| 2 beaten eggs | 2 teaspoons sugar |
| 1 cup milk | 1 teaspoon instant coffee |
| 1 cup light cream | crystals |
| ¼ cup coffee liqueur | Ground coriander *or* |
| 2 tablespoons whiskey | ground nutmeg |

In saucepan combine beaten eggs, milk, cream, coffee liqueur, whiskey, sugar, and coffee crystals. Cook over medium heat, stirring constantly, till mixture just begins to coat a metal spoon. Pour the hot eggnog into heatproof glasses or cups. Sprinkle ground coriander or ground nutmeg atop each serving. Serve the eggnog immediately. Makes 5 (4-ounce) servings.

## Daiquiri Punch

| | |
|---|---|
| 1 46-ounce can unsweetened pineapple juice, chilled | 2 16-ounce bottles lemon-lime carbonated beverage, chilled |
| 2½ cups light rum | Lime slices |
| 6 envelopes daiquiri cocktail mix | |

In punch bowl combine pineapple juice, rum, and dry daiquiri mix; stir to dissolve daiquiri mix. Carefully pour carbonated beverage down side of bowl. Mix gently. Float lime slices atop punch. Makes 18 (5-ounce) servings.

## Mock Champagne Punch

| | |
|---|---|
| 1 6-ounce can frozen lemonade concentrate | 1 28-ounce bottle ginger ale, chilled |
| 1 6-ounce can frozen pineapple juice concentrate | 1 25-ounce bottle sparkling white Catawba grape juice, chilled |
| 3 cups cold water | |

In large pitcher combine frozen lemonade and pineapple concentrates with water; stir till dissolved. Carefully stir in the chilled ginger ale and Catawba grape juice. Serve the punch over ice. Makes 22 (4-ounce) servings.

## Cranberry Punch

| | |
|---|---|
| 1 48-ounce bottle cranberry juice cocktail | 1 28-ounce bottle lemon-lime carbonated beverage, chilled |
| 1 6-ounce can frozen orange juice concentrate | 1 cup cranberries |

Combine cranberry juice and frozen orange juice concentrate; stir till orange juice dissolves. Chill. When ready to serve, pour chilled juices into punch bowl. Carefully pour in the chilled lemon-lime carbonated beverage; garnish punch with cranberries. Makes 20 (4-ounce) servings.

*Menu*

*Assorted Cheeses*
*Assorted Fresh Fruit*
*Hot Coffee Eggnog*
*Daiquiri Punch*
*Mock Champagne Punch*
*Cranberry Punch*

*For a simple and unusual holiday party, try a beverage buffet. Make several kinds using anything from eggnog to lemonade. For spiked-punch admirers, provide Daiquiri Punch and Hot Coffee Eggnog. Also offer Mock Champagne Punch and Cranberry Punch for a delicious holiday refresher. Complete your menu with assorted fresh fruits and cheeses.*

*Today's entertaining almost inevitably includes spreads and dips of some kind. Cheese is a common denominator for many appetizers and why not? The flavor is pleasant and appealing to most munchers.*

## Cheese-Ham Ball

1 8-ounce package cream cheese
1 cup shredded sharp American cheese (4 ounces)
⅓ cup dairy sour cream
1 4½-ounce can deviled ham
2 tablespoons finely chopped canned pimiento
1 teaspoon grated onion
1 tablespoon milk
Assorted crackers

Have cheeses at room temperature. Combine *half* of the cream cheese, American cheese, and sour cream; beat with electric mixer till blended. Beat in deviled ham; stir in pimiento and onion. Chill 1 hour. Form into an igloo shape on serving plate. Combine remaining cream cheese and milk; beat smooth. Spread over ham mixture; chill well. Sprinkle with snipped parsley, if desired. Serve with crackers. Makes about 2½ cups.

## Cheese and Bean Dunk

1 6-ounce roll garlic cheese food
1 11½-ounce can condensed bean with bacon soup
1 cup dairy sour cream
2 tablespoons sliced green onion
Crackers or chips

Cut cheese food into chunks. Place in saucepan with soup. Heat slowly, stirring constantly, till blended. Stir in sour cream and onion. Heat through over low heat; do not boil. Serve with crackers or chips. Makes 2⅔ cups.

## Green and Red Dip

4 avocados, seeded, peeled, and mashed
¼ cup finely chopped onion
2 to 4 tablespoons finely chopped canned green chili peppers
2 to 3 tablespoons lemon juice
1 teaspoon salt
1 teaspoon Worcestershire sauce
Few drops bottled hot pepper sauce
• • •
2 medium tomatoes, seeded and finely chopped
Corn chips

Combine all ingredients except tomatoes and corn chips. Season to taste. Stir in tomatoes. Chill. Serve with corn chips. Makes 2⅓ cups.

## Apple-Lemon Sparkle

8 cups apple juice *or* apple cider, chilled
1 6-ounce can lemonade concentrate
1 28-ounce bottle ginger ale, chilled
Ice

Combine apple juice and lemonade concentrate; stir to dissolve. Carefully pour in chilled ginger ale. Serve over ice. Makes 24 (4-ounce) servings.

## Party Tuna Cups

1 6½- *or* 7-ounce can
  tuna, drained
3 tablespoons finely
  chopped radish
3 tablespoons sweet
  pickle relish
⅓ cup mayonnaise *or*
  salad dressing

1½ teaspoons prepared
  mustard
1 unsliced loaf white *or*
  whole wheat bread
Mayonnaise *or* salad
  dressing
Radish slices

In mixing bowl combine tuna, chopped radish, and pickle relish. Mix in the ⅓ cup mayonnaise and mustard. Chill. Cut bread into 1-inch thick slices. Cut slices into rounds with a 1½-inch cutter. To make cups, hollow out rounds with kitchen shears, *leaving about ¼ inch on sides and bottoms.* Brush inside of bread cups with mayonnaise. Fill each cup with about 1 teaspoon tuna mixture. Garnish with radish slices. Makes 40.

## Christmas Banana Bread

¾ cup sugar
½ cup butter *or* margarine
2 medium bananas, mashed
  (⅔ cup)
2 eggs
2 teaspoons grated
  orange peel
¼ cup orange juice

2 cups all-purpose flour
1 teaspoon baking powder
½ cup finely chopped
  candied pineapple
½ cup chopped pecans
⅓ cup finely chopped red
  candied cherries

*Liven the color and enhance the flavor of banana bread during the holiday season by adding candied fruits and nuts. Guests will rave when they taste the unuslal flavor combination.*

In mixing bowl cream together the sugar and butter or margarine. Beat in mashed banana. Add eggs, grated orange peel, and juice; mix well. Stir together flour and baking powder; stir into the banana mixture. Fold in candied pineapple, chopped pecans and red candied cherries. Fill five well-greased and floured 10½-ounce soup cans *or* five 4½x2½x1½-inch loaf pans *or* four 6x3x2-inch loaf pans. Place on baking pan. Bake at 350° till done, 45 to 50 minutes. Allow bread to cool 5 minutes; remove from cans or pans. Cool thoroughly; wrap bread loaves separately in foil till ready to serve. Slice thinly to serve. Makes 4 or 5 small loaves.

## Sparkling Fruit Punch

1 3-ounce package lemon-
  flavored gelatin
1 cup boiling water
8 cups pineapple-orange
  fruit drink

1 28-ounce bottle lemon-lime
  carbonated beverage,
  chilled
1 quart orange sherbet

Dissolve the gelatin in boiling water. Add pineapple-orange drink. Chill well. Pour into punch bowl. Carefully pour in the chilled carbonated beverage. Spoon sherbet atop punch. Makes about 35 (4-ounce) servings.

# Christmas Foods

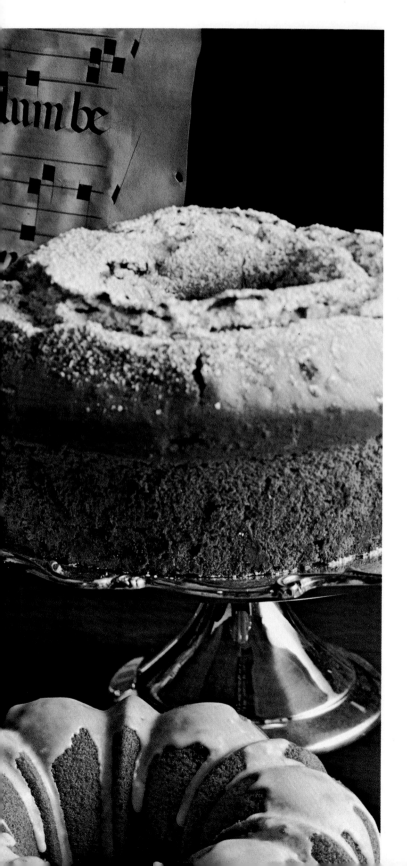

The deliciously long holiday season starts back in November and bumps into the New Year before the last fancy cookie or cup of eggnog disappears. In between are gala parties, hungry carolers, friends who drop in, and a round of activities that are gladdened by something festive to eat.

Every hostess has one or two specialties she always prepares. But, "what do you serve this year that you haven't served before—to the same guests?" It's an annual problem.

The delectable solution can be found in the following pages. Here Christmas foods are grouped for easy reference under headings such as Cookies and Candies, Main Dishes, Beverages, and so on. The luscious assortment is varied to suit any yuletide occasion.

Baking festive breads, cakes, and other goodies is part of the fun of holiday preparations. Shown top left is a *Gumdrop Nut Wreath;* center left is a *Holiday Sweet Bread;* and bottom left is *Christmas Kringle.* Pictured at top right is a *Spicy Fruit Ring.* At bottom right is a *Lemon European Cake.* (See index for recipe pages.)

# Cookies and Candies

## Dutch Letters (see photo, pages 4-5)

(see photo, pages 4-5)

*December 6th is St. Nicholas Day, a time of Christmas gift-giving in Holland. After exchanging presents, the family enjoys a snack of botterletter, or St. Nicholas Day Letters and hot chocolate or warm punch. The "letters" are little almond cakes in the shape of each family member's initials. Dutch-Americans today enjoy Dutch Letters anytime during the Christmas season.*

1 8-ounce can almond paste
1 egg
¼ cup sugar
• • •
3 cups all-purpose flour

¾ teaspoon salt
1½ cups butter *or* margarine
½ to ⅔ cup ice water
1 egg yolk

Combine almond paste, egg, and sugar; mix well and chill. Stir together flour and salt. Cut butter into flour till mixture resembles coarse crumbs. Add ice water, a tablespoon at a time, stirring till dough is well moistened. Shape into ball; cover and let stand 30 minutes. Divide dough into three parts. Roll each part on lightly floured surface to 8-inch square. Cut each into four 8x2-inch strips. For each of the 12 strips roll about 1 tablespoon filling into an 8-inch roll. Moisten dough edges with water. Close dough over filling; seal edges and ends. Shape into S shapes. Place on ungreased cookie sheets. Combine egg yolk and 1 tablespoon water; brush on letters. Bake at 375° for 30 to 35 minutes. Cool. Makes 12.

## Candy Window Cookies (see photo, pages 4-5)

(see photo, pages 4-5)

½ cup sugar
⅓ cup butter *or* margarine
1 egg
½ teaspoon vanilla
1¼ cups all-purpose flour

½ teaspoon baking powder
¼ teaspoon salt
3 ounces hard sour candy, crushed

Cream together sugar, butter or margarine, egg, and vanilla. Stir together flour, baking powder, and salt. Stir into creamed mixture. Chill 1 hour. Roll dough ⅛ inch thick on lightly floured surface. Cut in desired shapes; cut out centers, leaving a ½-inch wall. Place on foil-lined cookie sheet. Put ½ teaspoon candy in each cutout cookie center. Bake at 375° till candy melts, 6 to 7 minutes. Cool; peel off foil. Makes 3½ dozen cookies.

## Rolled Sugar Cookies

1 cup sifted powdered sugar
¾ cup butter *or* margarine
1 egg

1 teaspoon vanilla
2 cups all-purpose flour
1 teaspoon baking powder

Cream together sugar and butter. Beat in egg and vanilla. Stir together flour and baking powder. Stir into creamed mixture. Divide dough in half. Chill at least 1 hour. Roll *half* dough ⅛ inch thick on lightly floured surface. (Keep remaining dough chilled.) Cut with cookie cutters. Place on ungreased cookie sheet. Sprinkle with sugar, if desired. Bake at 375° for 6 to 8 minutes. Remove from pan. Repeat with remaining dough. Makes 48.

## Rosettes

| | |
|---|---|
| 2 eggs | 1 cup milk |
| 1 tablespoon granulated sugar | 1 teaspoon vanilla |
| ¼ teaspoon salt | Fat for frying |
| 1 cup all-purpose flour | Powdered sugar |

In mixing bowl combine the eggs, granulated sugar, and salt; beat well. Add flour, milk, and vanilla and beat till smooth. Heat a rosette iron in deep hot fat (375°). Dip the hot rosette iron into the batter, *being careful* batter only comes ¾ of the way up the side of iron.

Fry rosette in the hot fat till golden, about ½ minute. Lift iron out and tip slightly to drain off any excess fat. With fork, carefully push rosette off iron onto paper towels placed on rack. Reheat iron; make the next rosette. Sift powdered sugar over the cooled rosettes. Makes 3½ dozen.

*This old-fashioned Scandinavian recipe is called* sockerstruvor *in Swedish. Still popular among Scandinavians in Minnesota and Wisconsin, the "rosettes" are delicious "flowers" fried on a special iron in hot fat. The hot iron is dipped into the batter and then in the hot fat till the cookie is golden. You can purchase rosette irons at most Scandinavian stores.*

## Almond-Coconut Bars (see photo, pages 4-5)

| | |
|---|---|
| 1 cup all-purpose flour | ½ cup semisweet chocolate |
| ½ cup sifted powdered sugar | pieces |
| ½ cup shredded coconut | 1 package coconut-almond |
| ½ teaspoon salt | frosting mix |
| • • • | (for 2-layer cake) |
| ½ cup butter *or* margarine | ½ cup chopped almonds |

In mixing bowl thoroughly stir together the flour, sifted powdered sugar, shredded coconut, and salt. Cut in the butter or margarine till the mixture resembles coarse crumbs. Pat the coconut mixture in bottom of an ungreased 13x9x2-inch baking pan. Bake at 375° for 10 to 12 minutes.

Immediately sprinkle baked layer with the chocolate pieces. When the chocolate softens, spread lightly with spatula to cover the baked layer. Prepare the coconut-almond frosting mix according to the package directions. Stir in chopped almonds; spread carefully over the chocolate layer. Bake at 375° till topping is golden brown, about 20 minutes. Cool thoroughly in pan before removing. Cut into bars. Makes about 4 dozen bars.

## Krumkake (kroom′ kah kuh)

| | |
|---|---|
| ½ cup butter *or* margarine | 1 teaspoon vanilla |
| 3 eggs | • • • |
| ½ cup sugar | ½ cup all-purpose flour |

Melt butter; set aside. Beat eggs and sugar till well blended. Blend in cooled butter and vanilla. Beat in flour till smooth. Heat krumkake iron on medium-high heat. Drop small amount batter onto hot, ungreased iron (for 6-inch iron use about ½ tablespoon batter); close gently (do not squeeze). Bake till pale golden, 15 to 20 seconds; turn iron over and bake 15 to 20 seconds more. Remove cookie with narrow spatula; immediately roll into a cigar shape on wooden or metal form. Cool, seam side down, for 30 seconds; remove form. Repeat with remaining batter. Makes about 24.

*Christmas has been called the Scandinavian "antidote to darkness." As part of that antidote, homemakers bake a seemingly endless supply of cookies for holiday visitors. Krumkake, a Norwegian specialty, is baked on a special iron engraved with Christmas and Nativity scenes, then rolled on a wooden or metal roller.*

## Ginger Cookie Boys

| | |
|---|---|
| 1½ cups sugar | 2 teaspoons ground cinnamon |
| 1 cup butter *or* margarine | 1 teaspoon ground ginger |
| 1 egg | ½ teaspoon salt |
| 2 tablespoons dark corn syrup | ½ teaspoon ground cloves |
| 4 teaspoons grated orange peel | Confectioners' Icing (see recipe, page 119) |
| 3 cups all-purpose flour | Raisins |
| 2 teaspoons baking soda | |

Thoroughly cream together sugar and butter or margarine. Add egg; beat till light and fluffy. Add corn syrup and orange peel; mix well. Stir together flour, baking soda, cinnamon, ginger, salt, and cloves. Stir into creamed mixture. Chill dough thoroughly. On lightly floured surface roll the dough ¼ inch thick. Cut with gingerbread man cookie cutter.

Place cookies 1 inch apart on ungreased cookie sheet. Bake at 375° for 8 to 10 minutes. Cool 1 minute before removing from pan. Cool on rack. To decorate cookies put Confectioners' Icing into cake decorator. Pipe icing onto cookies; add raisins for eyes and buttons. Makes about 2 dozen.

*Pictured opposite:* Hang Christmas stockings and fill them with *Ginger Cookie Boys* and colorful peppermint sticks and candy canes. For an added treat, let everyone help himself to the sweets in the glass apothecary jars set on the fireplace mantel. Clockwise from the back: *Caramel Crunch* (see recipe, page 87), *Candied Grapefruit Peel* (see recipe, page 82), *Cherry Divinity* (see recipe, page 85), *Tiny Red Mints* (see recipe, page 82), and *Coconut-Fruit Balls* (see recipe, page 85).

## Spritz Cookies

| | |
|---|---|
| 1 cup butter *or* margarine | 1 egg |
| 1 cup sugar | • • • |
| 1 teaspoon vanilla *or* ½ teaspoon almond extract | 2⅓ cups all-purpose flour |
| | ½ teaspoon baking powder |
| | ¼ teaspoon salt |

Thoroughly cream together butter or margarine and sugar. Add vanilla or almond extract and egg; beat till light and fluffy. Stir together flour, baking powder, and salt. Stir into creamed mixture; mix well. Divide dough in half. Place half in cookie press. Press in desired shapes onto ungreased cookie sheet. Bake at 400° for 7 to 8 minutes. Makes about 6 dozen.

*Although Scandinavian in origin, these cookies are now firmly rooted in American Christmas tradition. The light, delicious dough is shaped into stars, trees, wreaths, and many other designs by forcing it through a cookie press. Enhance the cookies by tinting some of the dough with food coloring so that the Christmas tree shapes turn out green.*

## Christmas Chocolate Cutout Cookies

| | |
|---|---|
| ¾ cup granulated sugar | ½ cup semisweet chocolate pieces, melted and cooled |
| ½ cup packed brown sugar | |
| ½ cup butter *or* margarine | 2 cups all-purpose flour |
| • • • | ¼ teaspoon baking soda |
| 2 eggs | ⅛ teaspoon salt |
| ½ teaspoon vanilla | |

Cream together granulated sugar, brown sugar, and butter or margarine. Beat in eggs and vanilla. Blend in cooled chocolate. Stir together flour, baking soda, and salt. Stir into the creamed chocolate mixture. Cover and chill several hours or overnight. On lightly floured surface roll the dough ⅛ inch thick. Cut in desired shapes with cookie cutters. Place on ungreased cookie sheet. Bake at 350° for 8 minutes. Makes 5 dozen.

## Applesauce-Oatmeal Cookie Trio

1 cup butter *or* margarine
1 cup packed brown sugar
½ cup granulated sugar
2 eggs
1 cup applesauce
1 teaspoon vanilla
2 cups regular rolled oats
1½ cups all-purpose flour
1 cup chopped walnuts
½ teaspoon baking soda
½ teaspoon baking powder
½ cup flaked coconut
½ cup finely snipped pitted dates
½ cup semisweet chocolate pieces, melted and cooled
⅓ cup chopped maraschino cherries
1 cup chopped mixed candied fruits and peels

Cream butter and sugars. Add eggs; mix well. Mix in applesauce and vanilla. Stir together oats, flour, nuts, soda, baking powder, and ¼ teaspoon salt. Stir into applesauce mixture. Divide dough into thirds. To one third, mix in coconut and dates. To second third, chocolate and cherries. To remaining third, mix in fruits and peels. Drop teaspoonsful onto ungreased cookie sheets. Bake at 350° till done, 15 to 18 minutes. Makes 8 to 9 dozen.

## Fruit-Studded Drop Cookies

¾ cup sugar
½ cup butter *or* margarine
1 egg
½ teaspoon vanilla
1¾ cups all-purpose flour
1 teaspoon baking powder
½ teaspoon ground cinnamon
½ teaspoon ground cloves
¼ teaspoon baking soda
⅔ cup buttermilk
1 cup snipped pitted dates
1 cup sliced candied cherries
1 cup chopped pecans

Cream together sugar and butter or margarine. Add egg and vanilla, beat till light and fluffy. Stir together flour, baking powder, cinnamon, cloves, soda, and dash salt; add alternately with buttermilk to creamed mixture, mixing well. Stir in dates, candied cherries, and pecans. Drop teaspoonsful onto greased cookie sheet. Bake at 350° for 12 to 15 minutes. Makes about 4 dozen.

## Old-Fashioned Raisin-Nut Cookies

¾ cup packed brown sugar
½ cup butter *or* margarine
2 eggs
1 teaspoon vanilla
1½ cups all-purpose flour
½ teaspoon baking soda
¼ teaspoon ground cinnamon
1 cup raisins
1 cup chopped pecans
½ cup chopped candied cherries
½ cup chopped mixed candied fruits and peels

Cream together sugar and butter. Add eggs and vanilla; beat till light and fluffy. Stir together flour, baking soda, and cinnamon. Stir into the creamed mixture; beat till well blended. Stir in the raisins, chopped pecans, and candied fruits. Drop teaspoonsful onto greased cookie sheet. Bake at 350° for 8 to 10 minutes. Makes about 4 dozen cookies.

## Spiced Ginger Cookies

1 cup butter *or* margarine
¾ cup granulated sugar
¾ cup packed brown sugar
1 egg
1 tablespoon molasses
1½ tablespoons grated orange peel
1 tablespoon water

3½ cups all-purpose flour
2 teaspoons baking soda
2 teaspoons ground cinnamon
1 teaspoon ground ginger
½ teaspoon ground cloves
Granulated sugar
⅓ cup blanched almonds, halved

Cream together butter, ¾ cup granulated sugar, and brown sugar. Add egg; beat till light and fluffy. Add molasses, grated orange peel, and water to the creamed mixture; mix well. Stir together flour, baking soda, cinnamon, ginger, and cloves. Stir into creamed mixture. Chill thoroughly. Shape in 1-inch balls. Roll in granulated sugar and place 2 inches apart on ungreased cookie sheet. Top each cookie with almond half. Bake at 375° till lightly browned, 8 to 10 minutes. Makes 6 to 7 dozen cookies.

## Poinsettia Balls

1 cup butter *or* margarine
⅔ cup honey
2 egg yolks
2 tablespoons grated orange peel
3 tablespoons orange juice
3 cups all-purpose flour

½ teaspoon baking soda
½ teaspoon salt
¼ teaspoon ground nutmeg
2 slightly beaten egg whites
1½ cups finely chopped pecans
6 ounces red candied cherries

Cream butter and honey. Add egg yolks; mix well. Stir in orange peel and juice. Stir together flour, soda, salt, and ground nutmeg. Stir into creamed mixture. Chill thoroughly 1 hour. Form into 1-inch balls. Dip in egg whites; roll in nuts. Place 2 inches apart on ungreased cookie sheet. Cut each cherry into 6 to 8 petals. Place 4 or 5 petals on top of each ball. Bake at 325° for 18 to 20 minutes. Makes about 6 dozen cookies.

## Rum-Coffee Cookies

1 cup packed brown sugar
½ cup butter *or* margarine
2 eggs
½ teaspoon rum extract
1 teaspoon instant coffee crystals

1 tablespoon boiling water
1½ cups all-purpose flour
1½ teaspoons baking powder
¼ teaspoon salt
1 cup finely chopped pecans

Cream together sugar and butter. Add eggs and rum extract; beat well. Dissolve coffee crystals in boiling water; stir into creamed mixture. Stir together flour, baking powder, and salt. Stir into creamed mixture. Chill. drop teaspoonsful into nuts; roll to coat. Place on greased cookie sheet 2 inches apart. Bake at 350° for 8 to 10 minutes. Makes 4 dozen.

*The always-popular shaped cookies are formed by hand and require some special handling. Since the dough is pliable and quite soft, chill it thoroughly. Roll a small amount of dough into a smooth ball with the palms of the hands and then place on the cookie sheet. Make the cookies holiday-special by decorating either before or after baking. To decorate before baking, roll in granulated sugar and top with a nut half or dip in egg whites and roll in finely chopped nuts. As a final touch use scissors to cut red candied cherries into poinsettia petals and place on top of cookie. To decorate after baking, dip the baked cookies into icing and sprinkle with colored sugar or flaked coconut.*

## Candied Grapefruit Peel (see photo, page 78)

| | |
|---|---|
| 2 medium white grapefruit | ¼ teaspoon salt |
| Cold water | 1 3-ounce package lime- |
| 1½ cups sugar | flavored gelatin |
| ¾ cup water | Green sugar crystals |

Score grapefruit peel in 4 lengthwise sections with sharp point of knife. Loosen the peel from pulp with bowl of spoon. Remove most of the white membrane from peel. Cut the peel into ¼-inch-wide strips. Place the peel strips in large saucepan and cover generously with cold water. Boil 20 minutes; drain. Repeat the boiling process twice using fresh cold water each time. Drain thoroughly. In medium saucepan combine sugar, the ¾ cup water, and salt. Cook and stir till the sugar completely dissolves.

Add the peel; bring to boiling. Reduce the heat and simmer till the peel is just translucent, about 20 minutes. Gradually add the lime-flavored gelatin, stirring over low heat till the gelatin is dissolved. Remove fruit peel from gelatin mixture; drain. Roll each strip in green sugar crystals. Let the strips dry thoroughly on rack. Store in covered jar. (Use any flavor of gelatin, depending on the color desired. Also, try orange or lemon peel.)

## Tiny Red Mints (see photo, page 78)

*The versatile fondant is the basis for mint patties, fillings to stuff dates, or chocolate-dipped candies. Traditional cooked fondant is made of sugar and water with corn syrup and cream of tartar added for creaminess. There are also easy-to-make uncooked versions which are useful in home candymaking. Both varieties can be flavored and colored. The recipes here use peppermint or orange extract, but for other variations choose lemon, cherry, vanilla, wintergreen, or maple flavorings. Red, green, yellow, and pink are popular fondant colors.*

| | |
|---|---|
| Butter *or* margarine | ⅛ teaspoon cream of tartar |
| 2 cups sugar | Red food coloring |
| ½ cup light corn syrup | Peppermint extract |

Butter sides of a heavy 2-quart saucepan. Combine sugar, corn syrup, cream of tartar, and ½ cup water. Cook to the thread stage (232° on candy thermometer), stirring only till sugar dissolves. Immediately remove from the heat and cool for 10 minutes, without stirring the mixture.

Tint with a few drops red food coloring; blend in well. Mix in a few drops peppermint extract. Beat the mixture with spoon till creamy, about 10 minutes. Drop the mixture from a teaspoon onto waxed paper forming patties, swirling the tops. *Keep the saucepan over very hot water while forming patties* (the mixture hardens when cooled). Store the mints in a tightly covered container. Makes about 4 dozen mints.

## Fondant Stuffed Dates

| | |
|---|---|
| 1 cup sifted powdered sugar | 3 to 4 drops orange extract |
| 1 tablespoon butter *or* | 1 8-ounce package pitted |
| margarine, softened | dates |
| 2 teaspoons milk | Walnut halves |

In small mixing bowl cream together ½ *cup* of the powdered sugar, butter or margarine, milk, and the orange extract. Stir in the remaining ½ cup of powdered sugar; mix thoroughly. Divide the fondant in half. Roll each fondant half to pencillike rope about 14 inches long. Slice and stuff fondant into dates. Top each date with a walnut half. Makes about 36.

Next time the occasion calls for a fancy holiday mint, fix *Mint Whirls*. Place a rectangular layer of green fondant over a white layer and roll up. Next, chill and slice into bite-size pieces. Wrap these pieces in clear plastic and store in an attractive glass jar.

## Mint Whirls

| | |
|---|---|
| 1 3-ounce package cream cheese, softened | 2½ cups sifted powdered sugar |
| ½ teaspoon peppermint extract | Few drops green food coloring |

In small mixing bowl combine the softened cream cheese and the peppermint extract; stir till thoroughly mixed. Gradually add the sifted powdered sugar, mixing till the cream cheese mixture is smooth in texture (knead in the last of the sifted powdered sugar with hands). To ½ *cup* of the fondant add a few drops food coloring. Knead till the green color is evenly distributed.

Divide the green fondant in half. Pat each half out on a separate piece of waxed paper to a 5x4-inch rectangle; cover fondant with waxed paper. Divide the white fondant in half. On separate pieces of waxed paper pat each half to a 5-inch square. Remove top layer of waxed paper from green fondant. Place one rectangle of green fondant, paper side up, over a rectangle of white fondant; leave 1-inch margin of white at the top edge. Carefully peel off the remaining layer of waxed paper from green fondant.

Beginning at the bottom edge roll up the fondant jelly-roll fashion. Seal the seam. Repeat the procedure to form the second roll. Wrap the rolls in foil; chill thoroughly. Slice the roll carefully into ½-inch pieces; wrap each piece in clear plastic wrap. Makes 25 to 30 fondant pieces.

*Fondant will keep fresh and creamy for several weeks if tightly wrapped in clear plastic wrap, waxed paper, or foil. In fact, the fondant flavor improves when stored and allowed to ripen. Store the candy in an airtight container in a cool, dry place.*

## Easy Chocolate Fudge

½ cup butter *or* margarine
1 5½- or 6-ounce package
  *regular* chocolate
  pudding mix

½ cup milk
4¾ cups sifted powdered sugar
½ cup chopped walnuts
½ teaspoon vanilla

In medium saucepan melt butter or margarine; stir in dry chocolate pudding mix and milk. Bring to boiling; boil for 1 minute, stirring constantly. Remove from heat; beat in powdered sugar. Stir in chopped walnuts and vanilla. Turn into buttered 10x6x2-inch dish. Garnish with walnut halves, if desired. Chill; cut into 1½-inch squares. Makes 1¾ pounds.

## Double-Decker Fudge

Combine 4½ cups sugar; one 7-, 9-, or 10-ounce jar marshmallow creme; two 5⅓-ounce cans evaporated milk; ½ cup butter *or* margarine; and dash salt. Cook and stir over medium heat till mixture boils. Boil gently, stirring frequently, for 5 minutes. Divide mixture in half. *To one half* add one 6-ounce package semisweet chocolate pieces; stir till melted and blended. Pour into buttered 13x9x2-inch pan. *To remaining half,* add one 6-ounce package butterscotch pieces, beating till smooth. (If necessary, beat butterscotch mixture with rotary beater till pieces are melted and mixture is smooth.) Pour over chocolate layer; cool. Cut in 54 pieces.

## Honey Crunch Candy

Carob has a flavor that resembles a mild milk chocolate and also is called locust, locust pod, or St. John's Bread. The Holy Bible refers in the gospel of St. Mark to John the Baptist feeding upon "locusts" and wild honey. Although locusts were eaten in Israel during John's time, historians believe the "locusts" were actually carob pods — an edible, fleshy seedpod. Today, carob pods are ground fine and used in candies, cakes, cookies, and icings. Carob is imported to the United States from several European countries, and is available in health food stores.

1 cup honey
1 cup peanut butter
1 cup carob powder
1 cup shelled sunflower seed

½ cup toasted sesame seed
½ cup flaked coconut
½ cup chopped walnuts
½ cup raisins

In large saucepan heat honey and peanut butter, stirring constantly just till smooth. Remove from heat; stir in carob powder. Mix well. Add sunflower seed, sesame seed, coconut, walnuts, and raisins. Press into buttered 8x8x2-inch pan. Chill several hours or overnight. Cut into 1-inch squares. Store candy in the refrigerator. Makes 2¼ pounds.

## Quick French Chocolates (see photo, pages 4-5)

1 12-ounce package semisweet
  chocolate pieces
1 14-ounce can *sweetened
  condensed* milk

1 cup chopped walnuts
1 teaspoon vanilla
1½ cups grated coconut *or*
  flaked coconut, chopped

In saucepan melt chocolate pieces over medium heat. Remove from heat and stir in sweetened condensed milk, walnuts, and vanilla. Cool. Butter hands; shape rounded teaspoonsful of the cooled mixture into balls. Roll each ball in coconut to cover. Store in refrigerator. Makes 8 dozen balls.

## Cherry Divinity (see photo, page 78)

| | |
|---|---|
| 2½ cups sugar | 1 teaspoon vanilla |
| ½ cup light corn syrup | ½ cup chopped maraschino |
| 2 egg whites | cherries, well drained |

In 2-quart saucepan combine sugar, syrup, ½ cup water, and ¼ teaspoon salt. Cook to hard-ball stage (260° on candy thermometer); stir only till sugar dissolves. Meanwhile, beat egg whites till stiff peaks form. Gradually pour hot syrup over egg whites, beating at high speed on electric mixer. Add vanilla; beat till mixture holds its shape, 4 to 5 minutes. Quickly stir in cherries; drop by teaspoonful onto waxed paper. Makes 40 pieces.

*What would a southern Christmas be like without a fancy dish of divinity on the table for nibbling through the day? Custom has it that either cherries are folded into the beaten candy to add a special festive touch, or pecan halves are used to decorate the top.*

## Maple Sponge Candy

| | |
|---|---|
| 1 cup maple-flavored syrup | 2 teaspoons white vinegar |
| ½ cup sugar | 2 teaspoons baking soda |

Combine syrup, sugar, and vinegar in heavy 2-quart saucepan. Bring to boiling over medium heat; stir till sugar dissolves. Continue cooking, without stirring, to hard-crack stage (300° on candy thermometer). Remove from heat; quickly sift in soda; mix well. Immediately pour into buttered 9x9x2-inch pan. Do not spread. Cool; break into pieces. Makes about ½ pound.

*For the best success with cooked candies, use a candy thermometer. If you don't have one, judge the doneness by dropping hot candy mixture from a spoon into a small bowl of cold water. With fingers form into a ball. Use the following guides: Soft-ball (234-240°F) — ball flattens when removed from water; firm-ball (244-248°F) — ball does not flatten when removed; hard-ball (250-266°F) — ball is hard, yet pliable; soft-crack (270-290°F) — mixture separates into non-brittle threads; and hard-crack (300-310°F) — mixture separates into hard, brittle threads.*

## Butter Toffee

| | |
|---|---|
| 2 cups sugar | 1 cup coarsely chopped |
| 1 cup butter *or* margarine | almonds, toasted |
| 1 tablespoon light corn syrup | ½ cup semisweet chocolate |
| 1 cup chopped walnuts | pieces |

Combine sugar, butter, corn syrup, ½ cup water, and dash salt. Cook, stirring occasionally, to hard-crack stage (300° on candy thermometer). Watch carefully after reaching 280°. Quickly stir in *half* of the walnuts and all of the almonds. Spread in buttered 13x9x2-inch pan. Cool 5 minutes. Top with chocolate; allow to soften. Spread over surface. Sprinkle remaining walnuts over top. Cool, then chill. Break into pieces. Makes 2 pounds.

## Coconut-Fruit Balls (see photo, page 78)

| | |
|---|---|
| 1½ cups pitted dates | 1 cup walnuts |
| 1 cup dried prunes, cooked | ¼ cup sugar |
| and pitted | 2 3½-ounce cans flaked |
| 1 cup dried apricots | coconut |
| 1 cup raisins | Yellow food coloring |

Grind fruits and walnuts with coarse blade of food grinder. Add sugar; mix well. Chill 2 to 3 hours. Form into 1-inch balls. Tint coconut with food coloring; roll each ball in the coconut to cover. Makes 4 dozen.

## Popcorn Snowman

| | |
|---|---|
| 16 cups popped corn | 1 teaspoon vinegar |
| 2 cups sugar | ½ teaspoon salt |
| 1½ cups water | 1 teaspoon vanilla |
| ½ cup light corn syrup | Assorted candies |

Keep the popped corn warm in 300° oven. Cover the outside of an empty 8-ounce coffee can with brown wrapping paper and secure with tape. Turn the paper-covered coffee can right side up and place on waxed paper.

Butter the sides of a large saucepan. Thoroughly combine sugar, water, light corn syrup, vinegar, and salt. Cook and stir the mixture to dissolve the sugar. Continue cooking, without stirring, to the soft-crack stage (280° on candy thermometer). Stir vanilla into the cooked syrup.

Pour hot syrup slowly over popped corn, tossing the corn just to mix thoroughly. Butter hands lightly; *working quickly,* use about ⅔ *of the mixture* to shape the snowman's "body" around the covered can. Fill in additional popcorn to curve over edges of can. Shape the remaining popcorn mixture into a ball for the "head." Use assorted candies for the face and features. Fill the can inside with assorted candies, if desired. Put the head atop body; add a yarn "scarf." Top with a hat made from red felt.

The clownish snowman of song and story—who led the youngsters such a merry chase—can come to life in your kitchen in the form of this *Popcorn Snowman.* Decorate his popped corn body and head with gumdrops. Complete the snowman masterpiece by adding a colorful yarn scarf and top with a red felt hat.

## Buttery Peanut Brittle (see photo, pages 4-5)

| | |
|---|---|
| 2 cups sugar | 1 cup butter *or* margarine |
| 1 cup light corn syrup | 2 cups peanuts, chopped |
| ½ cup water | 1 teaspoon baking soda |

Heat and stir sugar, syrup, and water in 3-quart saucepan till sugar dissolves. When syrup boils, blend in butter. Continue cooking; stir often after mixture reaches 230° on candy thermometer. Add nuts when mixture reaches 280°; cook and stir till it reaches hard-crack stage (300°). Remove from heat. Quickly stir in soda. Pour onto 2 buttered cookie sheets. Stretch thin by lifting and pulling with forks. Cool. Break up. Makes 2¼ pounds.

*Candy and Christmas—a combination as comfortable as peas-in-a-pod. Christmas is traditionally a time for special indulgence in all the forbidden sweets of the rest of the year. This peanut brittle is especially suited to holiday nibbling.*

## Caramel Crunch (see photo, page 78)

| | |
|---|---|
| 8 cups popped corn | 1⅓ cups sugar |
| 1 cup pecan halves, toasted | 1 cup butter *or* margarine |
| 1 cup whole unblanched almonds, toasted | ½ cup light corn syrup |
| | 1 teaspoon vanilla |

Combine popped corn and nuts on buttered shallow baking pan. In saucepan combine sugar, butter, and light corn syrup. Bring to boiling over medium heat, stirring constantly. Continue boiling, stirring occasionally, till mixture turns caramel color. Remove from heat and stir in vanilla. Pour syrup over corn-nut mixture. Separate into clusters with two forks. Store in tightly closed bag or container. Makes about 2 pounds.

## Peanut Candy Roll

| | |
|---|---|
| 1 cup salted peanuts | ⅓ cup light corn syrup |
| 6 tablespoons butter *or* margarine, softened | 1 teaspoon maple flavoring |
| | 4½ cups sifted powdered sugar |

Chop ½ *cup* of the nuts finely and remaining ½ *cup* coarsely. In mixing bowl blend together butter, corn syrup, maple flavoring, and ½ teaspoon salt. Stir in powdered sugar all at once; knead till smooth. Add a few drops of water, if necessary. Knead in finely chopped peanuts. Shape mixture into two rolls; brush with a little additional corn syrup and roll immediately in coarsely chopped peanuts. Wrap; chill. Makes 1½ pounds.

## Slovakian Nut Candy

| | |
|---|---|
| 1 cup sugar | 1 teaspoon vanilla |
| 1 cup finely chopped pecans | ⅛ teaspoon salt |

In 10-inch skillet heat and stir sugar till melted and golden brown. Stir in pecans, vanilla, and salt. Pour immediately onto buttered cookie sheet. Roll quickly with buttered rolling pin to 8x8-inch square. Immediately cut into diamonds or squares or break into small pieces. Makes ½ pound.

# Main Dishes

## Savory Quail

| | |
|---|---|
| 8 4- to 6-ounce ready-to-cook quail | ½ cup dry white wine |
| ¼ cup all-purpose flour | 2 tablespoons sliced green onion |
| 1 teaspoon salt | ½ cup light cream |
| ⅛ teaspoon pepper | 2 egg yolks |
| ¼ cup butter *or* margarine | |

Tie legs of each quail together with string. In plastic bag combine flour, salt, and pepper. Add quail 2 or 3 at a time; shake thoroughly to coat. In skillet brown quail in butter. Add wine and onion. Cover and simmer till birds are tender, 25 to 30 minutes. Remove quail to warm platter; keep warm. Reserve ½ cup pan juices in skillet. Beat cream with egg yolks, ¼ teaspoon salt, and dash pepper; slowly stir into pan juices. Cook and stir till thickened. (Do not boil.) Serve over quail. Makes 4 servings.

## Pheasants Jubilee

*If you aren't lucky enough to have a hunter in the family, you can purchase frozen quail, pheasant, squab, duck, or goose from a game farm or from large local supermarkets.*

Wash two 1½- to 3-pound ready-to-cook pheasants; pat dry. Salt cavities. Stuff *each* bird with 1 bay leaf, 1 clove garlic, 1 slice lemon, and a few celery leaves. Cover breast of *each* pheasant with 3 or 4 slices of bacon; tie drumsticks to tail. Place on rack in shallow roasting pan. Roast at 350° till done, 1 to 2½ hours. Remove birds from pan; set aside 1 tablespoon drippings. Remove strings; discard stuffing. Keep birds warm. In saucepan combine reserved drippings and 1 tablespoon cornstarch. Drain one 16-ounce can pitted light sweet cherries; reserve syrup. Halve cherries. Combine reserved syrup, ¼ cup dry white wine, and ¼ teaspoon salt; stir into cornstarch mixture. Cook and stir till thick and bubbly. Stir in cherries and 1 tablespoon butter. Heat through. Serve over birds. Makes 4 to 6 servings.

## Mexican Squab

| | |
|---|---|
| 4 12- to 14-ounce ready-to-cook squabs | ½ cup chopped onion |
| ⅔ cup all-purpose flour | 2 tablespoons chopped green chili peppers |
| ¼ cup cooking oil | 1 tablespoon snipped parsley |
| • • • | 1 clove garlic, minced |
| 1 16-ounce can tomatoes, cut up | ½ teaspoon dried oregano, crushed |
| ½ cup uncooked long grain rice | |

Halve birds lengthwise; coat with mixture of flour and 2 teaspoons salt. Brown in hot oil; remove and set aside. Drain off fat. In same skillet mix remaining ingredients, 1 cup water, and ¼ teaspoon salt. Add birds. Cover; cook till birds and rice are done, about 45 minutes; stir often. Makes 8 servings.

## Burgundy-Basted Duckling

*Dress up roasted poultry
with a basting sauce or glaze.
These mixtures of fruit
or wine add to the flavor of
the poultry and give the
meat an attractive glossy
appearance. For best results
brush the bird with sauce
or glaze several times
during the roasting period.*

1 4- to 5-pound ready-to-cook
    duckling
¼ cup Burgundy
¼ cup lemon juice
¼ cup butter *or* margarine,
    melted
1 tablespoon Worcestershire
    sauce
1 clove garlic, minced

1 teaspoon salt
1 teaspoon dried marjoram,
    crushed
¼ teaspoon pepper
¼ teaspoon bottled hot pepper
    sauce
1 small onion, sliced and
    separated into rings

Place duckling, breast side up, on a rack in a shallow roasting pan. Prick skin all over. Combine Burgundy, lemon juice, butter, Worcestershire, garlic, salt, marjoram, pepper, and pepper sauce. Brush inside cavity with some of the sauce; fill with onion. Do not tie legs. Brush duck with more sauce. Roast, uncovered, at 375° for 1½ to 2 hours; brush frequently with additional wine sauce. Drain off excess fat as necessary. Makes 3 or 4 servings.

## Chicken with Raspberry Glaze

1 3- to 4-pound ready-to-cook
    whole roasting chicken
    Cooking oil
¼ cup red raspberry jelly
1 tablespoon lemon juice

1 tablespoon butter *or*
    margarine
1½ teaspoons cornstarch
    Dash ground cinnamon
1 tablespoon vinegar

Place chicken, breast side up, on rack in shallow roasting pan. Rub skin with oil. Insert meat thermometer in center of inside thigh muscle not touching bone. Roast, uncovered, at 375° till thermometer registers 185°, 1½ to 2 hours. Heat and stir together jelly, lemon juice, and butter till jelly melts. Combine cornstarch, cinnamon, and ¼ teaspoon salt; blend in vinegar. Stir into jelly mixture. Cook and stir till thickened and bubbly. Brush on chicken several times; roast 15 minutes more. Makes 4 servings.

## Turkey with Stuffing Croquettes

1 2½-pound frozen boneless
    turkey roast
3 slices bacon
½ cup finely chopped celery
¼ cup finely chopped onion
1 beaten egg

¼ cup chicken broth
1 tablespoon snipped parsley
¼ teaspoon poultry seasoning
¼ teaspoon rubbed sage
6 cups bread cubes (9 slices
    bread)

Roast turkey on a rack in 13x9x2-inch baking pan according to package directions. Cook bacon; drain, reserving drippings. Crumble; set aside. Cook celery and onion in drippings till tender. Combine egg, broth, parsley, seasonings, bacon, and vegetables. Pour over bread; toss to mix. Using ½ cup for each, form stuffing into balls. About 20 minutes before roast is done, arrange balls on rack; roast 20 minutes more. Makes 6 servings.

# Roasting Chart for Domestic Poultry

*Preparation:* For generous holiday servings, plan on 3 or 4 servings for a large roasting chicken, 1 pound per serving for duck or goose, and ½ to ¾ of a pound per serving for turkey. Prepare the bird for roasting by rinsing, draining, and patting dry. Then, rub the inside cavity with salt, if desired. (Omit salt if stuffing will be added.) Do not stuff the bird until just before cooking. If possible, spoon some of the stuffing loosely into the wishbone cavity. Pull the neck skin to the back and fasten securely with a small skewer. Then spoon remaining stuffing into the tail cavity. Tuck turkey legs under band of skin or tie securely to tail.

*Roasting Directions:* Place bird, breast side up, on a rack in a shallow roasting pan. Rub the skin of chicken, capon, and turkey with cooking oil. (Do not use oil on duck or goose.) Insert a meat thermometer in the center of inside thigh muscle without touching bone. Roast poultry, uncovered, following the temperature and time on chart. When bird is ⅔ done, cut skin or string between legs and continue roasting till done.

*Test for Doneness:* The meat thermometer should register 185°. Also, the thickest part of the drumstick should feel very soft when pressed between fingers protected with paper toweling. The drumstick should move up and down and twist easily in the socket.

*Carving:* Remove bird from oven; let stand 15 minutes to firm up. Place bird on meat board with wing tips folded back. Pull leg out. Cut through meat between thigh and back. Disjoint leg. Make a deep horizontal cut into the breast close to wing before carving the white meat. Cut slices from top down to the horizontal cut. Repeat steps with other side of the bird.

| Poultry | Ready-to-Cook Weight | Oven Temp. | Guide to Roasting Time | Special Instructions |
|---|---|---|---|---|
| Chicken | 1½-2 lbs.<br>2½-3 lbs.<br>3½-4 lbs.<br>4½-5 lbs. | 400°<br>375°<br>375°<br>375° | 1-1¼ hrs.<br>1¼-1½ hrs.<br>1¾-2 hrs.<br>2¼-2½ hrs. | Brush dry areas of skin occasionally with pan drippings. Cover the chicken loosely with foil. |
| Capon | 4-7 lbs. | 375° | 1½-2 hrs. | Same as above. |
| Turkey | 6-8 lbs.<br>8-12 lbs.<br>12-16 lbs.<br>16-20 lbs.<br>20-24 lbs. | 325°<br>325°<br>325°<br>325°<br>325° | 3½-4 hrs.<br>4-4½ hrs.<br>4½-5½ hrs.<br>5½-6½ hrs.<br>6½-7½ hrs. | Cover loosely with foil. Press lightly at end of drumsticks and neck, leaving air space between bird and foil. Last 45 minutes, cut band of skin or string between legs. Roast, uncovered, till done. |
| Foil-wrapped Turkey | 7-9 lbs.<br>10-13 lbs.<br>14-17 lbs.<br>18-21 lbs.<br>22-24 lbs. | 450°<br>450°<br>450°<br>450°<br>450° | 2¼-2½ hrs.<br>2¾-3 hrs.<br>3-3¼ hrs.<br>3¼-3½ hrs.<br>3¼-3¾ hrs. | Place skewered turkey, breast up, in center of greased, wide, heavy foil. Bring ends of foil up over breast; overlap fold and press up against ends of turkey. Place bird in shallow pan (no rack). Open foil last 20 minutes. |
| Domestic Duck | 3-5 lbs. | 375° | 1½-2 hrs. | Prick skin well all over to allow fat to escape. Do not rub with oil. |
| Domestic Goose | 7-9 lbs.<br>9-11 lbs.<br>11-13 lbs. | 350°<br>350°<br>350° | 2½-3 hrs.<br>3-3½ hrs.<br>3½-4 hrs. | Prick legs and wings with fork so fat will escape. During roasting, spoon off fat in pan. Do not rub with oil. |
| Cornish Game Hen | 1-1½ lbs. | 375° | 1½ hrs. | Roast, loosely covered, for ½ hour, then roast, uncovered, till done, about 1 hour. If desired, baste occasionally with butter the last hour. |

## Fluffy Stuffing

*Try any of the dressings on these two pages in any type of poultry. To determine how much stuffing you'll need, plan on using ¾ cup stuffing for every pound the bird weighs. So, a 3-pound duck will need 2¼ cups dressing and a 10-pound turkey, 7½ cups.*

1 cup chopped onion
¼ cup butter *or* margarine
8 cups soft bread cubes
　　(12 slices bread)

4 cups crisp rice cereal
2 teaspoons poultry
　　seasoning
1½ cups chicken broth

In skillet cook onion in butter or margarine till tender but not brown. Add bread cubes, cereal, and poultry seasoning; pour chicken broth over mixture. Toss lightly to mix. Use to stuff poultry *or* bake, covered, in a 2-quart casserole at 375° for 30 to 35 minutes. Makes 8 cups stuffing.

## Wild Rice and Oyster Stuffing

1 6-ounce package long grain
　　and wild rice mix
1 cup chopped onion
2 tablespoons butter

1 8-ounce can oysters,
　　drained and chopped
1 cup chopped fully cooked ham
¾ cup fine dry bread crumbs

Cook rice mix according to package directions. In skillet cook onion in butter till tender but not brown. Add cooked rice mix, oysters, ham, and bread crumbs. Toss gently to mix. Use to stuff poultry *or* bake, covered, in 1½-quart casserole at 350° for 40 to 45 minutes. Makes 5 cups stuffing.

## Bean and Sausage Stuffing

6 fully cooked smoked sausage
　　links, thinly sliced
1 cup chopped onion
1 16-ounce can dark red kidney
　　beans

1 10½-ounce can condensed
　　beef broth
3 tablespoons snipped parsley
1 8-ounce package herb-
　　seasoned stuffing mix

In skillet cook sausage and onion till onion is tender; drain off fat. Stir in undrained beans, broth, and parsley. Pour over stuffing mix and toss lightly to mix. Use to stuff poultry *or* bake, covered, in a 1½-quart casserole at 375° for 30 to 35 minutes. Makes 6 cups stuffing.

## Potato Dressing

*The Pennsylvania Dutch serve many traditional foods including cracker pudding, mincemeat, and plum pudding for Christmas. One special favorite is a recipe they call potato filling. It goes well with many types of poultry — especially duck.*

¾ cup chopped onion
¼ cup chopped celery
¼ cup butter *or* margarine
2 medium potatoes, cooked and
　　mashed (2 cups)

1½ cups soft bread crumbs
2 beaten eggs
2 tablespoons snipped parsley
½ teaspoon dried marjoram,
　　crushed

In skillet cook onion and celery in butter or margarine till tender but not brown. Combine with remaining ingredients, ¾ teaspoon salt, and ⅛ teaspoon pepper; mix thoroughly. Use to stuff poultry *or* bake, covered, in a 1-quart casserole at 375° for 45 minutes. Makes 3 cups dressing.

## Corn Stuffing Balls

| | |
|---|---|
| 8 slices bacon | ½ teaspoon ground sage |
| 1 cup chopped celery | ¼ teaspoon pepper |
| ½ cup chopped onion | 3 cups coarsely crumbled |
| 1 8¾-ounce can cream-style | corn bread |
| corn | 3 cups slightly dry bread |
| 1 teaspoon poultry seasoning | cubes (4 slices) |
| ½ teaspoon salt | 2 beaten eggs |

*Corn Stuffing Balls are an easy variation of traditional corn bread stuffing. You will find they go well with meats other than poultry such as roast, lamb, pork chops, or pot roast.*

In skillet cook bacon till crisp; drain, reserving ⅓ cup drippings. Crumble bacon and set aside. Cook celery and onion in the reserved bacon drippings till tender but not brown. Stir in bacon, cream-style corn, poultry seasoning, salt, sage, and pepper. Pour the mixture over the crumbled corn bread and dry bread cubes. Add the beaten eggs and toss lightly to mix. Using a ½-cup measure, firmly pack stuffing into cup. Turn out of cup and gently form into a ball. Repeat with remaining stuffing. Place stuffing balls in a shallow baking pan. Bake at 375° for 15 minutes. Makes 10 stuffing balls.

## Meaty Rice Stuffing

| | |
|---|---|
| ½ pound ground beef | 1 teaspoon salt |
| ½ cup chopped onion | ½ teaspoon dried savory, |
| ¼ teaspoon salt | crushed |
| 3 cups water | ¼ teaspoon dried thyme, |
| 2½ cups quick-cooking rice | crushed |
| 2 cups chopped celery | ¼ teaspoon ground sage |
| ½ cup chopped celery leaves | ¼ teaspoon pepper |

In saucepan cook beef, onion, and ¼ teaspoon salt till meat is browned and onion is tender. Drain. Stir in water, rice, celery, celery leaves, 1 teaspoon salt, savory, thyme, sage, and pepper. Bring quickly to a boil. Cover and remove from heat. Let stand 10 minutes. Use to stuff poultry *or* bake, covered, in a 2-quart casserole at 325° for 1 hour. Makes 8 cups stuffing.

## Holiday Apple Stuffing

| | |
|---|---|
| 1 cup finely chopped onion | ¾ teaspoon ground sage |
| 2 tablespoons butter *or* | ½ teaspoon salt |
| margarine | ⅛ teaspoon pepper |
| 2 cups chopped peeled apple | 2 beaten eggs |
| 1 5-ounce can water chestnuts, | ½ cup chicken broth |
| drained and sliced | 4 cups dry bread cubes (about |
| 3 tablespoons snipped parsley | 5½ slices bread) |

In a skillet cook onion in butter or margarine till tender but not brown. Stir in apple, water chestnuts, snipped parsley, sage, salt, and pepper. Stir in eggs and chicken broth. Pour the egg-apple mixture over the bread cubes. Toss lightly to mix. Use to stuff poultry *or* bake, covered, in a 1½-quart casserole at 375° for 30 to 35 minutes. Makes 4½ cups stuffing.

## Beef Wellington

1 4-pound beef tenderloin
  roast
2 cups all-purpose flour
½ teaspoon salt
⅔ cup shortening
⅓ to ½ cup cold water
2 2¾-ounce cans liver pâté
1 beaten egg

1½ cups water
2 beef bouillon cubes
½ cup cold water
¼ cup all-purpose flour
⅓ cup Burgundy
½ teaspoon dried basil,
  crushed
Parsley sprigs

Place roast on a rack in a shallow roasting pan. Insert meat thermometer. Roast at 425° till meat thermometer registers 130°, about 45 minutes. Reserve drippings. Cool meat. Stir 2 cups flour and salt together; cut in shortening till mixture resembles coarse crumbs. Slowly add ⅓ to ½ cup cold water, tossing with fork till moistened. Form into a ball. Roll to 14x12-inch rectangle; spread pâté to within ½ inch of edges. Center meat, top down, on pastry. Draw up long sides; overlap. Brush with egg; seal. Trim ends; fold up. Brush with egg; seal. Place on greased baking sheet, seam down. Brush with egg. Bake at 425° for 35 minutes. Meanwhile for gravy, in saucepan combine reserved drippings, 1½ cups water, and bouillon cubes. Heat and stir till bouillon dissolves. Blend ½ cup cold water into ¼ cup flour; add to pan with Burgundy and basil. Cook and stir till thickened and bubbly. Season to taste with salt and pepper. Trim beef with parsley; serve with gravy. Makes 12 servings.

## Vegetable-Stuffed Sirloin

¼ cup chopped celery
¼ cup chopped onion
¼ cup shredded carrot
2 tablespoons butter *or*
  margarine
• • •
1 teaspoon salt
1 teaspoon dried savory,
  crushed
½ teaspoon dried basil,
  crushed

¼ teaspoon dried thyme,
  crushed
⅛ teaspoon pepper
1 3- to 4-pound beef sirloin
  tip roast
¾ cup dry red wine
½ cup water
½ cup water
⅓ cup all-purpose flour
½ teaspoon Kitchen Bouquet

In a small skillet cook celery, onion, and carrot in butter or margarine till vegetables are tender but not brown; cool slightly. Combine salt, savory, basil, thyme, and pepper. Cut a horizontal pocket in the meaty end of the roast. Rub the herb mixture on all surfaces of the meat including the pocket. Stuff pocket with vegetable mixture; skewer closed. Place roast on rack in a shallow roasting pan. Combine wine and first ½ cup water; pour over meat. Cover and cook in 350° oven till meat is tender, 2 to 2½ hours. Remove meat to warm platter. Skim excess fat from pan juices. Add enough water to pan juices to equal 2½ cups liquid. Blend together remaining ½ cup water, flour, and Kitchen Bouquet; stir into pan juice mixture. Cook, stirring constantly, over medium heat till mixture is thickened and bubbly. Serve the gravy with the stuffed roast. Makes 10 to 12 servings.

## Beef with Yorkshire Pudding

Place one 8-pound beef standing rib roast, fat side up, in a shallow roasting pan. Season with salt and pepper. Insert meat thermometer avoiding bone. Roast, uncovered, at 325° till meat thermometer registers 140° for rare, 160° for medium, and 170° for well-done, Allow about 3¼ hours for rare, 4 hours for medium, and 4¾ hours for well-done. Remove meat from pan. Cover; keep warm. Reserve ¼ cup meat drippings. Increase oven temperature to 400°. Combine 4 eggs, 2 cups all-purpose flour, 2 cups milk, and 1 teaspoon salt. Beat 1½ minutes with rotary beater or electric mixer. Pour *half* reserved drippings into *each* of two 9x9x2-inch baking pans. Pour *half* batter into each pan. Bake at 400° for 30 minutes. Serve with roast. Makes 12 servings.

*Some say Beef with Yorkshire Pudding came to America via the fashionable cooks who settled in the Carolinas and Maryland; others claim that English-Canadians introduced it into our border states. Certainly it is a great favorite among Anglo-Americans even today any time, but especially as a festive main course for Christmas dinner.*

## Veal Roast à la Bleu

| | |
|---|---|
| 1 4- to 6-pound veal sirloin<br>    roast | 2 tablespoons dry sauterne<br>¼ cup cold water |
| 1 8-ounce can tomatoes, cut up | 2 tablespoons cornstarch |
| ¾ cup finely chopped fully<br>    cooked ham | ½ cup shredded Swiss cheese<br>    (2 ounces) |

Place roast, fat side up, on rack in shallow roasting pan. Mix undrained tomatoes, ham, wine, and dash pepper; pour over roast. Cover and cook in 350° oven till meat is tender, 2 to 2½ hours. Uncover and continue cooking 15 minutes more. Remove meat to platter. Blend water into cornstarch; stir into pan juices. Cook and stir till thickened and bubbly. Add cheese and stir over low heat till melted. Serve with roast. Makes 6 to 8 servings.

## Cranberry-Pork Crown Roast

*For holiday meals that call for something extra special try serving Cranberry-Pork Crown Roast. It features a meat cut you may not be familiar with, the pork crown roast. Your butcher probably will need a few days to get the roast, so be sure to order several days ahead.*

| | |
|---|---|
| 1 5½- to 6-pound pork crown roast (12 to 16 ribs) | 2 18-ounce cans vacuum-packed sweet potatoes |
| ½ cup cranberry juice cocktail | Cranberry-Apricot Sauce |
| 2 tablespoons light corn syrup | Gravy |

Place roast in a shallow roasting pan, bone ends down. Insert meat thermometer making sure it does not rest on bone. Roast at 325° till thermometer reads 170°, 3 to 3½ hours. Meanwhile, combine cranberry juice and corn syrup; use to baste roast 4 times during last hour of roasting.

Drain sweet potatoes; place in a 2-quart casserole. Pour *half* Cranberry-Apricot Sauce over potatoes; reserve remaining sauce. Cover; bake along with roast during last 45 minutes. To serve roast, place on warm platter, reserving drippings. Arrange potatoes in crown center and around roast. Spoon hot reserved Cranberry-Apricot Sauce over potatoes. Slice between ribs allowing one rib per person. Serve with Gravy. Serves 12 to 16.

*Cranberry-Apricot Sauce:* In saucepan combine one 8-ounce can whole cranberry sauce, ½ cup apricot preserves, ¼ cup cranberry juice cocktail, ¼ teaspoon salt, and ¼ teaspoon ground cinnamon. Bring to boiling.

*Gravy:* Skim fat from reserved pan drippings; add enough water to make 2 cups. In saucepan blend 1 tablespoon cold water into 2 tablespoons cornstarch. Add meat drippings mixture. Cook and stir till thickened and bubbly.

## Pork Chops with Prunes

| | |
|---|---|
| 4 pork loin chops, cut ½ inch thick | ¾ cup dry white wine |
| 8 ounces pitted dried prunes | 2 tablespoons currant jelly |
| | ¼ cup dairy sour cream |

Trim fat from chops. In skillet cook trimmings till 1 tablespoon fat accumulates; discard trimmings. Brown chops in hot fat; season with salt and pepper. Add ¼ cup water. Cover; simmer till tender, about 45 minutes. Simmer prunes in wine for 25 to 30 minutes; drain, reserving liquid. Transfer prunes and chops to heated platter; reserve pan drippings. Add reserved prune liquid to drippings; cook till mixture measures about ⅓ cup. Stir in jelly till melted. Stir some of the hot mixture into sour cream; return to skillet. Heat, *but do not boil.* Spoon sauce over chops. Makes 4 servings.

## Glazed Ham Loaf

Combine 2 eggs, ¾ cup quick-cooking *or* regular rolled oats, and ½ cup milk. Add ¾ pound ground fully cooked ham (3 cups) and ¾ pound ground pork; mix thoroughly. Shape mixture into a loaf and place in a 10x6x2-inch baking dish. Bake at 350° for 1 hour. Meanwhile, in a saucepan combine ⅔ cup apricot nectar, ⅓ cup packed brown sugar, ⅓ cup dark corn syrup, 2 tablespoons vinegar, 1 tablespoon all-purpose flour, 1 teaspoon dry mustard, and 6 whole cloves. Cook, stirring constantly, till mixture is slightly thickened. Remove cloves. Pour *half* the apricot sauce over the ham loaf and bake 15 minutes more. Pass remaining sauce. Makes 6 to 8 servings.

## Cranberry-Orange Ham

| | |
|---|---|
| ½ cup sugar | 2 cups cranberries, ground |
| 3 tablespoons cornstarch | 1 8-pound boneless fully |
| 1 12-ounce jar orange | cooked ham, cut into ¼ |
| marmalade | inch thick slices |

In a small saucepan blend sugar and cornstarch together. Stir in the orange marmalade and ground cranberries. Cook and stir over low heat till sugar is dissolved and mixture thickens and bubbles. Cool. Spread mixture on every other ham slice, using about 1 tablespoon mixture for each slice. Reassemble ham to its original shape. Tie slices together and place on a rack in a shallow roasting pan. Roast at 325° for 2¼ to 2½ hours. If desired, baste ham with pan juices during the last 15 minutes of roasting time. To serve, place ham on a warm platter and carefully remove string. Makes 24 servings.

## Noel Ham

| | |
|---|---|
| 1 5-pound canned ham | 1 16-ounce jar spiced crab |
| Whole cloves | apples *or* 1 14-ounce jar |
| ½ cup packed brown sugar | spiced apple rings |

Score top of ham in a diamond pattern; stud with whole cloves. Place ham on a rack in a shallow roasting pan. Insert meat thermometer. Bake ham at 325° till meat thermometer registers 140°, about 1½ hours. Meanwhile, measure sugar into saucepan. Drain apples, reserving syrup. Stir reserved apple syrup into brown sugar; bring to boiling. Reduce heat and simmer 2 minutes. About 30 minutes before end of baking, place apples around ham; baste ham and apples with some of the brown sugar mixture. Continue baking; baste ham and apples frequently with remaining mixture. Makes 14 servings.

## Lobster Newburg

| | |
|---|---|
| Pastry Petal Cups | 3 beaten egg yolks |
| 6 tablespoons butter *or* | 1 5-ounce can lobster, drained |
| margarine | and broken into pieces |
| 2 tablespoons all-purpose | 3 tablespoons dry white wine |
| flour | 2 teaspoons lemon juice |
| 1½ cups light cream | Paprika |

Prepare Pastry Petal Cups. Melt butter or margarine in a saucepan; blend in flour. Add cream all at once. Cook and stir till sauce thickens and bubbles. Stir a moderate amount of hot mixture into egg yolks; return to remaining hot mixture. Cook and stir till mixture thickens. Stir in lobster; heat through. Stir in wine, lemon juice, and ¼ teaspoon salt. Serve in Pastry Petal Cups. Sprinkle lobster mixture with paprika. Makes 5 servings.

*Pastry Petal Cups:* Prepare 1 stick piecrust mix according to package directions. Roll ⅛ inch thick; cut into twenty-five 2¼-inch rounds. In each of 5 muffin cups, place one round in bottom; overlap 4 rounds on sides. Press together. Prick. Bake at 450° for 10 to 12 minutes. Cool.

*Lobster Newburg was created at Delmonico's, a famous New York City restaurant of the 1890's. The chef named the dish for a frequent patron named Wenburg. The fame of the dish spread and it is now thoroughly enjoyed in many parts of the country— especially in New England, where it is a traditional favorite for festive meals.*

Add a touch of elegance to your holidays by serving *Leg of Lamb Italian.* Garnish this flavorful roast with pear halves filled with strawberry jelly, twisted orange slices, and a sprig of parsley.

## Red Snapper with Crab Stuffing

*Red Snapper with Crab Stuffing is ideal for meatless Christmas Eve meals or for a change of pace on Christmas Day. You can substitute another mild-flavored whole fish, like white fish or flounder.*

¼ cup chopped onion
¼ cup chopped celery
¼ cup butter *or* margarine
1 7½-ounce can crab meat, drained and cartilage removed
1 3-ounce can chopped mushrooms, drained

½ cup coarsely crushed saltine crackers (11)
Dash pepper
1 3- to 3½-pound red snapper, boned and dressed
Salt
Cooking oil
Cheese-Wine Sauce

Cook onion and celery in butter till tender but not brown. Stir in crab, mushrooms, saltine cracker crumbs, and pepper. Sprinkle the red snapper both inside and out with salt. Brush a large shallow roasting pan lightly with cooking oil. Place fish in pan. Fill the inside of the snapper *loosely* with the crab mixture; fasten the opening with several wooden picks. Brush the top side of the snapper with cooking oil. Spoon the remaining crab mixture into a small casserole or baking dish; cover. Bake fish and extra stuffing at 350° till fish flakes easily when tested with fork, 35 to 40 minutes; brush occasionally with cooking oil. Lift fish to warm platter; remove wooden picks. Serve fish immediately with Cheese-Wine Sauce. Makes 4 to 6 servings.

*Cheese-Wine Sauce:* In a saucepan melt 2 tablespoons butter *or* margarine. Blend in 2 tablespoons all-purpose flour, ¼ teaspoon salt, and dash pepper. Add 1 cup milk all at once. Cook and stir till mixture is thickened and bubbly. Stir in ½ cup shredded sharp American cheese (2 ounces) and 2 tablespoons dry white wine. Heat till cheese is melted, stirring constantly.

# Leg of Lamb Italian

| | |
|---|---|
| ⅓ cup lemon juice | 1 teaspoon dry mustard |
| ¼ cup cooking oil | ½ teaspoon garlic powder |
| 1 tablespoon dried oregano, crushed | 1 5- to 6-pound lamb leg |
| 2 teaspoons chopped anchovies | ¼ cup all-purpose flour |

Combine lemon juice, oil, oregano, anchovies, mustard, garlic powder, and 1 teaspoon salt. Place lamb in large plastic bag; set in a deep bowl. Pour marinade over lamb in bag and close. Marinate in refrigerator overnight, pressing bag against meat occasionally. Drain, reserving marinade. Place meat, fat side up, on rack in shallow roasting pan. Insert meat thermometer, making sure it does not touch bone. Roast at 325° till meat thermometer registers 175° to 180°, for 3 to 3½ hours. Baste occasionally with reserved marinade. Remove lamb to serving platter. Skim fat from pan drippings; pour drippings into measuring cup. Add enough of the remaining marinade to measure 2¼ cups liquid. Blend ¼ cup cold water into flour; stir into marinade mixture. Cook and stir till thickened and bubbly. Makes 8 to 10 servings.

# Lamb Chops with Cranberry Stuffing

| | |
|---|---|
| 6 lamb shoulder chops, cut ¾ inch thick (about 2¼ pounds total) | ¼ cup chopped onion |
| Cooking oil | ½ cup butter *or* margarine |
| 2 cups whole cranberries, chopped | 1 8-ounce package herb-seasoned stuffing mix |
| ⅓ cup sugar | 1 cup water |
| ½ cup chopped celery | 2 medium oranges, sectioned and chopped |
| | ½ cup chopped pecans |

In a large skillet brown the lamb chops slowly in a small amount of cooking oil for 10 to 15 minutes. Remove chops from pan; drain off excess fat. Meanwhile, combine cranberries and sugar; let stand a few minutes. Cook celery and onion in butter till tender but not brown. Remove from heat; stir in stuffing mix and water. Mix thoroughly. Stir in cranberries, oranges, and pecans. Turn into 13x9x2-inch baking dish. Top with lamb chops. Sprinkle with salt and pepper. Cover; bake at 350° for 45 minutes. Uncover and bake till desired doneness, about 15 minutes more. Makes 6 servings.

# Grilled Cheese and Pork Sandwiches

| | |
|---|---|
| 12 slices sharp American cheese | ¾ cup applesauce |
| 12 thin slices cooked pork | 12 slices white bread |
| Ground cinnamon | Butter, softened |

Place 1 slice cheese, 2 slices pork, dash cinnamon, dash salt, 2 tablespoons applesauce, and a second slice cheese on each of *6 slices* of bread. Top with remaining bread slices. Spread outside of sandwiches with butter; place on a hot griddle. Cook till golden, 10 to 12 minutes. Makes 6 servings.

*Using leftover meats from holiday meals can be a problem. So, to add zest to after-the-holiday menus try this recipe and those on the next two pages.*

## Denver Scramble

Denver Scramble is a sophisticated version of the Denver sandwich. This egg, leftover ham, onion, and green pepper combination was created by the pioneers out West to use up the last of the eggs. Now, it makes a tasty dish for late-night entertaining and snacks.

1 cup finely chopped fully
   cooked ham
1 2-ounce can mushroom stems
   and pieces, drained
¼ cup chopped onion

2 tablespoons chopped green
   pepper
2 tablespoons butter
8 beaten eggs
⅓ cup milk

In a medium skillet cook ham, mushrooms, onion, and green pepper in butter till vegetables are tender but not brown, about 5 minutes. Combine the eggs and milk; add to skillet, folding eggs over with wide spatula so the uncooked part goes to the bottom. Cook till eggs are set throughout but are still fluffy and moist, 5 to 8 minutes. Makes 6 servings.

## Beef and Broccoli Casserole

1 10-ounce package frozen
   cut broccoli
½ cup long grain rice
   • • •
½ cup chopped onion
¼ cup butter *or* margarine
3 tablespoons all-purpose
   flour
¾ teaspoon salt

⅛ teaspoon pepper
2¼ cups milk
1 cup shredded sharp American
   cheese (4 ounces)
2 cups cubed cooked beef
1 cup herb-seasoned stuffing
   mix
⅓ cup water

Cook broccoli and rice according to package directions. Drain both; set aside. In a saucepan cook onion in *2 tablespoons* of the butter till tender but not brown. Blend in flour, salt, and pepper. Add milk. Cook and stir till sauce is thickened and bubbly. Add cheese; stir till melted. Stir in cooked rice, broccoli, and beef. Turn into 2-quart casserole. Melt remaining butter. Add herb-seasoned stuffing mix and water. Sprinkle over all. Bake, uncovered, at 350° till heated through, 35 to 40 minutes. Makes 6 servings.

## Turkey Chowder

2 cups cubed potatoes
1 10-ounce package frozen baby
   lima beans
½ cup chopped onion
½ cup sliced celery
¼ teaspoon salt
1 10½-ounce can condensed
   cream of chicken soup

1 16-ounce can tomatoes,
   cut up
1½ cups chopped cooked
   turkey *or* chicken
½ teaspoon poultry seasoning
¼ teaspoon garlic salt
⅛ teaspoon pepper
½ cup shredded Cheddar cheese

In 3-quart saucepan, combine potatoes, beans, onion, celery, and salt. Blend 2 cups water into soup; add to vegetables. Cook, covered, till vegetables are tender, 35 to 45 minutes. Add undrained tomatoes, turkey, poultry seasoning, garlic salt, and pepper. Simmer 15 minutes. Serve in bowls; sprinkle *1 tablespoon* cheese over each serving. Serves 8.

## Curried Turkey Open-Facers

1 large apple, cored
1 tablespoon butter *or*
    margarine
1 envelope sour cream
    sauce mix
1 teaspoon curry powder

3 English muffins, split and
    toasted
Butter *or* margarine,
    softened
12 thin slices cooked turkey
    *or* chicken

Cut apple into 12 wedges; cook in 1 tablespoon butter 1 to 2 minutes on each side. Prepare sauce mix according to package directions; stir in curry. Spread cut side of muffins with butter and a little sauce. Keep remaining sauce warm. Overlap 2 turkey slices atop each muffin half. Top with 2 apple wedges. Wrap sandwiches in foil. Bake at 400° for 15 to 20 minutes. Unwrap onto serving plates. Spoon remaining sauce over. Makes 6.

*With the high cost of meat, smart shoppers know that one way to save money is to plan ahead — even during the holidays. Take advantage of the lower cost per pound of large whole turkeys and roasting chickens. Buy the largest bird you can cook and store. Then wrap and freeze the leftovers to use later in recipes like Curried Turkey Open-Facers.*

## Chicken-Cranberry Pinwheel Bake

¼ cup chopped onion
¼ cup butter *or* margarine
⅓ cup all-purpose flour
1 13¾-ounce can chicken broth
1⅓ cups milk
3 cups chopped cooked chicken
    *or* turkey

1 3-ounce can sliced
    mushrooms, drained
2 cups packaged biscuit mix
½ cup milk
½ cup cranberry-orange relish
2 teaspoons sugar

In saucepan cook onion in butter till tender but not brown. Blend in flour; add chicken broth and 1⅓ cups milk. Cook and stir till thickened and bubbly. Stir in chicken or turkey and mushrooms. Keep hot. Combine biscuit mix and ½ cup milk. Stir till well blended. Turn out on lightly floured surface; knead 5 or 6 times. Roll out to 10-inch square. Combine cranberry relish and sugar; spread over dough, leaving ½-inch edge. Roll up jelly-roll fashion. Moisten edge with a little water to seal; cut into 8 slices. Turn chicken mixture into 12x7½x2-inch baking dish. Arrange pinwheels, cut side down atop chicken mixture. Bake at 425° for 25 minutes. Makes 8 servings.

## Chicken-Macaroni Molds

1 3-ounce package lemon-
    flavored gelatin
1 cup boiling water
½ cup cold water
2 tablespoons wine vinegar
1 tablespoon chopped onion

⅓ cup mayonnaise
1 cup cooked macaroni
1 cup diced cooked chicken
    *or* turkey
½ cup diced celery
Lettuce

Dissolve gelatin in boiling water. Stir in cold water, vinegar, onion, 1 teaspoon salt, and dash pepper. Gradually stir gelatin mixture into mayonnaise; beat till smooth. Chill till partially set. Fold in macaroni, chicken, and celery. Turn into six ½-cup molds. Chill till firm, 3 to 4 hours. Unmold onto lettuce-lined plates. Garnish with tomato wedges, if desired. Serves 6.

# Salads and Vegetables

*Pictured opposite:* Enhance your holiday menus with colorful *Cherry Blossom Muffins* (see recipe, page 118), *Cranberry-Whipped Cream Salad,* and festive red and green layered *Fruited Holiday Wreath.*

●

## Cranberry-Whipped Cream Salad

1 8¼-ounce can crushed
    pineapple
1 3-ounce package raspberry-
    flavored gelatin
1 16-ounce can whole
    cranberry sauce

1 teaspoon grated orange peel
1 11-ounce can mandarin
    orange sections, drained
1 cup whipping cream
    ● ● ●
Frosted Fruit

Drain pineapple; reserve syrup. Add boiling water to reserved syrup to make 1 cup. Dissolve gelatin in hot liquid. Stir in cranberry sauce and orange peel; chill till partially set. Fold in orange sections and pineapple. Whip cream; fold into fruit mixture. Pour into 6-cup mold. Chill till set. Unmold; garnish cranberry salad with Frosted Fruit. Makes 8 to 10 servings.

*Frosted Fruit:* Break 1 pound green grapes into small clusters. Dip grapes and ½ pound cranberries into beaten egg white. Drain; dip fruit in granulated sugar to coat. Place fruit on rack to dry for 2 hours.

*To unmold a gelatin salad, loosen with the tip of a knife and then dip the mold for a few seconds just to the rim in warm water. Rinse the platter with cold water and place face down over top of mold. Hold tightly together and invert. Then lift off the mold. If you want lettuce or other greens around the mold, tuck pieces under the edges of the mold on the serving plate.*

## Fruited Holiday Wreath

1 8-ounce package cream
    cheese, softened
¼ cup chopped walnuts
    ● ● ●
1 3-ounce package lime-
    flavored gelatin
2 cups boiling water
2½ cups cold water
½ cup chopped celery
1 envelope unflavored gelatin

1 6-ounce can frozen lemonade
    concentrate, thawed
¼ cup sugar
1 cup mayonnaise *or* salad
    dressing
1 16-ounce can fruit cocktail
1 3-ounce package cherry-
    flavored gelatin
½ cup whipping cream

Form cream cheese into balls. Roll in walnuts; set cream cheese balls aside. Dissolve lime-flavored gelatin in *1 cup* boiling water; stir in *1 cup* cold water and celery. Chill lime mixture till partially set. Pour a little of the lime mixture into 8½-inch fluted tube pan or 9½-cup ring mold; chill till almost set. Carefully arrange cheese balls in mold. Slowly pour remaining lime gelatin over cheese balls being careful not to disturb arrangement; chill till just firm.

Soften unflavored gelatin in ½ *cup* cold water; stir over low heat till gelatin is dissolved. Add ½ *cup* lemonade concentrate, sugar, and remaining 1 cup cold water. Beat in ½ *cup* mayonnaise. Chill till second layer is partially set. Carefully pour over lime layer. Chill again till almost firm. Drain fruit cocktail; reserve syrup. Add enough water to syrup to make 1 cup. Dissolve cherry gelatin in remaining 1 cup boiling water; stir in syrup mixture. Chill till partially set. Fold in fruit cocktail; carefully pour over lemonade layer. Chill till firm. Unmold. Combine remaining mayonnaise and remaining lemonade concentrate. Whip cream; fold into mayonnaise mixture; serve with salad. Makes 12 to 14 servings.

*Many fruit gelatin salads also can serve as the dessert course. For a meal that calls for a substantial dessert, use a gelatin salad that's rich with fruit and whipped cream. If you need a light dessert, serve a whipped fruit-flavored gelatin.*

## Cranberry-Cheese Squares

1 envelope unflavored gelatin
1 7-ounce bottle ginger ale
1 16-ounce can whole cranberry
 sauce
2 tablespoons lemon juice
¼ teaspoon ground allspice
⅛ teaspoon ground nutmeg
1 11-ounce can mandarin orange
 sections, drained

1 3-ounce package raspberry-
 flavored gelatin
1 cup boiling water
1 3-ounce package cream
 cheese, softened
1 cup cranberry juice
 cocktail
• • •
½ cup whipping cream

Soften the unflavored gelatin in ¼ *cup* of the ginger ale; dissolve over hot water. Combine the whole cranberry sauce, lemon juice, allspice, nutmeg, and remaining ginger ale; stir in the softened unflavored gelatin. Pour into an 8x8x2-inch dish. Arrange the drained mandarin orange sections in the gelatin; chill till almost firm.

Dissolve the raspberry-flavored gelatin in the boiling water. Blend into the cream cheese; beat smooth. Stir in the cranberry juice cocktail; chill till partially set. Whip the cream till soft peaks form; fold into chilled raspberry mixture. Pour over cranberry layer. Chill till firm, 5 to 6 hours or overnight. Cut in squares to serve. Makes 9 servings.

## Creamy Cranberry Mold

1 8¼-ounce can crushed
 pineapple
1 teaspoon grated orange peel
2 medium oranges
 Water

1 3-ounce package raspberry-
 flavored gelatin
1 16-ounce can whole
 cranberry sauce, cut up
½ cup whipping cream

Drain pineapple, reserving syrup. After grating orange peel, section oranges over bowl to catch juice. Dice sections; set aside. Combine reserved pineapple syrup and orange juice; add water to make ¾ cup. Heat to boiling. Dissolve raspberry gelatin in boiling liquid. Beat in cranberry sauce. Chill till partially set. Fold in orange peel, oranges, and pineapple. Whip cream till soft peaks form; fold into gelatin mixture. Pour into a 5-cup mold. Chill till set. Unmold. Makes 8 to 10 servings.

## Cran-Apple Salad Molds

1 6-ounce package strawberry-
 flavored gelatin
2 cups boiling water
1 8½-ounce can applesauce

1 16-ounce can whole
 cranberry sauce
½ cup port
¼ cup chopped walnuts

Dissolve the strawberry-flavored gelatin in 2 cups boiling water. Stir in the applesauce, cranberry sauce, and port. Chill mixture till partially set; fold in chopped walnuts. Pour into ten 5-ounce individual molds. Chill till firm, 5 to 6 hours or overnight. Makes 10 servings.

## Frozen Cheesecake Salad

| | |
|---|---|
| 1 10¾- *or* 11-ounce package cheesecake mix | 10 drops red food coloring |
| 1 8¼-ounce can crushed pineapple | 1 cup cranberries, chopped |
| 1 cup milk | ½ cup chopped nuts |
| | ½ cup snipped pitted dates |

Reserve graham cracker crumb portion of cheesecake mix for use another time. In small mixing bowl blend together dry cheesecake mix, *undrained* pineapple, milk, and food coloring; beat till slightly thickened. Fold in cranberries, nuts, and dates. Turn mixture into foil-lined 3-cup refrigerator tray. Freeze. Remove from pan; cut into wedges. Makes 6 servings.

## Cranberry Relish Salad

| | |
|---|---|
| 1 3-ounce package cream cheese, softened | 1 14-ounce jar cranberry-orange relish |
| 2 cups frozen whipped dessert topping, thawed | 1½ cups tiny marshmallows |
| • • • | 1 8¼-ounce can crushed pineapple, drained |
| 1 11-ounce can mandarin orange sections, drained | ⅓ cup chopped nuts |
| | Lettuce leaves |

Beat cream cheese into dessert topping. Reserve a few mandarin oranges for garnish. Stir remaining oranges, relish, marshmallows, pineapple, and nuts into topping mixture. Chill several hours. Serve on lettuce-lined plates; garnish with reserved mandarin oranges. Makes 6 to 8 servings.

*Cranberries, America's gift to the holiday table, find their way into most holiday meals. Preserve this tradition but avoid monotony by serving this zesty fruit in various ways. You'll find taste-tempting recipes for salads and relishes using cranberries in all forms on these pages.*

## Cranberry-Orange Relish

| | |
|---|---|
| 1 16-ounce package cranberries | 1 teaspoon grated orange peel |
| 2 cups sugar | 1¼ cups orange juice |

In saucepan combine cranberries, sugar, grated orange peel, and orange juice. Bring to boiling; reduce heat. Boil gently, uncovered, till cranberry skins pop, 8 to 10 minutes. Stir once or twice. Cool. Store in covered container in refrigerator till ready to serve. Makes about 4 cups.

## Cranberry-Date Relish

| | |
|---|---|
| 2 cups cranberries | 2 tablespoons vinegar |
| 1 cup water | ⅛ teaspoon ground cinnamon |
| ½ cup sugar | ⅛ teaspoon ground ginger |
| ¼ cup light raisins | 1 cup snipped pitted dates |

In medium saucepan combine all ingredients except dates. Bring to boiling. Boil gently, uncovered, until cranberry skins pop, 8 to 10 minutes; stir occasionally. Stir in dates. Chill. Makes about 2 cups.

*Add color and flavor to meals by using relishes — those with cranberries are especially enjoyed during the holidays. Use them as an accompaniment for meat or poultry or as an addition to a relish tray.*

## Vegetable Juice-Shrimp Aspic

3½ cups vegetable juice
    cocktail
1¼ cups chopped celery
⅓ cup chopped onion
2 tablespoons packed
    brown sugar

2 bay leaves
1 teaspoon salt
2 envelopes unflavored gelatin
2 tablespoons lemon juice
1 4½-ounce can shrimp,
    drained and chopped

Combine *2 cups* of the vegetable juice cocktail with ¼ cup of the celery, onion, brown sugar, bay leaves, and salt. Cover and simmer 5 minutes; strain. Soften gelatin in *1 cup* cold vegetable juice cocktail; dissolve in hot mixture. Stir in remaining vegetable juice cocktail and lemon juice. Chill till partially set. Fold in remaining celery and shrimp. Pour into 5-cup star mold. Chill till firm. Unmold. Makes 8 to 10 servings.

## Christmas Vegetable Salad Mold

1 envelope unflavored
    gelatin
1½ cups tomato juice
1 tablespoon sugar
1 tablespoon finely
    chopped onion
1 large tomato, peeled
2 tablespoons vinegar

1 medium cucumber, peeled
    and chopped
¼ cup chopped celery
¼ cup chopped carrot
¼ teaspoon garlic salt
¼ teaspoon dried basil,
    crushed
Lettuce

In saucepan soften gelatin in *1¼ cups* tomato juice; stir in sugar and onion. Heat and stir till gelatin dissolves. Chop tomato, reserving juice; set tomato aside. Combine reserved juice, remaining ¼ cup tomato juice, and vinegar. Add water to make ½ cup liquid. Add tomato juice mixture to gelatin mixture; blend well. Chill till partially set. Fold in tomato, cucumber, celery, carrot, garlic salt, basil, and dash pepper. Pour into 4-cup mold; chill till firm. Unmold on lettuce-lined plate. Makes 6 servings.

## Pimiento Salad Molds

1 4-ounce can whole pimientos
1 3-ounce package lemon-
    flavored gelatin
1¾ cups boiling water
1 3-ounce package cream
    cheese, softened

1 tablespoon lemon juice
½ cup chopped cucumber
½ cup chopped celery
¼ cup mayonnaise
1 tablespoon chopped onion
Lettuce

Oil 6 individual salad molds. Drain pimientos and open pods; cut into 24 petals. Line each mold with 4 petals; chill. Dissolve gelatin in boiling water; beat in cream cheese and lemon juice. Chill till partially set. Stir in cucumber, celery, mayonnaise, and onion. Spoon into pimiento-lined molds. Chill molds till set. Unmold onto lettuce-lined plates. Garnish each salad with a dollop of mayonnaise, if desired. Makes 6 servings.

## Cranberry-Pear Coleslaw

¼ cup dairy sour cream
2 tablespoons mayonnaise *or*
    salad dressing
2 teaspoons sugar
    • • •
3 cups shredded cabbage

2 fresh medium pears, cored
    and cubed
½ cup chopped celery
1 8-ounce can jellied cranberry
    sauce, chilled
Lettuce

*Cranberries add a bright wintery touch to the cabbage salad standby in Cranberry-Pear Coleslaw. Pears add fresh fruit flavor. And sour cream seasons the mayonnaise.*

Combine sour cream, mayonnaise or salad dressing, and sugar. Combine the cabbage, pears, and chopped celery. Cube cranberry sauce and reserve a few cubes to use for garnish. Add cranberry cubes and sour cream mixture to cabbage mixture. Toss gently. Serve in lettuce-lined salad bowl. Garnish with the reserved cranberry cubes. Makes 6 to 8 servings.

## Gourmet Asparagus Salad

1 10-ounce package frozen
    asparagus spears
2 7-ounce cans artichoke
    hearts, drained and
    halved
Freshly ground pepper
⅓ cup olive oil *or* salad oil

¼ cup lemon juice
1 clove garlic, halved
½ teaspoon salt
    • • •
4 lettuce leaves
¼ cup sliced pitted ripe
    olives

Cook frozen asparagus according to package directions; drain. In mixing bowl combine cooked asparagus and drained artichoke hearts; sprinkle with the freshly ground pepper. Combine olive oil or salad oil, lemon juice, garlic, and salt; pour over vegetables. Cover and chill several hours; toss once or twice. Drain and remove garlic. Arrange vegetables on lettuce leaves; garnish with the sliced ripe olives. Makes 4 servings.

## Mexican Frijoles Salad (free' holez)

2 tablespoons salad oil
2 tablespoons vinegar
1 small clove garlic, minced
½ teaspoon chili powder
    Dash pepper
1 16-ounce can pinto beans,
    drained
1 16-ounce can red beans,
    drained

¾ cup diced celery
¼ cup small white
    onion rings
2 tablespoons sweet pickle
    relish
    • • •
Lettuce
Small white onion rings

*Frijoles is the Mexican word for beans. And that's just what this is — a bean salad. The addition of chili powder adds an extra perky touch making it different from other bean salads.*

In mixing bowl combine salad oil, vinegar, minced garlic, chili powder, and pepper for marinade; beat thoroughly with rotary beater. Set aside. Combine pinto beans, red beans, celery, the ¼ cup onion rings, and pickle relish. Pour marinade over bean mixture; toss lightly. Cover and chill several hours or overnight, stirring occasionally. Serve in lettuce-lined bowl. Garnish with the additional onion rings. Makes 6 to 8 servings.

## Pineapple-Green Peas

*Liven the flavor of canned peas by adding pineapple. This tasty combination in a tart-sweet sauce is particularly good when the holiday main dish is a baked ham or pork roast.*

1 8¼-ounce can pineapple
   tidbits
2 tablespoons sliced green onion
1 tablespoon butter *or*
   margarine
3 tablespoons packed brown
   sugar

4 teaspoons cornstarch
¼ teaspoon salt
   Dash pepper
2 tablespoons vinegar
   Water
2 17-ounce cans peas,
   drained

Drain pineapple, reserving syrup. Cook onion in butter till tender but not brown. Remove from heat; stir in sugar, cornstarch, salt, and pepper. Combine reserved syrup, vinegar, and enough water to make 1 cup. Stir into onion mixture. Return to heat. Cook and stir till thickened and bubbly. Stir in pineapple and peas. Heat through. Makes 8 servings.

## Acorn Squash Wedges with Creamed Onions

3 acorn squash, quartered
1 tablespoon butter *or*
   margarine
1 tablespoon all-purpose
   flour
   Dash salt

¾ cup milk
1 15½-ounce can boiled
   onions, drained
2 tablespoons chopped
   pimiento

Arrange squash in single layer in large shallow baking dish; season with salt and pepper. Cover; bake at 350° till tender, 35 to 40 minutes. Meanwhile, melt butter in saucepan. Stir in flour and salt. Add milk all at once. Cook and stir till thickened and bubbly. Stir in onions and pimiento. Serve sauce and vegetables with squash. Makes 8 servings.

*Take advantage of acorn squash and onions while they are in season. Acorn Squash Wedges with Creamed Onions are ideal to serve with Thanksgiving or Christmas meals. Pimiento cut in stars gives added good flavor and a bright touch of color.*

## Creamy Herbed Green Beans

2 9-ounce packages frozen
　Italian green beans
¼ cup chopped onion
3 tablespoons butter *or*
　margarine
1 cup herb-seasoned stuffing mix

⅓ cup water
• • •
1 cup dairy sour cream
½ cup milk
½ cup shredded American
　cheese (2 ounces)

Cook beans according to package directions. Meanwhile, in small saucepan cook onion in the butter or margarine till tender. Add stuffing mix and water; toss to mix. Set aside. Drain cooked beans. Stir in the sour cream, milk, and shredded American cheese; heat through. Add ⅔ *of the stuffing* mixture to the beans; mix well. Turn into a serving bowl; sprinkle with the remaining stuffing mixture. Makes 8 servings.

## Ivy League Beets

1 16-ounce can sliced beets
　*or* 1 pound fresh beets
• • •
1 tablespoon cornstarch
¼ teaspoon salt
¼ teaspoon pumpkin pie spice

⅓ cup cold water
¼ cup strawberry jam
2 tablespoons lemon juice
2 tablespoons butter *or*
　margarine

Drain canned beets. (Or, in covered saucepan cook the whole fresh beets in a small amount of boiling salted water till tender, about 35 minutes. Drain, peel, and slice beets.) In saucepan combine cornstarch, salt, and pumpkin pie spice; stir in cold water, jam, and lemon juice. Cook and stir over medium heat till cornstarch mixture is thickened and bubbly; stir in the sliced beets and the butter. Continue cooking till heated through. Makes 4 servings.

## Cheesy Carrot Bake

2 pounds carrots
• • •
2 tablespoons butter *or*
　margarine
2 tablespoons all-purpose
　flour
¾ teaspoon dry mustard

½ teaspoon salt
¼ teaspoon paprika
⅛ teaspoon pepper
2 cups milk
¼ cup grated Parmesan cheese
½ cup canned French-fried
　onions

Peel carrots; slice crosswise on the bias. Cook, covered, in boiling salted water till just tender, about 20 minutes; drain. Set aside. In a small saucepan melt butter or margarine; blend in the flour, dry mustard, salt, paprika, and pepper. Add milk all at once. Cook, stirring constantly, till mixture is thickened and bubbly. Stir in cheese. Combine the drained, cooked carrots and sauce; turn into a 1½-quart casserole. Bake, covered, at 350° for 30 minutes. Uncover; sprinkle the French-fried onions over carrot mixture. Return to the oven for 3 to 5 minutes more. Makes 8 servings.

*By the time the holiday bird, stuffing, and rolls are in the oven there's often no more room. When this is the case, choose a vegetable that is prepared atop the range. Fit vegetable casseroles into holiday meals when oven space allows. You'll find a variety of both types of vegetables in this section.*

## Broccoli-Onion Deluxe

*Preserve the texture of vegetable casseroles by being careful not to overcook the vegetables, rice, or pasta used. They will finish cooking after the casserole is in the oven.*

2 10-ounce packages frozen
  cut broccoli
2 cups frozen whole small
  onions

• • •

¼ cup butter or margarine
2 tablespoons all-purpose
  flour

¼ teaspoon salt
  Dash pepper
1 cup milk
1 3-ounce package cream
  cheese, cut up
1 cup soft bread crumbs
¼ cup grated Parmesan cheese

Cook broccoli according to package directions; drain. Cook onions in boiling salted water till tender, about 10 minutes; drain. In saucepan melt *2 tablespoons* butter; blend in flour, salt, and pepper. Add milk. Cook and stir till thickened and bubbly. Reduce heat; blend in cream cheese, stirring till melted. Stir in vegetables; turn into 1½-quart casserole. Bake, uncovered, at 350° for 20 minutes. Melt remaining butter; toss with crumbs and Parmesan. Sprinkle atop casserole; bake 15 to 20 minutes more. Serves 10.

## Broccoli-Corn Bake

1 16-ounce can cream-style
  corn
1 10-ounce package frozen
  chopped broccoli, cooked
  and drained
¾ cup coarsely crumbled
  saltine crackers

3 tablespoons butter *or*
  margarine, melted
1 beaten egg
1 tablespoon instant minced
  onion
½ teaspoon salt
  Dash pepper

Mix cream-style corn, broccoli, ½ *cup* of the crumbled crackers, *2 tablespoons* of the butter, egg, onion, salt, and pepper. Turn into 1-quart casserole. Sprinkle with a mixture of the remaining crumbled crackers and remaining butter. Bake, uncovered, at 350° for 35 to 40 minutes. Serves 6.

## Spinach-Rice Casserole

1 cup long grain rice
1 10-ounce package frozen
  chopped spinach

• • •

½ cup chopped onion
2 tablespoons butter *or*
  margarine

2 beaten eggs
1¾ cups milk
½ cup grated Parmesan cheese
½ teaspoon salt
¼ teaspoon dried basil,
  crushed

Cook rice in boiling salted water for 15 minutes. Cook spinach according to package directions. Drain both well. In a saucepan cook onion in butter till tender but not brown. Combine onion mixture, rice, and spinach. Combine eggs, milk, Parmesan cheese, salt, and basil; stir into rice mixture. Turn into 8x8x2-inch baking dish. Cover; bake at 350° till a knife inserted off-center comes out clean, 30 to 35 minutes. Makes 8 or 9 servings.

## Nutty Sweet Potato-Peach Bake

| | |
|---|---|
| 4 medium sweet potatoes | ¼ teaspoon ground ginger |
| • • • | 1 cup diced canned peaches, |
| ⅓ cup packed brown sugar | well drained |
| ⅓ cup broken cashew nuts | 2 tablespoons butter *or* |
| ½ teaspoon salt | margarine |

Scrub sweet potatoes thoroughly. Cut off woody portions; do not peel. Cook whole sweet potatoes, covered, in boiling salted water till just done, about 30 minutes. Drain; peel and slice. In small mixing bowl blend together the brown sugar, cashew nuts, salt, and ginger. In 1½-quart casserole layer *half* the sliced sweet potatoes, *half* the diced peaches, and *half* the brown sugar-cashew mixture. Repeat layers. Dot with butter or margarine. Bake, covered, at 350° about 30 minutes. Uncover and bake 10 minutes more. Garnish with sliced canned peaches, if desired. Makes 6 servings.

## Stuffed Sweet Potatoes

| | |
|---|---|
| 6 medium sweet potatoes | 1 tablespoon grated orange |
| ½ cup raisins | peel |
| ¼ cup butter *or* margarine | ½ teaspoon salt |
| ¼ cup chopped walnuts | Orange juice |

Prick potatoes and bake at 400° till done, 40 to 45 minutes. Cut a long slice from the top of each potato. Scoop out potato, reserving shells. Mash the potato. Add raisins, butter or margarine, chopped walnuts, grated orange peel, salt, and enough orange juice to moisten; mix well. Pile lightly into the reserved shells. Place in shallow baking dish and return to 400° oven. Bake till heated through, about 20 minutes longer. Makes 6 servings.

## Sweet Potato Soufflé

| | |
|---|---|
| 1¼ pounds sweet potatoes | Dash ground nutmeg |
| (about 2 large) | Dash pepper |
| 2 tablespoons chopped onion | ¾ cup milk |
| ¼ cup butter *or* margarine | • • • |
| ¼ cup all-purpose flour | 4 well-beaten egg yolks |
| 1 teaspoon salt | 4 stiffly beaten egg whites |

In a saucepan cook sweet potatoes in boiling water till tender, 30 to 40 minutes. Peel sweet potatoes. Mash sweet potatoes; measure 2 cups and set aside. In a saucepan cook chopped onion in butter or margarine till tender but not brown. Blend in the flour, salt, nutmeg, and pepper. Stir in the milk. Cook, stirring constantly, till mixture is thickened and bubbly. Stir in the mashed sweet potatoes; mix well. Add a moderate amount of hot mixture to the beaten egg yolks, stirring constantly. Return to remaining hot mixture; mix well. Fold in the stiffly beaten egg whites. Spoon mixture into a 1½-quart soufflé dish. Bake at 350° till knife inserted just off-center comes out clean, about 45 minutes. Makes 6 servings.

*Sweet potatoes are festive whether eaten seasoned with butter, salt, and pepper, or prepared in a special manner for a special time of the year. During the holidays, serve sweet potatoes in addition to or for a welcome change from white potatoes. Cook them with fruits and sweet-sour sauces for flavor additions to make eating the vegetable a pleasure. Or, include elegant Sweet Potato Soufflé in your menu.*

# Breads

## Twistree Bread

2¾ to 3 cups all-purpose flour
1 package active dry yeast
¼ teaspoon baking soda
1 cup buttermilk
¼ cup shortening

¼ cup sugar
1 egg
2 tablespoons butter, softened
1 tablespoon *each* red and
    green sugar crystals

*Pictured opposite:* Can you imagine a more festive show-off for your Christmas bread-making than *Twistree Bread?* Shaping breads into a holiday design takes only a few minutes and the result is spectacular. Use sugar crystals to decorate the trees and, if desired, frost with Confectioners' Glaze.

Combine *1½ cups* of the flour, yeast, and baking soda. Heat buttermilk, shortening, sugar, and 1 teaspoon salt till warm (115-120°), stirring constantly. Add to dry mixture; add egg. Beat at low speed of electric mixer for ½ minute, scraping bowl. Beat 3 minutes at high speed. By hand, stir in enough remaining flour to make moderately stiff dough. Knead on lightly floured surface till smooth (5 minutes). Cover; let rest 10 minutes. Halve dough. Roll one half to 14x6-inch rectangle. Spread with *1 tablespoon* butter; sprinkle with red sugar crystals. Fold in half to make 14x3-inch rectangle. Cut into fourteen 1-inch-wide strips. Twist each dough strip; arrange on greased baking sheet in tree shape (see photo at right for shaping guide). Repeat with remaining dough, butter, and green sugar crystals. Let rise 1 hour. Bake at 375° for 15 minutes; cool. Makes 2 trees.

## German Stollen

¾ cup raisins
½ cup chopped mixed candied
    fruits and peels
¼ cup dried currants
¼ cup rum

• • •

4 to 4½ cups all-purpose flour
2 packages active dry yeast
1 cup milk
½ cup butter *or* margarine

¼ cup sugar
1 teaspoon salt
2 eggs
2 tablespoons grated orange
    peel
1 tablespoon grated lemon peel
½ teaspoon almond extract
½ cup chopped blanched
    almonds
Confectioners' Glaze

*Many years ago, the German nut and fruit bread, stollen, was part of the German Christmas religious atmosphere. The oblong shape was used to represent the manger. In medieval times a small figure of Christ was placed on top of the stollen. Today a sprig of holly is usually the sole decoration for this heavily nutted and fruited holiday bread. To many German- and non-German-Americans alike, Christmas wouldn't be Christmas without stollen for breakfast.*

Soak first 3 ingredients in rum. Combine *1½ cups* of the flour and yeast. Heat and stir milk, butter, sugar, and salt till warm (115-120°). Add to dry mixture; add eggs, peels, and almond extract. Beat at low speed of electric mixer for ½ minute, scraping bowl. Beat 3 minutes at high speed. By hand, stir in fruit-rum mixture, nuts, and enough remaining flour to make soft dough. Knead on floured surface till smooth. Place in greased bowl; turn once. Cover; let rise till double (1¼ hours). Punch down; divide in half. Cover; let rest 10 minutes. Roll each half to 10x7-inch oval. Fold long side over to within ½ inch of opposite side; seal. Place on greased baking sheets. Cover; let rise till double (45 minutes). Bake at 375° for 15 to 20 minutes. While warm, glaze with Confectioners' Glaze. Makes 2.

*Confectioners' Glaze:* To make of desired consistency, add about 1½ tablespoons milk to 1 cup sifted powdered sugar. Add ¼ teaspoon vanilla.

## Christmas Kringle (see photo, pages 74-75)

*Christmas Kringle is traditional in Denmark during the holidays. This buttery-rich, yeast-raised coffee cake is a special treat for family and friends when stuffed with a sweet raisin or date filling. Adorn the flaky coffee bread with mouth-watering garnishes such as sugar and chopped almonds.*

¾ cup butter, softened
2¾ to 3 cups all-purpose flour
1 package active dry yeast
1 cup milk
½ cup sugar

2 eggs
Sweet Filling *or* Date Filling
¾ cup finely chopped blanched almonds

Roll butter out between sheets of waxed paper to 10x6-inch rectangle; chill. Combine 1¼ *cups* flour and yeast. Heat milk, ¼ cup sugar, and 1 teaspoon salt till warm (115-120°). Add to flour mixture; add *1 egg.* Beat at low speed of electric mixer for ½ minute, scraping bowl. Beat 3 minutes at high speed. By hand, stir in enough remaining flour to form a moderately stiff dough. Knead on lightly floured surface 3 to 5 minutes. Cover; let rest 10 minutes. Roll out to 12-inch square. Place chilled butter in center of square. Fold sides of dough over to cover butter; forming a 12x6-inch rectangle. Pinch edges to seal. Cover; let rest 10 minutes. Roll out again to 12-inch square; carefully fold in thirds. Wrap in foil; chill 30 to 60 minutes.

Repeat rolling, chilling, and folding twice more. Cut dough lengthwise into 3 strips, each 12 inches long. Roll first strip out to 18x4-inch rectangle. Mix together 1 egg and 1 tablespoon water; brush some on rectangle. Spread with *one-third* of the Sweet *or* Date Filling. Fold to form 18x2-inch roll; seal edges. Place, seam side down, on greased baking sheet, shaping into an oval. Seal ends together and flatten to ½-inch thickness. Repeat with remaining dough and filling to make 2 more ovals. Let kringles rest 30 minutes. Bake at 375° for 25 minutes. Remove to rack. Brush with remaining egg mixture; sprinkle with chopped almonds and remaining sugar. Makes 3.

*Sweet Filling:* Cream together 1½ cups sugar and ½ cup butter till fluffy. Stir in 1½ cups light raisins *or* 1½ cups coarsely chopped pecans.

*Date Filling:* Combine 2 cups snipped pitted dates, 1 teaspoon grated orange peel, ½ cup orange juice, ⅓ cup sugar, and ¼ teaspoon salt. Bring to boil; reduce heat. Cover. Simmer till thick, 5 minutes; stir often. Cool.

## Holiday Sweet Bread (see photo, pages 74-75)

5¼ to 5½ cups all-purpose flour
2 packages active dry yeast
1 cup milk
1 cup sugar

½ cup butter *or* margarine
¼ teaspoon salt
3 eggs
½ cup mashed cooked potatoes

In large mixing bowl combine *2½ cups* of the flour and yeast. Heat milk, sugar, butter, and salt till warm (115-120°), stirring constantly; add to dry mixture. Add eggs and potatoes. Beat at low speed of electric mixer for ½ minute, scraping bowl. Beat 3 minutes at high speed. By hand, stir in enough remaining flour to make moderately stiff dough. Knead on lightly floured surface till smooth (8 to 10 minutes). Place in greased bowl, turning once to grease surface. Cover; let rise till nearly double (1½ hours). Punch down; divide dough in half. Cover; let rest 10 minutes. Shape half into eight balls. Place around edge of greased 9x1½-inch round baking pan to form ring. Repeat with other half of dough. Let rise till almost double (45 to 60 minutes). Bake at 375° for 20 to 25 minutes. Remove from pans; cool. Makes 2.

## Brazilian King's Bread

3 to 3½ cups all-purpose flour
1 package active dry yeast
⅔ cup milk
6 tablespoons butter *or*
    margarine
⅓ cup sugar
2 eggs
2 tablespoons butter *or*
    margarine, melted
2 tablespoons sugar

½ teaspoon ground cinnamon
½ cup chopped Brazil nuts
⅓ cup chopped mixed candied
    fruits and peels
¼ cup raisins
1 tablespoon butter *or*
    margarine, melted
2 tablespoons finely chopped
    Brazil nuts
Sugar

In large mixing bowl combine *1½ cups* of the flour and the yeast. In saucepan heat the milk, 6 tablespoons butter, ⅓ cup sugar, and 1 teaspoon salt till warm (115-120°), stirring constantly. Add to dry mixture in mixing bowl; add eggs. Beat at low speed with electric mixer for ½ minute, scraping sides of bowl constantly. Beat 3 minutes at high speed. By hand, stir in enough remaining flour to make moderately soft dough.

Knead dough on lightly floured surface till smooth and elastic (8 to 10 minutes). Place in a greased bowl; turn once to grease surface. Cover; let dough rise in warm place till double (1 to 1½ hours). Punch down; turn out on lightly floured surface. Roll dough into a 20x12-inch rectangle. Brush with the 2 tablespoons melted butter. Combine the 2 tablespoons sugar and ground cinnamon; sprinkle over dough. Combine the ½ cup chopped Brazil nuts, mixed fruits and peels, and raisins. Sprinkle over dough. Roll as for jelly roll, beginning at long side; seal edge. Shape in ring and place, seam side down on greased baking sheet; seal end of the ring.

Cover; let rise in warm place till almost double (30 to 45 minutes). Bake at 375° for 25 to 30 minutes. Brush with 1 tablespoon melted butter. Sprinkle with 2 tablespoons nuts, then sprinkle lightly with sugar. Let stand few minutes; sprinkle again with more sugar. Makes 1 ring.

*On January 6th, Epiphany, the people of Brazil end Christmas with the Festival of the Three Kings. Inspired by this holiday celebration, they serve Brazilian King's Bread with fragrant Brazilian coffee. Made of rich yeast dough, candied fruits, and Brazil nuts, the regal ring is decorated with sugar and ground nuts. According to the Brazilian custom, a tiny doll is baked in the bread. Whoever finds this treasure in his portion is declared king or queen of the Epiphany celebration. Revive this tradition by replacing the tiny doll with a whole Brazil nut.*

## Gumdrop Nut Wreath (see photo, pages 74-75)

1 13¾-ounce package hot
    roll mix
½ cup snipped red and
    green gumdrops

½ cup chopped walnuts
Confectioners' Glaze
    (see recipe, page 112)
Gumdrop Holly

Prepare hot roll mix according to package directions. Stir in snipped gumdrops and walnuts. Cover; let rise in warm place till double (30 to 45 minutes). Punch down; divide dough in half and form each half into a ball. Cover; let rest 10 minutes. Roll each ball into a 24-inch long rope.

Twist the two ropes of dough together; transfer to greased baking sheet and form into a ring. Cover; let rise till almost double (30 to 45 minutes). Bake at 375° for 25 to 30 minutes. (Cover with foil after first 20 minutes if bread browns too quickly.) Remove from pan; cool. Frost with Confectioners' Glaze and decorate with Gumdrop Holly. Makes 1 ring.

*Gumdrop Holly:* Use red gumdrops for berries; roll green gumdrops flat with rolling pin and trim flattened pieces to leaf shapes.

When the holiday season arrives, have slices of *Festive Three C Bread* ready to serve your guests. The 'Three C' in the recipe title stands for three of the flavorful ingredients used—carrot, coconut, and cherries. For gift giving, wrap the loaf in clear plastic wrap, tie with a silver bow, and add a sprig of holly for a simple trim.

### Italian Panettone (pahn uh tone' ee)

*This most famous of Italy's many Christmas creations, panettone is claimed by Genoa, Milan, Venice, and Turin, but it is the Milanese version that is best known. Cutting a cross in the top is a traditional decoration. It is a delicious dessert or breakfast cake, served with wine or strong coffee.*

| | |
|---|---|
| 5½ to 6 cups all-purpose flour | ½ cup light raisins |
| 2 packages active dry yeast | ½ cup dried currants |
| 1 cup milk | ¼ cup chopped citron |
| ½ cup honey | 2 to 3 teaspoons crushed |
| ½ cup butter *or* margarine | aniseed |
| 1 teaspoon salt | 1 egg |
| 3 eggs | 1 tablespoon water |

In large mixing bowl combine *1½ cups* of the flour and yeast. Heat together milk, honey, butter or margarine, and salt just till warm (115-120°), stirring constantly. Add to dry mixture in mixing bowl; add 3 eggs. Beat at low speed of electric mixer for ½ minute, scraping sides of bowl constantly. Beat 3 minutes at high speed. By hand, stir in raisins, currants, citron, aniseed, and enough of the remaining flour to make a soft dough. Knead on lightly floured surface till smooth and elastic (8 to 10 minutes).

Shape into ball. Place in greased bowl; turn once. Cover; let rise in warm place till double (about 1½ hours). Punch down; divide in half. Cover; let rest 10 minutes. Shape into two round loaves; place on two greased baking sheets. Cut cross ½ inch deep in top of each loaf. Cover; let rise till double (about 45 minutes). Beat the 1 egg with water; brush tops. Bake at 350° for 35 to 40 minutes. Remove from pan; cool. Makes 2.

## Spicy Fruit Ring (see photo, pages 74-75)

| | |
|---|---|
| 1 13¾-ounce package hot roll mix | 3 eggs |
| 1 package 2-layer-size spice cake mix | ¼ cup cooking oil |
| | 2 cups raisins |
| 1 8-ounce can applesauce | 1½ cups snipped pitted dates |
| | 1 cup coarsely chopped pecans |

Soften yeast from roll mix in 1 cup warm water (110°). In large mixing bowl combine flour mixture from roll mix, the cake mix, applesauce, eggs, oil, and yeast. Blend on low speed of electric mixer; beat on medium speed for 5 minutes. Stir in remaining ingredients. Turn into greased and floured 10-inch tube pan. Bake at 350° about 65 minutes. Cool in pan 30 minutes. Turn out; cool on rack. If desired, dust with powdered sugar.

## Pineapple-Cream Cheese Coffee Cake

| | |
|---|---|
| 3 to 3¼ cups all-purpose flour | 1 teaspoon salt |
| 1 package active dry yeast | 1 egg |
| 1 3-ounce package cream cheese, cubed | 1 8¼-ounce can crushed pineapple |
| ½ cup milk | 1 cup sifted powdered sugar |
| ¼ cup sugar | • • • |
| 2 tablespoons butter | Maraschino cherries |

In large mixing bowl combine *1 cup* of the flour and yeast. Heat together cheese, milk, sugar, butter, and salt just till warm (115-120°), stirring constantly. Add to dry mixture; add egg. Beat at low speed of electric mixer for ½ minute scraping sides of bowl constantly. Beat 3 minutes at high speed. Drain pineapple, reserving syrup. By hand, stir in pineapple and remaining flour to make a soft dough. Knead on lightly floured surface (3 to 5 minutes). Place in greased bowl; turn once. Cover; let rise in warm place till double. Punch down. Shape dough into 22 balls. Arrange in tree shape on greased baking sheet by using 5 balls for first two rows, then decreasing one ball for remaining four rows; use 2 balls for trunk. Let rise till nearly double. Bake at 350° for 30 to 35 minutes. Combine powdered sugar and 3 to 4 teaspoons of reserved pineapple syrup. Drizzle over bread. Garnish with cherries. Makes 1.

## Festive Three C Bread

Stir together thoroughly 2½ cups all-purpose flour, 1 cup sugar, 1 teaspoon baking powder, 1 teaspoon baking soda, 1 teaspoon ground cinnamon, and ½ teaspoon salt. Combine 3 beaten eggs, ½ cup cooking oil, and ½ cup milk; add to the flour mixture and stir just till blended. Stir in 2 cups shredded carrot, one 3½-ounce can flaked coconut (1⅓ cups), ½ cup chopped maraschino cherries, ½ cup raisins, and ½ cup chopped pecans.

Turn into 4 well-greased and floured 16-ounce fruit or vegetable cans. Bake at 350° for 45 to 50 minutes. Remove from cans; cool thoroughly on rack. Wrap in foil; store in refrigerator. Makes 4 small loaves.

*Need a delightful treat or an easy-to-prepare gift? Then, bake an irresistible holiday bread. For nut breads, bake them a day ahead and then wrap and store them for one day. This allows the flavors to mellow and the bread will slice easier, too.*

## Christmas Plum Coffee Cake

½ cup milk
¼ cup butter *or* margarine
3 tablespoons granulated sugar
1 13¾-ounce package hot
   roll mix
2 beaten eggs

1 8¾-ounce can whole,
   unpitted purple plums
1 cup packed brown sugar
½ cup finely chopped almonds
½ cup fine dry bread crumbs
½ teaspoon ground cinnamon

Heat milk, butter, and granulated sugar; cool to 110°. Add yeast from roll mix; stir to soften. Add eggs and flour from roll mix; stir till smooth. Knead on lightly floured surface (3 to 5 minutes). Place in greased bowl, turning once to grease surface. Cover; let rise till double. Punch down; let rest 10 minutes. Meanwhile, drain plums; pit and chop. Combine plums, brown sugar, almonds, bread crumbs, and cinnamon. Divide dough in half. Roll one half to 12x8-inch rectangle. Spread half of the plum mixture on dough rectangle. Roll up long sides to meet in center. Place on greased baking sheet. With scissors, snip ⅔ of the way to the center at 1½-inch intervals on each side. Turn each section slightly to one side. Repeat with remaining dough and plum mixture. Cover; let rise till nearly double. Bake at 375° for 30 minutes; cover with foil last 15 minutes of baking time. Makes 2.

## Gumdrop Bread

3 cups all-purpose flour
¾ cup sugar
3½ teaspoons baking powder
1 teaspoon salt
1 beaten egg

1½ cups milk
2 tablespoons cooking oil
¾ cup snipped gumdrops
½ cup chopped walnuts

Stir together thoroughly flour, sugar, baking powder, and salt. Combine egg, milk, oil, gumdrops, and nuts; add to dry mixture. Stir just till moistened. Pour into greased and floured 9x5x3-inch baking pan. Bake at 350° till done, 1 hour. Remove from pan; cool on rack. Makes 1 loaf.

## Cherry Blossom Muffins (see photo, page 103)

1 egg
⅔ cup orange juice
2 tablespoons sugar
2 tablespoons cooking oil

2 cups packaged biscuit mix
½ cup chopped pecans
½ cup cherry preserves
Spicy Topping

Combine egg, orange juice, sugar, and oil. Add biscuit mix; beat vigorously 30 seconds. Stir in nuts. Grease 12 muffin pans or line with paper bake cups. Fill muffin pans ⅓ full with batter. Top *each* with 2 teaspoons cherry preserves. Cover with the remaining batter till ⅔ full. Sprinkle with Spicy Topping. Bake at 400° for 20 to 25 minutes. Makes 12 muffins.

*Spicy Topping:* In small mixing bowl stir ¼ cup sugar, 2 tablespoons all-purpose flour, and ½ teaspoon ground nutmeg together thoroughly. Cut in 1 tablespoon butter *or* margarine till mixture is crumbly.

## Ukrainian Christmas Eve Doughnuts

4½ cups all-purpose flour
2 packages active dry yeast
• • •
1 cup milk
⅓ cup sugar
¼ cup shortening
1 teaspoon salt

1 teaspoon vanilla
2 eggs
3 egg yolks
1 12-ounce can prune cake and
   pastry filling
Fat for frying
Confectioners' Icing

In large mixing bowl combine *2 cups* of the flour and yeast. In saucepan heat together the milk, sugar, shortening, and salt just till warm (115-120°), stirring constantly. Stir in the vanilla. Add to dry mixture in the mixing bowl; add the eggs and egg yolks. Beat at low speed of electric mixer ½ minute, scraping sides constantly. Beat 3 minutes at high speed. By hand, stir in enough remaining flour to make a moderately stiff dough. Turn the dough onto lightly floured surface; knead till smooth and elastic (4 to 5 minutes). Place in lightly greased bowl, turning once to grease surface.

Cover; let rise in warm place till double (about 1¼ hours). Punch down. Cover; let rest 10 minutes. Roll out dough to ⅛-inch thickness. Cut into circles with floured 2½-inch cutter. Place *1 teaspoon* of the prune filling on each of *half* of the circles; top with the unfilled circles. Moisten edges with water and press edges firmly to seal. Cover; let rise on floured surface till about double. Fry a few at a time in deep hot fat (375°) till golden, 1 to 1½ minutes on each side. Drain on paper toweling. When cool, frost with Confectioners' Icing. Makes about 24 doughnuts.

*Confectioners' Icing:* In small mixing bowl add enough milk (about ¼ cup) to 2 cups sifted powdered sugar to make icing of spreading consistency. Add dash salt and 1 teaspoon vanilla; mix thoroughly.

## Apple Dandy Rolls

1 13¾-ounce package hot
   roll mix
¾ cup warm water (110°)
1 egg
¼ cup sugar

½ teaspoon ground nutmeg
• • •
Cranberry-Apple Filling
Confectioners' Glaze
(see recipe, page 112)

Soften yeast from roll mix in warm water. Stir in egg, sugar, nutmeg, and flour mixture from hot roll mix; mix well. Cover and chill at least 2 hours. On lightly floured surface, roll the dough to 18x10-inch rectangle. Cut rectangle into eighteen 10x1-inch strips. Roll each strip into a rope; coil ropes loosely to form round rolls. Carefully place rolls on greased baking sheet.

Gently press center of *each* roll and fill with about *1 tablespoon* Cranberry-Apple Filling. Cover; let rise in warm place till almost double (30 to 45 minutes). Bake at 375° for 15 minutes. Remove from pan immediately; drizzle with Confectioners' Glaze while still warm. Makes 18 rolls.

*Cranberry-Apple Filling:* In small saucepan combine 1 cup chopped, peeled apple (1 medium), ½ cup fresh cranberries, and ½ cup sugar. Cook and stir over medium heat till apple is tender, 6 to 7 minutes. Remove from heat and stir in ¼ cup chopped walnuts and 1 tablespoon butter. Cool.

"Prosymo zavitaty," or "Welcome, with good will," is a Ukrainian greeting, especially heartfelt at Christmas time when the ovens have been busy baking all the Christmas breads, cakes, and goodies such as these festive doughnuts. All are important parts of a Ukrainian holiday welcome. The Ukraine is the breadbasket of Russia, and breadmaking among Ukrainian and Ukrainian-American women is an age-old skill. Each bread shape has a symbolic meaning. The circle is one of the major symbols, an ancient sign of prosperity, eternity, and good luck— highly appropriate for a year-end festival.

# Desserts

Pictured opposite: Buche de Noel, Royal Plum Dessert, and Christmas Kringle (see recipe, page 114) are rich, fancy desserts that family and friends expect amid the gaiety of the holiday season.

## Royal Plum Dessert

| | |
|---|---|
| 1 16-ounce can whole, unpitted purple plums | ½ cup chopped walnuts |
| 1 14½-ounce package ginger-bread mix | ¼ cup sugar |
| | 2 tablespoons cornstarch |
| 1 cup light raisins | 1 tablespoon lemon juice |
| | Fluffy Hard Sauce |

Drain plums; reserve syrup. Remove pits; cut plums in pieces. Prepare gingerbread mix following package directions, adding ½ teaspoon salt. Stir in plums, raisins, and nuts. Bake in well-greased 6-cup fluted tube pan at 375° for 1 hour. Meanwhile, add water to reserved plum syrup to make 1½ cups. Mix sugar and cornstarch. Stir in syrup mixture. Cook and stir till thick and bubbly; cook 1 minute more. Stir in lemon juice. Loosen cake edges and *immediately* unmold onto serving plate. Pour warm sauce over. Pass Fluffy Hard Sauce. Serves 10 to 12.

*Fluffy Hard Sauce:* Thoroughly cream together 2 cups sifted powdered sugar and ½ cup butter *or* margarine. Stir in 1 beaten egg yolk and 1 teaspoon vanilla. Fold 1 stiffly beaten egg white into mixture. Chill.

## Buche de Noel (boosh′ duh noel)

*Buche de Noel, light and elegant and frosted with chocolate, has long been a Christmas tradition in France and among French-Canadians and the Creoles of Louisiana. The chocolate-filled jelly roll is cut and the pieces placed to resemble a branching log—the Yule Log—making it a delightful holiday dessert.*

| | |
|---|---|
| 4 egg yolks | ½ teaspoon baking powder |
| ½ cup granulated sugar | ¼ teaspoon salt |
| ½ teaspoon vanilla | Powdered sugar |
| 4 egg whites | 2 tablespoons rum |
| ½ cup granulated sugar | Chocolate Filling |
| 1 cup sifted cake flour | |

Beat yolks till thick and lemon-colored. Gradually add ½ cup granulated sugar, beating constantly. Stir in vanilla. Beat egg whites till soft peaks form; gradually add ½ cup granulated sugar, beating till stiff peaks form. Fold in yolk mixture. Sift together flour, baking powder, and salt; fold into egg mixture. Bake in greased and floured 15½x10½x1-inch baking pan at 375° for 10 to 12 minutes. Promptly loosen edges; turn out onto towel sprinkled with powdered sugar. Sprinkle cake with rum. From long side roll cake and towel together; cool. Unroll cake; spread with *half* the Chocolate Filling. Reroll. Diagonally cut 4-inch piece from roll. Place cut edge of piece against longer roll on serving plate. Frost with remaining Chocolate Filling; mark with fork tines to resemble bark. Decorate as desired.

*Chocolate Filling:* Melt 1½ one-ounce squares unsweetened chocolate; cool. In small saucepan heat ⅔ cup granulated sugar and ⅓ cup water to boiling; cook to soft-ball stage (240°). In small mixing bowl beat 2 egg yolks till thick and lemon-colored. Very gradually add hot syrup, beating constantly; continue beating till mixture is completely cool. Beat in ½ cup softened butter, *1 tablespoon at a time.* Add chocolate, 1 tablespoon rum, and 1 teaspoon instant coffee crystals; beat till thick.

## Dark Fruitcake (see photo, pages 4-5)

Sometimes called Black Fruitcake, English Fruitcake, or Merry Christmas Cake, this rich nut-and-fruit-studded cake is a legacy of our English colonial past, though many European countries have their own versions of a special fruit-filled cake for the holidays. Often, the cake is baked 1 to 6 weeks before Christmas Day and aged with liquor. Because of the cake's richness, it is not served with Christmas dinner but as a specially-decorated "teatime" cake later in the day. Any leftover fruitcake is stored and eaten later—sometimes as late as July.

| | |
|---|---|
| 2 cups dark raisins | 1½ teaspoons baking powder |
| 2 cups pitted dried prunes, cooked and chopped | ¾ teaspoon salt |
| 2 cups chopped mixed candied fruits and peels | 1 cup butter *or* margarine |
| 1 cup light raisins | 1 cup granulated sugar |
| 1 cup chopped red candied cherries | ½ cup packed brown sugar |
| ½ cup chopped candied pineapple | 1½ teaspoons ground cinnamon |
| 1½ cups broken walnuts | 1 teaspoon ground cloves |
| 1½ teaspoons grated orange peel | 1 teaspoon ground mace |
| ¼ cup Burgundy | ½ teaspoon ground allspice |
| 2½ cups sifted cake flour | 5 eggs |
| | 1½ teaspoons vanilla |
| | • • • |
| | ½ cup brandy |
| | ½ cup light rum |

In large bowl combine fruits, walnuts, and orange peel. Pour Burgundy over and set aside. Sift together flour, baking powder, and salt; mix *half* the flour mixture with fruit mixture. In mixing bowl cream together butter, sugars, and spices till light and fluffy. Add eggs, one at a time; beat well after each. Stir in vanilla. Mix in remaining flour mixture. Pour over fruits; mix well. Pour batter into well-greased 10-inch tube pan. Bake at 275° till done, 3½ to 4 hours. Cool in pan slightly; unmold and cool completely. Combine ¼ cup *each* of the brandy and rum; use to soak several layers of cheesecloth. Wrap cake in soaked cheesecloth, then in foil. Store in refrigerator two to three days. Use remaining brandy and rum to re-moisten cheesecloth. Re-wrap and refrigerate cake two to six weeks. Garnish with halved almonds and candied cherries, if desired. Makes 1 fruitcake.

## Light Fruitcake Ring (see photo, pages 4-5)

The light fruitcake-dark fruitcake controversy continues in many households. A way to solve the dilemma is to make both at the holiday season, a light one such as this light ring for its devotees, a dark one for those who favor the heavier, fruitier flavor of the traditional English fruitcake.

| | |
|---|---|
| ¾ cup chopped candied cherries | ¼ cup chopped candied orange peel |
| ½ cup light raisins | 1½ cups all-purpose flour |
| ½ cup chopped candied pineapple | ½ cup butter *or* margarine |
| ½ cup chopped walnuts | ½ cup sugar |
| ¼ cup chopped mixed candied fruits and peels | 2 eggs |
| ¼ cup chopped candied lemon peel | 2 tablespoons light corn syrup |
| | 2 tablespoons orange juice |
| | Dry sherry |

Combine fruits, walnuts, and peels; mix with ½ *cup* of the flour. In mixing bowl cream butter and sugar till light; add eggs, one at a time, beating well after each. Combine corn syrup, orange juice, and *2 tablespoons* sherry; add to creamed mixture alternately with remaining flour. Fold in fruits and nuts. Spoon into well-greased 5½-cup ring mold. Bake at 275° for 1¼ to 1½ hours. Cool in pan slightly; unmold and cool completely. Wrap in sherry-soaked cheesecloth, then in foil. Store in airtight container in cool place. Re-moisten with sherry once a week. If desired, brush with sieved apricot preserves before serving. For even slicing, chill before serving. Makes 1.

## Lemon European Cake (see photo, pages 74-75)

1½ cups sugar
¾ cup butter *or* margarine
3 eggs
3 cups all-purpose flour
1 tablespoon baking powder
1 teaspoon salt
1 teaspoon ground mace

1 cup milk
¾ cup raisins
¾ cup broken walnuts
1½ teaspoons grated lemon peel
3 tablespoons lemon juice
1 teaspoon vanilla
Lemon Glaze

Cream together sugar and butter; add eggs, one at a time, beating well after each addition. Stir together flour, baking powder, salt, and mace; add to creamed mixture alternately with milk. Stir in raisins, nuts, lemon peel and juice, and vanilla; blend lightly. Turn into greased 10-inch fluted tube pan. Bake at 325° till done, about 1¼ hours. Cool 10 minutes; remove from pan and cool on rack. Drizzle with Lemon Glaze. Makes 1 cake.

*Lemon Glaze:* Add 1 teaspoon lemon juice to 1 cup sifted powdered sugar. Stir in enough milk to make glaze desired consistency.

*Fruitcake's flavor and texture improves when stored and allowed to age several weeks before using. Bake the cake, remove from pans, cool, and then wrap in brandy-, wine-, or fruit juice-soaked cheesecloth. Overwrap with foil or store in an airtight container and keep in a cool place. Each week the cheesecloth should be re-moistened.*

## Last Minute Fruitcake

¾ cup sugar
½ cup shortening
1 egg
2½ cups all-purpose flour
1 teaspoon baking soda
1 teaspoon salt
¼ teaspoon ground cinnamon
¼ teaspoon ground cloves

¼ teaspoon ground nutmeg
1 teaspoon instant coffee
  crystals
1 cup applesauce
2 cups chopped mixed candied
  fruits and peels
1 cup raisins
1 cup chopped nuts

Cream sugar and shortening till fluffy. Add egg; beat well. Stir together flour, soda, salt, and spices. Dissolve coffee crystals in ¼ cup water; stir in applesauce. Stir flour mixture into creamed mixture alternately with applesauce mixture. Fold in fruits and peels, raisins, and nuts. Spoon into 2 greased and lightly floured 7½x3½x2-inch loaf pans. Bake at 325° for 1 to 1¼ hours. Cool 10 minutes; remove from pans. Cool on rack. If desired, wrap in wine-soaked cheesecloth. Wrap in foil. Store in cool place at least 24 hours. Makes 2.

*Do you sometimes get a late start on fruitcake baking and then wish you had made some in time for it to mellow? Solve your problem by making Last Minute Fruitcake— just let it stand overnight.*

## Pineapple-Coconut Fruitcake

Combine 1½ cups chopped candied pineapple, 1½ cups light raisins, one 7-ounce package flaked coconut, 1 cup chopped walnuts, and ½ cup chopped candied orange peel. Cream 1 cup sugar and ½ cup butter *or* margarine till fluffy. Add 4 eggs, one at a time, beating well after each. Stir in ½ cup pineapple juice. Stir together 2½ cups all-purpose flour, 1 teaspoon baking powder, and ½ teaspoon salt. Add to sugar mixture. Fold into fruit mixture. Spoon into 7 greased and floured 10½- or 12-ounce cans. Bake at 300° for 1½ hours. Cool. Remove from cans. Wrap separately in brandy-soaked cheesecloth, then in foil. Store in cool place at least 2 weeks. Re-moisten once or twice with brandy. Makes 7 small fruitcakes.

## Apricot-Cream Cheese Fruitcake

| | |
|---|---|
| ½ cup snipped dried apricots | 1 cup butter *or* margarine |
| ½ cup light raisins | 1½ teaspoons vanilla |
| ¼ cup sugar | 4 eggs |
| 1½ cups sugar | 2¼ cups sifted cake flour |
| 1 8-ounce package cream cheese, softened | 1½ teaspoons baking powder |
| | ½ cup chopped pecans |

Combine apricots, raisins, the ¼ cup sugar, and 2 cups water in saucepan; bring to boiling. Reduce heat; cover and simmer 15 to 20 minutes. Drain well; set aside. Cream together the 1½ cups sugar, cream cheese, butter, and vanilla. Add eggs, one at a time, beating well after each. Sift together cake flour and baking powder. Add to creamed mixture and blend well. Fold in apricot mixture and pecans. Spoon into well-greased and floured 10-inch fluted tube pan. Bake at 325° for 65 to 70 minutes. Cool completely. Remove from pan. Wrap cake in foil; store overnight. Makes 1.

## Plain Pastry

*Pastry and pies have evolved from heavy concoctions to light, melt-in-your-mouth delicacies. Although pies are delicious and in season all year, holidays are special times to make and enjoy all types—from fruit to chiffon.*

| | |
|---|---|
| 2 cups all-purpose flour | ⅔ cup shortening |
| 1 teaspoon salt | 5 to 7 tablespoons cold water |

Stir flour and salt together; cut in shortening till crumbly. Sprinkle *1 table-spoon* water over part of mixture. Gently toss with fork; push to side of bowl. Repeat to moisten all. Form into ball. Roll out on lightly floured surface till ⅛-inch thick. Makes one 2-crust 8-, 9-, or 10-inch pie, two 8-, 9-, or 10-inch pastry shells, or 6 to 8 tart shells.

*For Baked Pastry Shell:* Fit pastry into pie plate; trim ½ to 1 inch beyond edge of plate. Fold under and flute edge. Prick bottom and sides well with fork. Bake at 450° till golden, 10 to 12 minutes. Cool.

## Cherry Christmas Pie (see photo, pages 4-5)

| | |
|---|---|
| 1 envelope unflavored gelatin | 2 egg whites |
| ½ cup sugar | ⅛ teaspoon cream of tartar |
| ¼ cup all-purpose flour | ¼ cup sugar |
| 1½ cups milk | 1 cup flaked coconut |
| ¾ teaspoon vanilla | ⅓ cup finely chopped maraschino cherries |
| Few drops almond extract | 1 *baked* 9-inch pastry shell |
| ½ cup whipping cream | |

In saucepan blend together gelatin, the ½ cup sugar, flour, and dash salt. Stir in milk and ½ cup water. Cook and stir till gelatin is dissolved and mixture is thick and bubbly. Chill till partially set. Beat till smooth. Stir in vanilla and almond extract. Whip cream. Beat egg whites and cream of tartar to soft peaks. Gradually add the ¼ cup sugar, beating till stiff peaks form. Fold whipped cream, egg white mixture, coconut, and cherries into gelatin mixture. Spoon into pastry shell. Chill till firm. Garnish with candied or maraschino cherries, if desired.

## Homemade Mincemeat Pie

| | |
|---|---|
| 1 pound beef stew meat | 1 teaspoon grated orange peel |
| 4 pounds apples, peeled, cored, and cut up | 1 cup orange juice |
| | 1 teaspoon grated lemon peel |
| 4 ounces suet | ¼ cup lemon juice |
| 1 15-ounce package raisins | 1 teaspoon salt |
| 2½ cups sugar | ½ teaspoon ground nutmeg |
| 2 cups dried currants | ¼ teaspoon ground mace |
| ½ cup diced mixed candied fruits and peels | Pastry for 2-crust 9-inch pie (see recipe, page 124) |

Simmer beef, covered, in water till tender, about 2 hours. Drain. Cool. Put beef, apples, and suet through coarse blade of food chopper. Combine with remaining ingredients *except* pastry in large kettle. Stir in 2½ cups water. Cover and simmer 1 hour; stir often. Line 9-inch pie plate with pastry; fill with 3 cups mincemeat. Adjust top crust. Seal; flute. Bake at 400° for 35 to 40 minutes. Freeze remaining in 3-cup portions. Makes enough for 4 pies.

*Originally Middle Eastern, mince pies were brought to Europe by the Crusaders and soon became associated with Christmas. Baked in the shape of a manger, with a figure of Christ on top, the spicy pies symbolized the gifts of the Magi. It was a challenge to an Englishman to eat twelve pies in the twelve nights of Christmas, since it was said, "You will have as many happy months in a year as the mince pies you taste at Christmas-time."*

## Eggnog Custard Pie

In mixing bowl blend together 4 beaten eggs, ⅓ cup sugar, ½ teaspoon rum flavoring, ¼ teaspoon salt, and ¼ teaspoon vanilla. Gradually stir in 3 cups canned *or* dairy eggnog. Pour into one unbaked 9-inch pastry shell. Sprinkle with ground nutmeg. Bake at 350° until a knife inserted just off-center comes out clean, 45 to 50 minutes. Cool; then chill well.

## Apple Butter-Pumpkin Pie

| | |
|---|---|
| 1 cup canned pumpkin | 3 slightly beaten eggs |
| 1 cup apple butter | 1 5⅓-ounce can evaporated milk |
| ¾ cup packed brown sugar | |
| ½ teaspoon ground cinnamon | ⅓ cup milk |
| ½ teaspoon salt | 1 unbaked 9-inch pastry shell |

Thoroughly mix pumpkin, apple butter, sugar, cinnamon, and ½ teaspoon salt. Blend in eggs and milks. Turn into unbaked pastry shell. Bake at 400° till knife inserted just off-center comes out clean, 45 to 50 minutes. Cool.

## Lemon-Pineapple Pie

| | |
|---|---|
| 1 20-ounce can crushed pineapple | 1 2-ounce package dessert topping mix |
| 1 3⅝- *or* 3¾-ounce package *instant* lemon pudding mix | • • • |
| | 1 9-inch graham cracker crust |

In bowl stir together undrained pineapple and dry pudding mix. Prepare topping mix following package directions; fold into pineapple mixture. Turn into crust. Chill thoroughly. Garnish with more whipped topping, if desired.

*The creamy, elegant, and super-rich layer cakes known as tortes are a specialty of Vienna, and Austrian-Americans find them especially appropriate for the Christmas table. This easy-to-make version of a chocolate torte is a holiday delight.*

## Easy Viennese Torte

| | |
|---|---|
| 1 6-ounce package semisweet chocolate pieces | 4 slightly beaten egg yolks |
| ½ cup butter *or* margarine | 2 tablespoons powdered sugar |
| ¼ cup water | 1 teaspoon vanilla |
| | 1 frozen loaf pound cake |

Heat and stir chocolate, butter, and water till blended; cool slightly. Stir in next 3 ingredients till smooth. Chill till spreading consistency. Slice cake horizontally into 6 layers. Spread each layer with *2 tablespoons* chocolate mixture; stack. Frost with remaining chocolate. Chill; slice.

## Fruitcake Torte

| | |
|---|---|
| 3 cups crumbled fruitcake | 1 quart vanilla ice cream, |
| ¼ cup brandy | slightly softened |

Line 8½x4½x2½-inch loaf pan with foil; extend foil 4 to 5 inches over sides of pan. Sprinkle fruitcake with brandy. Press *1 cup* crumbs into pan; spread *2 cups* ice cream over. Repeat. Cover with remaining crumbs. Fold foil over top. Freeze till ice cream is firm. Lift torte from pan; remove foil. Slice.

The slightly sweet yeast dough made with lots of butter and eggs makes brioche a delight for any meal when used as a bread or dessert. *Mandarin Rum Brioche* becomes an elegant dessert when glazed and filled with fruit and cream.

## Snowy Vanilla Torte

| | |
|---|---|
| 1½ cups finely crushed vanilla wafers | 2 egg whites |
| 6 tablespoons butter *or* margarine, melted | ¼ teaspoon grated lemon peel |
| ¼ teaspoon ground nutmeg | 1 tablespoon lemon juice |
| ¾ cup sugar | ½ teaspoon vanilla |
| 1 envelope unflavored gelatin | 1 2-ounce package dessert topping mix |
| 1¼ cups water | 1 cup dairy sour cream |
| | Ground nutmeg |

For crust, combine vanilla wafer crumbs, butter, and ¼ teaspoon nutmeg. Press firmly onto bottom and sides of 9-inch springform pan; chill. In saucepan combine sugar, gelatin, and dash salt; stir in water. Cook and stir over medium heat till gelatin dissolves. Chill till partially set. Add egg whites, lemon peel, lemon juice, and vanilla; beat till very fluffy, 5 to 7 minutes. Chill till partially set. Prepare dessert topping mix according to package directions; fold into gelatin mixture along with sour cream. Pile mixture into crust; sprinkle lightly with ground nutmeg. Chill till vanilla torte is firm, several hours or overnight. Makes 12 to 14 servings.

## Mandarin Rum Brioche

| | |
|---|---|
| 1 package active dry yeast | 2 eggs |
| ⅓ cup warm water (110°) | 1½ cups all-purpose flour |
| ¼ cup butter *or* margarine | Rum Syrup |
| 3 tablespoons sugar | Raspberry Glaze |
| ¼ teaspoon salt | Fruit Filling |

Soften yeast in water. Thoroughly cream butter, sugar, and salt. Blend in yeast, eggs, and ½ *cup* of the flour. Add remaining flour; beat 2 minutes. Turn into greased bowl. Cover and let rise in warm place till nearly double, 45 to 50 minutes. Stir down; turn into well-greased and floured 6-cup fluted mold. Cover and let rise till nearly double, about 20 minutes. Bake at 375° till done, about 20 minutes. Remove from mold; cool. Slice ¾-inch thick piece off top of brioche; cut piece removed into 4 pie-shaped wedges. Place wedges upside down on cooling rack over tray. Hollow out remaining part of brioche, leaving a ¾-inch wall. (Use interior as snack.)

Pour Rum Syrup over the brioche and pie-shaped wedges. Brush some of the Raspberry Glaze over outside of brioche. Fill center with Fruit Filling. Set pie-shaped wedges atop filling. Brush wedges with remaining Raspberry Glaze. If desired, garnish with mandarin orange sections. Chill 1 to 2 hours. Cut into wedges to serve. Makes 4 to 6 servings.

*Rum Syrup:* Drain one 11-ounce can mandarin orange sections, reserving liquid. Set oranges aside for Fruit Filling. In saucepan combine reserved mandarin liquid, 1 cup water, and ¾ cup sugar; heat and stir till sugar dissolves. Remove from heat and stir in ½ cup rum.

*Raspberry Glaze:* Sieve ⅔ cup raspberry preserves into saucepan. Stir in 2 tablespoons sugar and heat mixture to boiling. Remove from heat.

*Fruit Filling:* Sprinkle reserved mandarin orange sections with 1 tablespoon sugar. Whip 1 cup whipping cream till soft peaks form; fold in oranges.

*Add glamour to any meal by ending it with a torte dessert. Tortes have a cake or meringue base, are filled with custard or fruit filling, and are frosted with a light icing, whipped cream, or meringue. The only requirement is that they be rich and delicious.*

## Cream Puff Christmas Tree

*No need to hurry to make the Cream Puff Christmas Tree at the last minute. Make it early in the day and refrigerate. Bring it out when you're ready — maybe to use as your table's centerpiece during the meal. Use candied cherries as ornaments on this tree.*

In saucepan melt ½ cup butter *or* margarine in 1 cup boiling water. Stir together 1 cup all-purpose flour and ¼ teaspoon salt; add all at once to butter-water mixture. Beat till a ball forms that doesn't separate. Remove from heat; cool slightly. Add 4 eggs, one at a time, beating well after each. Drop mixture from tablespoon onto greased baking sheet in 24 mounds, 2 inches apart. Bake at 400° till golden and puffy, 30 to 35 minutes. Cool. Split; remove moist webbing from inside. Prepare two 2-ounce packages dessert topping mix following package directions; stir in 2 tablespoons rum and ½ teaspoon ground nutmeg. Fill puffs with topping mixture. Frost with Confectioners' Glaze (see recipe, page 112) tinted with few drops green food coloring. Arrange puffs on serving plate, pyramid style, with 9 puffs as base. Trim with candied cherries. Chill. Makes 24 puffs.

## Ginger Pumpkin Soufflés

| | |
|---|---|
| 1 cup canned pumpkin | ¼ teaspoon ground nutmeg |
| ¼ cup packed brown sugar | 3 beaten egg yolks |
| 2 tablespoons butter *or* margarine | 3 egg whites |
| ¼ teaspoon ground ginger | 2 tablespoons packed brown sugar |

In saucepan combine pumpkin, the ¼ cup brown sugar, butter, ginger, nutmeg, and dash salt. Cook and stir till butter is melted. Stir moderate amount of hot mixture into beaten egg yolks; return to saucepan. Cook and stir 2 minutes more over low heat. Remove from heat. Beat egg whites to soft peaks; gradually add the 2 tablespoons brown sugar, beating till stiff peaks form. Fold into pumpkin mixture. Turn into four 1-cup soufflé dishes. Place in shallow baking pan. Pour hot water in pan to depth of 1 inch. Bake at 350° till knife inserted off-center comes out clean, 25 to 30 minutes. Garnish with snipped candied ginger, if desired. Makes 4 servings.

## Date-Almond Shortcake

| | |
|---|---|
| 1 8-ounce package pitted dates | 1 cup milk |
| 3 cups all-purpose flour | ¾ cup butter *or* margarine, melted |
| 4 teaspoons baking powder | ¾ cup sliced almonds, toasted |
| 1 teaspoon ground cinnamon | 1½ cups whipping cream |
| ½ teaspoon salt | 3 tablespoons powdered sugar |
| ½ cup packed brown sugar | ½ teaspoon vanilla |
| 1 beaten egg | |

Halve *four* of the dates; snip remaining. Stir together flour, baking powder, cinnamon, and salt. Stir in brown sugar. Combine egg, milk, and butter; stir into flour mixture with snipped dates and ½ *cup* almonds. Spread in 2 greased 9x1½-inch round baking pans. Bake at 450° for 15 to 20 minutes. Remove from pans; cool. Whip together cream, powdered sugar, and vanilla; spread *half* atop one layer. Top with second layer; spread with remaining whipped cream. Garnish with remaining almonds and dates. Serves 8.

## Date-Macaroon Mold

| | |
|---|---|
| 1 envelope unflavored gelatin | 1 cup snipped pitted dates |
| ¼ cup sugar | 1 cup finely crumbled soft |
| 1 cup milk | coconut macaroons |
| 2 beaten egg yolks | 2 stiffly beaten egg whites |
| ⅓ cup orange juice | 1 cup whipping cream |

In saucepan mix gelatin and sugar; stir in milk and yolks. Cook and stir over medium-low heat till slightly thickened, 10 to 12 minutes. Remove from heat; stir in juice. Chill till partially set. Add dates and macaroon crumbs; fold in egg whites. Whip cream till soft peaks form; fold into date mixture. Turn into 5½-cup mold. Chill till set. Makes 8 servings.

## Eggnog-Macaroon Molds

| | |
|---|---|
| 1 envelope unflavored gelatin | 2 tablespoons rum |
| 2 cups canned *or* dairy eggnog | 1 cup whipping cream |
| ¼ cup sugar | ⅓ cup sliced maraschino |
| ½ cup crumbled soft coconut | cherries |
| macaroons | 8 whole maraschino cherries |

In saucepan combine gelatin, eggnog, and sugar; heat and stir till gelatin is dissolved. Stir in macaroon crumbs and rum. Chill till partially set. Whip cream till soft peaks form; fold into eggnog mixture with sliced cherries. Pour into individual ½-cup molds. Chill till firm. Unmold into small serving bowls. Garnish each with a whole cherry. Makes 8 servings.

## Strawberry Cake Roll

| | |
|---|---|
| ¾ cup sifted cake flour | 1 3-ounce package strawberry- |
| ¾ teaspoon baking powder | flavored gelatin |
| ¼ teaspoon salt | 1 cup boiling water |
| 4 eggs | 1 10-ounce package frozen |
| 1 teaspoon vanilla | strawberries |
| ¾ cup granulated sugar | 1 2-ounce package dessert |
| Powdered sugar | topping mix |

Sift together flour, baking powder, and salt. Beat together eggs and vanilla till thick and lemon-colored. Gradually add granulated sugar, beating till fluffy. Fold in flour mixture. Spread batter evenly in greased and lightly floured 15½x10½x1-inch baking pan. Bake at 400° till lightly browned, 10 to 12 minutes. Immediately loosen sides; turn out onto towel sprinkled with powdered sugar. Starting at narrow end, carefully roll cake and towel together; cool 30 minutes on rack. Chill thoroughly.

Meanwhile, dissolve gelatin in boiling water; stir in frozen berries till thawed. Chill till partially set. Unroll cake; remove towel. Spread with gelatin mixture; chill till gelatin is almost set, about 10 minutes. Carefully reroll cake. Chill well. Prepare dessert topping mix following package directions; use to frost cake roll. Chill cake roll till served. Makes 10 servings.

*Use the shape of molds to advantage when you prepare a gelatin dessert. Fill the center of a ring mold with fruit or whipped cream. Use a tower mold when you want to capture the attention of all with elegant height. Or, add a different touch to each guest's dessert with individual molds.*

Petit fours don't have to be cube-shaped. For holiday entertaining attract attention with *Starlight Cakes*. Compliments you'll receive from your family and guests will make the little extra effort worth every minute.

## Apple Strudel

*Special and festive as a Christmas dessert, strudel is a seasoned traveler. Strudel is a German and Austrian word derived from the German word meaning "whirlpool." The specialty began as a delicate honeyed Turkish pastry, baklava, traveled to Hungary and was stuffed with nuts and apples—becoming a darling dessert. According to those familiar with the dessert, a good strudel dough is as thin as onionskin—so thin you can read through it.*

| | |
|---|---|
| 3 cups all-purpose flour | 2 teaspoons ground cinnamon |
| ½ cup butter *or* margarine | 6 cups very thinly sliced |
| 1 beaten egg | peeled tart apples* |
| ⅔ cup warm water | ½ cup dried currants* |
| ¾ cup butter, melted | 1 beaten egg white |
| ⅔ cup granulated sugar* | Powdered sugar |

Stir together flour and ½ teaspoon salt; cut in the ½ cup butter till crumbly. Mix beaten egg and water; add to flour and stir well. Turn onto lightly floured surface; knead 5 minutes. Halve dough. Cover; let stand 1 hour.

Cover large table with floured cloth. On cloth, roll *half* dough to 15-inch square. Brush with *2 tablespoons* melted butter; let stand few minutes. Starting from middle of square, *carefully* work underneath dough using backs of hands to gently stretch from one corner to the next till dough is *paper thin* and about 36 inches square. Brush with ¼ *cup* melted butter.

Mix granulated sugar and cinnamon. Trim edges of dough: put *half* the apples along one side, 6 inches from edge. Pour *half* the sugar mixture over apples; top with *half* the currants. Gently fold the 6-inch piece of dough over filling. Slowly and evenly raise cloth behind filling making dough roll away from you into tight roll. Seal ends. Place on lightly greased 15½x10½x1-inch baking pan; curve slightly to form crescent. Repeat with remaining dough. Brush tops of strudels with egg white. Bake at 350° for 45 to 50 minutes. Remove from pan; cool on rack. Sprinkle with powdered sugar. Makes 2.

*\*Note:* For Cranberry Strudel use one 16-ounce package cranberries, chopped, instead of apples; 2 cups sugar; and pecans instead of currants.

## Starlight Cakes

| | |
|---|---|
| ¾ cup shortening | 1 cup milk |
| 1½ cups granulated sugar | 5 stiffly beaten egg whites |
| 1½ teaspoons vanilla | Milk |
| 2¼ cups sifted cake flour | 6 cups sifted powdered sugar |
| 1 tablespoon baking powder | 1 teaspoon vanilla |
| 1 teaspoon salt | Silver decorator candies |

In large mixing bowl cream shortening and granulated sugar. Add 1½ teaspoons vanilla. Sift together flour, baking powder, and salt. Add to creamed mixture alternately with the 1 cup milk, beating after each addition. Beat 2 minutes at medium speed of electric mixer. Fold in beaten egg whites. Pour into well-greased and floured star-shaped molds (individual gelatin molds), using ¼ cup batter in each. Bake at 375° for 20 to 25 minutes. Cool 5 minutes before removing from pans. Stir enough milk (⅓ to ½ cup) into powdered sugar to make pouring consistency. Stir in the 1 teaspoon vanilla and ⅛ teaspoon salt. Place cakes on rack over baking sheet; spoon icing evenly over cakes. Decorate with silver decorator candies. Makes 20 cakes.

## Burnt Sugar Angel Cake

| | |
|---|---|
| ½ cup sugar | 1 cup chopped pecans, toasted |
| 1 package angel cake mix | Burnt Sugar Icing |

Cook and stir sugar till melted and golden brown. Stir in ½ cup water; boil till syrupy and reduced to ⅓ cup, 5 to 10 minutes. Cool. Prepare cake mix following package directions *except* use ¼ *cup* syrup mixture for ¼ cup of the water called for on package; reserve remaining syrup. Stir nuts into batter. Bake in *ungreased* 10-inch tube pan at 375° for 30 to 40 minutes. Invert cake. Cool; remove from pan. Spoon Burnt Sugar Icing over top.

*Burnt Sugar Icing:* In bowl combine 1 cup sifted powdered sugar, 2 tablespoons softened butter *or* margarine, 2 tablespoons milk, and the remaining syrup mixture from the cake; mix till smooth.

*Convenient angel cake mix cuts costs and time for you. Add a delightful flavor by melting and caramelizing sugar to make a syrup to use in both cake and icing.*

## Crème de Cherry Tarts

| | |
|---|---|
| 1 envelope unflavored gelatin | 3 stiffly beaten egg whites |
| ½ cup sugar | 1 cup whipping cream |
| ½ cup water | ⅓ cup maraschino cherries, |
| 3 egg yolks | drained and chopped |
| ¼ cup crème d'almond | 10 *baked* 3-inch tart shells *or* |
| 4 drops red food coloring | 1 *baked* 9-inch pastry shell |

In saucepan combine gelatin, sugar, and dash salt. Beat together water and egg yolks; add to gelatin mixture. Cook and stir till slightly thickened. Remove from heat; stir in crème d'almond and food coloring. Chill till partially set. Fold in egg whites. Whip cream; fold into gelatin mixture. Fold in cherries. Chill till mixture mounds slightly. Pile gelatin mixture into tart shells or pastry shell. Chill till filling is firm. Makes 10 tarts or 1 pie.

# Beverages

## Champagne Party Punch

Fresh cranberries
Green grapes
Oranges, cut in wedges

• • •

2 ⅘-quart bottles sauterne,
chilled

3 cups cognac, chilled
6 ⅘-quart bottles champagne,
chilled
8 cups carbonated water,
chilled (2 quarts)

Place cranberries, green grapes, and orange wedges on a foil-lined baking sheet. Freeze fruit. Before serving, combine sauterne and cognac in a punch bowl. Resting bottle on rim of bowl, carefully pour in champagne and carbonated water. Add frozen fruits. Makes about 60 (5-ounce) servings.

## Apple Brandy Brew

1 lemon, sliced
4 ⅘-quart bottles apple-
flavored pop wine, chilled

1 32-ounce can apple cider,
chilled (4 cups)
1 pint peach brandy, chilled

Fill a ring mold half full with water; freeze firm. Arrange lemon slices atop; add enough additional water to anchor lemon slices. Freeze firm. Before serving, mix wine, cider, and brandy in punch bowl. Unmold ice ring; float atop wine mixture. Makes about 30 (5-ounce) servings.

## Merry Party Punch

2 cups water
½ cup sugar
½ teaspoon whole cloves

• • •

4 cups unsweetened grape juice
1 6-ounce can frozen pink
lemonade concentrate

½ cup unsweetened pineapple
juice
4 to 6 drops red food coloring
Festive Ice Chips
1 28-ounce bottle carbonated
water, chilled
Artificial holly

In saucepan mix water with sugar and cloves. Bring to boiling; cover and simmer 5 minutes. Set aside to cool; strain. Combine grape juice, lemonade concentrate, pineapple juice, and food coloring. Add cooled sugar mixture. Chill. Before serving, pour grape mixture over Festive Ice Chips in a punch bowl. Gently pour carbonated water down side of bowl. Garnish with artificial holly, if desired. Makes about 20 (5-ounce) servings.

*Festive Ice Chips:* Combine 4 cups water, 1 cup unsweetened grape juice, ½ of a 6-ounce can frozen pink lemonade concentrate, ¼ cup unsweetened pineapple juice, and a few drops red food coloring. Pour into two 3-cup refrigerator trays and freeze till firm. Before using, break frozen mixture into large chips with an ice pick.

*Pictured opposite:* Add elegance and color to all types of holiday parties with punches. At your next gathering, try serving a wine-based punch such as *Champagne Party Punch* (front) or *Apple Brandy Brew* (left).

## Sparkling Cranberry Drink

*To add a festive note to Sparkling Cranberry Drink, try freezing cranberries in ice cubes. First fill half a refrigerator tray with water; freeze firm. Then add a fresh cranberry to each cube and finish filling tray with water; freeze solid.*

2 16-ounce cans jellied
   cranberry sauce
1½ cups orange juice
½ cup lemon juice

Ice cubes
• • •
2 28-ounce bottles ginger
   ale, chilled (7 cups)

Beat the jellied cranberry sauce till smooth. Add orange and lemon juices; mix thoroughly. Place ice cubes in a large punch bowl; pour cranberry mixture over ice cubes. Resting bottle on rim of punch bowl, carefully pour in ginger ale. Serve immediately. Makes 20 (5-ounce) servings.

## Parsonage Punch

2 18-ounce cans unsweetened
   pineapple juice
3 cups orange juice
½ cup lemon juice

⅓ cup honey
3 pints pineapple sherbet
2 28-ounce bottles ginger
   ale, chilled

Combine fruit juices and honey; chill. Pour into punch bowl. Spoon in sherbet. Resting bottle on rim of punch bowl, carefully pour in ginger ale, stirring gently. Serve immediately. Makes 32 (4-ounce) servings.

## Holiday Nectar

1 46-ounce can apricot nectar
   (about 6 cups)
2 cups water
1 6-ounce can frozen orange
   juice concentrate

Few drops aromatic bitters
1 pint orange sherbet
2 10-ounce bottles lemon-lime
   carbonated beverage,
   chilled

Combine apricot nectar, water, orange juice concentrate, and bitters; chill. To serve, spoon *half* of the sherbet into a punch bowl; add some of the apricot nectar mixture. Muddle. Add remaining nectar mixture. Resting bottle on rim of bowl, carefully pour in the chilled lemon-lime carbonated beverage. Spoon in remaining sherbet. Makes about 16 (5-ounce) servings.

## Christmas Wine Punch

3 cups orange juice
1½ cups sugar
1½ cups lemon juice
• • •
1 ⅘-quart bottle sauterne,
   chilled

½ cup brandy
1 ⅘-quart bottle champagne,
   chilled
1 cup frozen whole straw-
   berries, halved
Orange slices

Combine orange juice, sugar, and lemon juice, stirring till sugar dissolves. Chill well. To serve, stir in sauterne and brandy; carefully pour in champagne. Garnish with berries and orange slices. Makes 24 (4-ounce) servings.

## Christmas Cooler

1 3-ounce package lime-flavored
    gelatin
1 cup boiling water
1 6-ounce can frozen limeade
    concentrate
½ teaspoon almond extract

½ teaspoon vanilla
8 large ice cubes (2 cups)
2 7-ounce bottles ginger
    ale, chilled
Red maraschino cherries
    with stems

Dissolve gelatin in boiling water; cool. In a blender container combine cooled gelatin mixture, frozen limeade concentrate, almond extract, and vanilla. Cover and blend at high speed, adding 1 ice cube at a time till smooth and frothy. Gently stir in the ginger ale and 2 cups cold water. Serve immediately. Garnish with cherries. Makes 16 (4-ounce) servings.

## Strawberry-Lemon Tea

2 10-ounce packages frozen
    sliced strawberries,
    thawed
4 cups pineapple-orange drink,
    chilled

4 cups strong black tea,
    chilled
¾ cup lemon juice
½ cup sugar
Ice cubes

Press strawberries through a sieve. Mix with pineapple-orange drink, tea, lemon juice, and sugar. Serve over ice. Makes 21 (4-ounce) servings.

*Dress up Strawberry-Lemon Tea by moistening the glass rims with a lemon slice. Then dip the rims in plain or colored sugar. For an extra special touch, garnish each serving with a fresh pineapple spear.*

## Brandy Milk Punch

2 cups milk
¾ cup brandy
¼ cup powdered sugar
3 tablespoons anisette

1 egg white
½ teaspoon vanilla
¼ teaspoon ground nutmeg
4 ice cubes

In a blender container, combine milk, brandy, sugar, anisette, egg white, vanilla, nutmeg, and ice cubes. Cover; blend till frothy. Pour into tall glasses; sprinkle with ground nutmeg, if desired. Makes 9 (5-ounce) servings.

## Brandy Eggnog Deluxe

6 egg yolks
¾ cup sugar
½ teaspoon vanilla
¼ teaspoon ground nutmeg
1½ cups brandy

⅓ cup bourbon
3 cups whipping cream, chilled
2 cups cold milk
6 egg whites
6 tablespoons sugar

Beat egg yolks till light. Gradually add ¾ cup sugar, vanilla, and nutmeg; beat constantly. Stir in brandy and bourbon; chill. Stir in cream and milk. Beat egg whites till soft peaks form; add remaining sugar, beating to stiff peaks. Fold into yolk mixture. Serve at once. Makes 24 (4-ounce) servings.

*So often did Anglo-Saxons toast one another with "Be of good health" or "Wassail," that the word came to mean the drink itself. The Wassail bowl was a Christmas mainstay in English homes throughout the twelve nights of the holiday. Carolers would come door-to-door, exchanging songs for a cup of hot punch. The toast floating on the surface gave rise to the expression "drinking a toast."*

## Wassail Bowl

| | |
|---|---|
| 1 medium orange, halved | ½ cup sugar |
| 10 whole cloves | • • • |
| 2 ⅘ -quart bottles claret | 4 inches stick cinnamon |

Stud orange halves with whole cloves. In a saucepan combine orange halves, claret, sugar, and cinnamon. Cover; simmer about 15 minutes. Remove cinnamon and orange halves. Serve hot in small punch bowl. If desired, float whole oranges studded with whole cloves atop. Makes 14 (4-ounce) servings.

## Ruby Spiced Toddy

| | |
|---|---|
| 1 32-ounce bottle cranberry juice cocktail | 1 cup apple cider *or* juice |
| 2 cups orange juice | ½ cup grenadine syrup |
| 1 cup unsweetened grapefruit juice | ¼ teaspoon ground cloves |
| | ¼ teaspoon ground nutmeg |
| | Stick cinnamon |

In a large saucepan combine cranberry juice cocktail, orange juice, grapefruit juice, apple cider, grenadine syrup, cloves, and nutmeg. Heat mixture just to boiling. To serve, pour hot cranberry mixture into mugs. Garnish each serving with stick cinnamon stirrer. Makes 8 (8-ounce) servings.

## Honey Buttered Wine

| | |
|---|---|
| 2 cups dry white wine | 4 teaspoons butter *or* |
| 3 tablespoons orange liqueur | margarine |
| 3 tablespoons honey | Lemon slices |
| 1 tablespoon sugar | Stick cinnamon |

In a small saucepan combine dry white wine, orange liqueur, honey, and sugar. Heat to boiling; pour wine mixture into four small mugs. Top each serving with *1 teaspoon* of the butter or margarine. Garnish with lemon slices and stick cinnamon stirrers. Makes 4 (5-ounce) servings.

## The Hot Apple

| | |
|---|---|
| 1½ cups apple juice | 1 21-ounce can baked apples, drained and halved |
| 2 tablespoons packed brown sugar | 3 thin slices lemon, halved |
| 12 whole cloves | 2 tablespoons butter *or* margarine |
| • • • | |
| 1½ cups brandy | |

In saucepan combine apple juice, brown sugar, and cloves; bring to boiling. Reduce heat; simmer, covered, for 15 minutes. Strain. Return to pan; add brandy and heat. Place *half* baked apple, *half* lemon slice, and *1 teaspoon* butter in *each* mug. Pour in juice mixture. Makes 6 (4-ounce) servings.

## Flaming Brandied Coffee

| | |
|---|---|
| 1½ cups brandy | 2 inches stick cinnamon |
| Peel of 1 lemon, cut up | 4 cups hot double-strength |
| 16 whole cloves | coffee |
| 8 sugar cubes | |

In a chafing dish combine brandy, lemon peel, cloves, sugar, and cinnamon; stir to dissolve sugar. Fill demitasse cups with coffee. Warm brandy mixture slightly; ignite, stirring to blend spices with brandy. Ladle into demitasse cups. Serve at once. Makes about 15 demitasse servings.

*Make double-strength coffee for Flaming Brandied Coffee by using two tablespoons of instant coffee crystals for each cup of boiling water.*

## Orange-Spiked Coffee

| | |
|---|---|
| 1⅓ cups hot coffee | ⅓ cup orange liqueur |
| ⅓ cup brandy | Whipped cream |

In saucepan mix coffee, brandy, and liqueur. Heat almost to boiling. Pour into coffee cups. Top with dollops of whipped cream; garnish with orange peel twists, if desired. Serve immediately. Makes 4 (5-ounce) servings.

## Lemon-Maple Christmas Punch

In large saucepan mix 4 cups lemon juice and 3 cups maple-flavored syrup. Heat just till boiling. Stir in 4 cups blended whiskey; heat through. *Do not boil.* Serve immediately in small mugs. Sprinkle with ground nutmeg and garnish with lemon slices, if desired. Makes 20 (4-ounce) servings.

## Spiked Grape Punch

| | |
|---|---|
| 4 cups grape juice | 1 6-ounce can frozen orange |
| 1 cup sugar | juice concentrate |
| 1 6-ounce can frozen lemonade | 4 inches stick cinnamon |
| concentrate | 1½ cups vodka |

In a saucepan combine grape juice, sugar, lemonade concentrate, orange juice concentrate, and 5½ cups water. Add cinnamon. Simmer about 15 minutes. Remove cinnamon; stir in vodka. Makes about 25 (4-ounce) servings.

## Hot Buttered Lemonade

| | |
|---|---|
| 4½ cups boiling water | ¾ cup lemon juice |
| ¾ cup sugar | 2 tablespoons butter |
| 1½ teaspoons grated lemon peel | Stick cinnamon |

In a saucepan combine water, sugar, lemon peel, and juice. Cook and stir till heated through. Pour into mugs; top each serving with *1 teaspoon* of the butter. Serve with stick cinnamon stirrers. Makes about 6 (8-ounce) servings.

Arrange your New Year's Eve midnight buffet around a centerpiece of decorated cupcakes. Be sure to include an assortment of appetizers, *Deviled Popcorn*, and hearty *Party Chicken-Ham-wiches*. Complete the menu with *Orange-Eggnog Punch*. (See complete menu on page 161.)

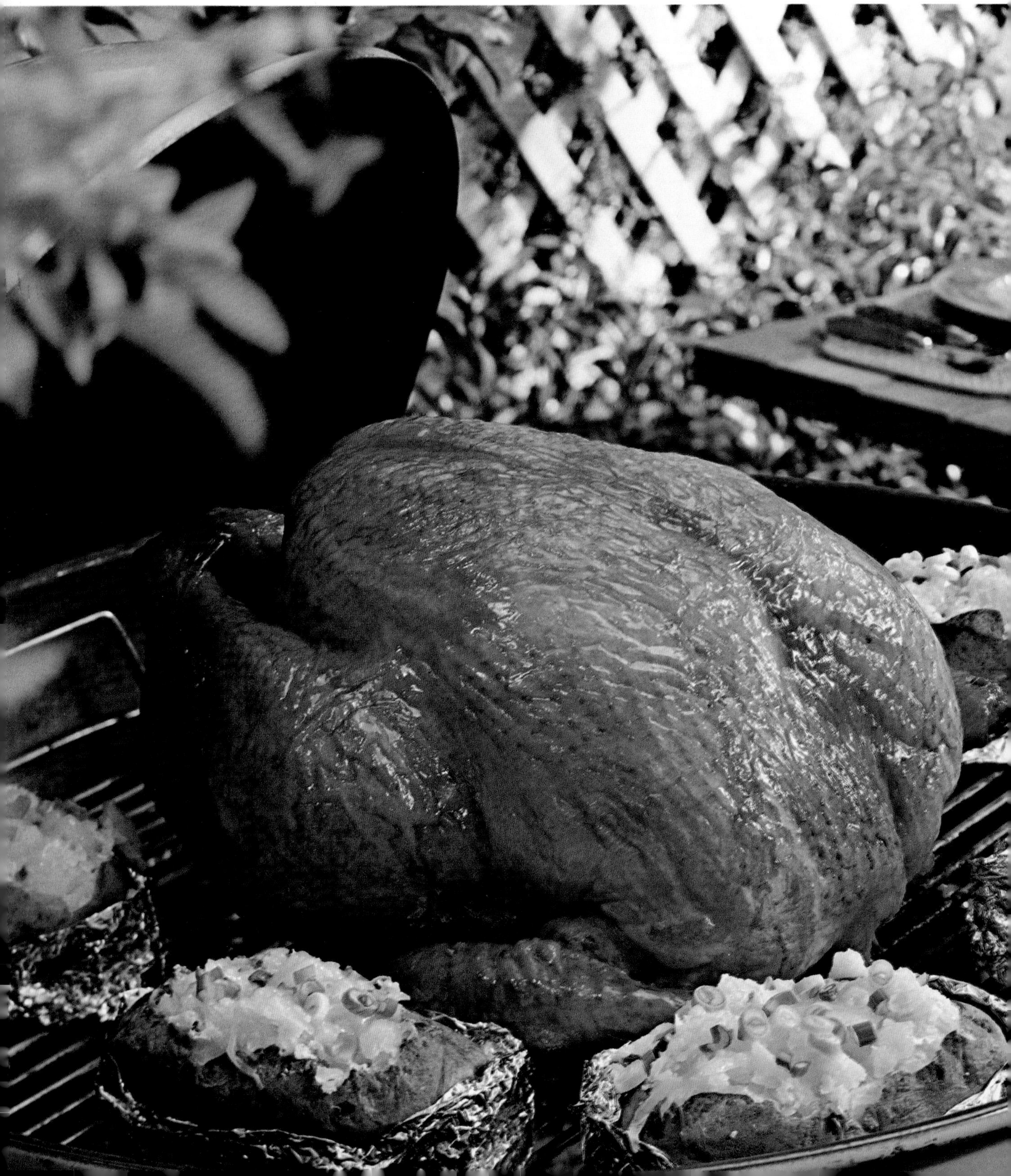

# Thanksgiving for Everyone

Thanksgiving Day is turkey day from New England's blustery coast to Florida's sunny shores and for all points west. There are bound to be cranberries too—whole in sauce, chopped in relish, molded in a salad, or baked in a pie. Additional foods reflect family lifestyles.

For some, Thanksgiving is a time when relatives gather after church to enjoy a traditional dinner and catch up on family doings. For others, the day's activities are more casual with the menu planned accordingly.

If you lean towards the traditional, you'll want to try the dishes appearing in the early American feast in this section. But perhaps you want something different to serve. If so, you'll find a tasty assortment of good foods under the heading of Thanksgiving Recipes.

*Hickory-Smoked Turkey* is Thanksgiving fare in Florida and elsewhere that an outdoor dinner is possible. Foil-wrapped *Whole Grilled Potatoes* cook along with the bird. They receive a cheese and onion topping just before serving. Other regional favorites are *Orange-Tomato Cocktail* and a *Fresh Fruit Salad* bursting with avocado. (See complete menu on page 146.)

# Early American Thanksgiving

## *Menu*

(see photo, page 145)

*Roast Turkey*
*(see chart, page 91)*
*Oyster Stuffing*
*Plymouth Succotash*
*Steamed Clams*
*Codfish Balls*
*Rye and Injun Bread*
*Butter    Jelly*
*Whipped Parsnips*
*Indian Pudding*
*Cranberry Tarts*
*Beverage*

Every autumn, on the last Thursday of November, Americans join together in a national celebration of our historic past. Although celebrated earlier in Virginia, the traditional Thanksgiving feast began in Massachusetts in 1621, as a celebration after the Pilgrims had survived a horrendous winter in which almost half their small band from the Mayflower succumbed to cold, disease, or starvation. To solidify relations with the neighboring Wampanoag Indians and to thank them for their help in showing the Pilgrims how to plant crops and which forest plants were edible, Governor Bradford of the Plymouth Colony invited Chief Massasoit and his braves to the feast.

It was an exuberant time after the bleakest year imaginable. In the bubbling pots were deer, turkey, ducks, geese, as well as oysters and other sea creatures. All the vegetables the Indians had taught the settlers to use were cooked—squash, pumpkins, and corn—as well as leeks and watercress. The women cracked corn for hominy, gathered cranberries, and baked corn bread and white bread. There were also crisp, cold apples, wild plums, and dried berries, and even wine from wild grapes. Oddly cranberry sauce and pumpkin pie were not on that first Thanksgiving menu. Despite the chilly weather, all food was prepared, and served outdoors.

For the settlers and the ninety Indians who attended, the feast was a great success. But the following year a drought caused a poor harvest, and there was little reason to repeat the festivities. It was not until 1623 that another Thanksgiving Day was ordained, and it was held in July—to give thanks for the safe passage of a ship with supplies and new settlers.

Records of succeeding Thanksgiving celebrations are scant. For two hundred years, Thanksgiving Day was set aside for fasting and prayer. In 1863, President Lincoln proclaimed a National Thanksgiving Day.

Now Thanksgiving is a family day when generations of a family travel great distances to feast and fete one another, to reminisce and to share the year's experiences. Through the decades the traditional Thanksgiving meal has remained more or less as it was for the first settlers—turkey or other game, numerous autumn vegetables, cranberries, pumpkin (now in pie form), and squash—a bounteous tribute to a generous fall harvest. Food preparation has come a long way from those first heavy iron pots and kettles used in the fireplace or outdoors, but the wholesome, abundant fruits-of-the-earth remain part of our Thanksgiving heritage.

## Whipped Parsnips

*Parsnips are a delicious part of our Early American Thanksgiving tradition. An old verse says: For pottage and puddings, and custards and pies, our pumpkins and parsnips are common supplies.*

| | |
|---|---|
| 1½ pounds parsnips | 2 tablespoons packed brown |
| 1½ pounds potatoes (4 or 5 | sugar |
| medium) | ½ teaspoon salt |
| ¼ cup butter *or* margarine | Milk, warmed |

Peel and dice parsnips and potatoes. Place vegetables in boiling salted water; cover. Cook till vegetables are tender, for 15 to 18 minutes. Drain well and mash. Stir in butter, sugar, salt, and enough warmed milk to make fluffy. Sprinkle with nutmeg, if desired. Makes 6 to 8 servings.

## Rye and Injun Bread

In mixing bowl combine 1½ cups all-purpose flour, ¾ cup cornmeal, and 1 package active dry yeast. In a saucepan heat 1 cup milk, ½ cup water, ¼ cup light molasses, and 1 teaspoon salt till just warm (115-120°); add to flour mixture in bowl. Beat at low speed of electric mixer for ½ minute, scraping sides of bowl constantly. Beat at high speed 3 minutes more. Stir in ¾ cup stirred rye flour and an additional ½ cup all-purpose flour. Cover; let rise in warm place till almost double (about 1 hour). Punch down; place in a greased 1½-quart casserole. Cover; let rise till almost double (about 45 minutes). Bake, uncovered, at 325° for 30 minutes; cover top of bread with foil. Continue baking 20 minutes more. Makes 1 loaf.

*Once commonplace in colonial homes, Rye and Injun Bread sounds rather exotic today. It was the staple dark bread of New England, a blend of rye flour and Indian cornmeal which was mixed, kneaded, and baked in the embers on the hearth.*

## Plymouth Succotash

| | |
|---|---|
| 1 pound dry navy beans | 1 cup chopped carrot |
| 1 3-pound ready-to-cook broiler-fryer chicken, cut up | 1 medium onion, sliced |
| | ½ teaspoon dried thyme, crushed |
| 1 2½-pound corned beef brisket | 2 14½-ounce cans golden hominy, drained |
| 4 ounces salt pork | |
| 3 cups sliced potatoes | Salt |
| 1 cup chopped turnip | Pepper |

Rinse beans. Place in a large kettle with 4 cups water. Bring to boiling; boil 2 minutes. Cover and let stand 1 hour. Meanwhile in a covered saucepan, cook chicken in 4 cups water over low heat till tender, 35 to 40 minutes. Drain chicken, reserving broth. Remove bones from chicken, refrigerate meat. Add corned beef, salt pork, and reserved chicken broth to beans. Cover and simmer 1 hour. Add potatoes, turnip, carrot, onion, and thyme. Cover and simmer 1 hour more. Remove corned beef and salt pork. Discard salt pork. Mash beans slightly. Dice corned beef; return to bean mixture. Add chicken and hominy. Season with salt and pepper. Continue simmering till chicken is heated through, about 15 minutes. Serves 10.

*The Pilgrims turned an Indian standby, succotash (corn and beans cooked together in the same pot) into a rather special stew by adding chicken, beef, or salt pork. They dubbed their version Plymouth Succotash. In Plymouth, Massachusetts, Forefathers' Day is celebrated every December 21, with a special feast that includes Plymouth Succotash, hot johnny cake, and Indian pudding, all New World creations.*

## Oyster Stuffing

| | |
|---|---|
| ½ cup chopped celery | 1 tablespoon snipped parsley |
| ½ cup chopped onion | 3 cups shucked oysters with liquid |
| 1 bay leaf | |
| ¼ cup butter *or* margarine | 2 beaten eggs |
| 6 cups dry bread crumbs (about 12 slices) | 1 teaspoon poultry seasoning |
| | 1 teaspoon salt |

Cook celery, onion, and bay leaf in butter till tender. Discard bay leaf. Add bread crumbs and parsley; mix well. Drain oysters, reserving liquid. Add oysters, eggs, poultry seasoning, salt, and dash pepper to crumb mixture; mix well. Stir in enough reserved oyster liquid to moisten. Makes enough stuffing to fill a 10- to 12-pound turkey; or bake, covered, in a 2-quart casserole at 375° for 30 to 35 minutes. Makes 6½ cups.

*Benjamin Franklin once uttered these wry words about the turkey: "I wish the Bald Eagle had not been chosen as the Representative of our country...
The turkey is a much more respectable bird, and withal a true original Native of America." Colonial wild turkeys sometimes weighed up to fifty pounds. Formidable birds indeed!*

## Steamed Clams

*Pictured Opposite:* For a holiday meal in the Pilgrim tradition prepare this Early American Thanksgiving feast (for complete menu, see page 142).

Thoroughly wash 24 soft-shelled clams in shells. Cover with salt water (⅓ cup salt to 16 cups cold water); let stand 15 minutes; then rinse. Repeat twice. Place clams on a rack in kettle with 1 cup hot water; cover tightly and steam just till shells open, about 5 minutes. Discard any that do not open. Loosen clams from shells; serve with melted butter. Serves 4.

## Codfish Balls

*Codfish once was designated the 'sacred cod' in Massachusetts, for at one time New England's economy rested largely on the cod. Cod was eaten many ways by the ingenious colonists. A favorite dish was Codfish Balls served at Sunday morning breakfast.*

|  |  |
|---|---|
| 8 ounces salt cod | 2 tablespoons butter *or* |
| 3 cups diced potatoes | margarine |
| ¼ cup chopped onion | ½ teaspoon Worcestershire |
| 1 egg | sauce |
| ¼ cup snipped parsley | Fat for frying |

Soak cod in water several hours or overnight; drain. Dice. Cook cod, potatoes, and onion in boiling water till tender, about 10 minutes; drain. Beat with electric mixer. Add egg, parsley, butter, Worcestershire, and ¼ teaspoon pepper; beat. Drop by heaping tablespoonsful into deep hot fat (375°). Fry till golden, 2 to 3 minutes, turning once. Drain. Makes 30.

## Indian Pudding

*Indian pudding is not derived from an Indian dish, but is purely a colonial invention, named for the cornmeal in it. Served warm, Indian Pudding is a filling, tasty, and economical dish — just right for a cold New England winter supper.*

|  |  |
|---|---|
| 3 cups milk | ¼ cup sugar |
| ⅓ cup molasses | 2 tablespoons butter |
| ⅓ cup cornmeal | ½ teaspoon ground ginger |
| 1 egg | ½ teaspoon ground cinnamon |

In saucepan combine milk and molasses; stir in cornmeal. Cook, stirring constantly, till thick, about 10 minutes. Remove from heat. Beat egg slightly with fork. Combine egg, sugar, butter, ginger, cinnamon, and ¼ teaspoon salt. Gradually stir in hot cornmeal mixture. Bake, uncovered, in a 1-quart casserole at 300° for about 1½ hours. Makes 6 servings.

## Cranberry Tarts

*The Indians called the shiny red berries* sassamanesh *and ate them raw, added them to dried meat and melted animal fat to make pemmican, and even used them as a poultice on wounds. Early colonists named them cranberries and found dozens of uses for them — in breads, muffins, and pies.*

|  |  |
|---|---|
| Pastry for a 2-crust pie | 2 tablespoons cornstarch |
| (see recipe, page 124) | 1 teaspoon vanilla |
| 3 cups cranberries | ¾ cup all-purpose flour |
| ½ cup raisins | ⅓ cup sugar |
| 1½ cups sugar | 6 tablespoons butter |

Roll pastry ⅛ inch thick. Cut into six 6-inch circles. Fit into tart pans; press out bubbles. In a saucepan combine cranberries, raisins, and 1 cup water. Simmer 3 minutes. Stir together 1½ cups sugar and cornstarch; stir into cranberries. Cook and stir till thickened and bubbly. Stir in vanilla. Spoon into tart shells. Combine flour and ⅓ cup sugar; cut in butter till crumbly. Sprinkle over tarts. Bake at 400°, 30 to 35 minutes. Makes 6.

# Outdoor Thanksgiving

In the warm-weather states, holidays take on their own particular coloration. In Florida, parts of California, and tropical Hawaii, an outdoor Thanksgiving celebration takes on a special look. Imagine a swim before Thanksgiving dinner—or dinner served on the porch, patio, beach, or near the pool— or perhaps after dark under the stars. This is not only *possible* in sleepy, sulfurous temperatures, but a frequent happening in places where the climate dictates such indulgences. Though Thanksgiving outdoors might seem ridiculous to people who live in colder regions of the country, the first Pilgrim Thanksgiving actually was held outdoors in chilly Massachusetts, hardly in a climate conducive to a holiday pre-dinner dip.

Actually, in our warmer climates, Thanksgiving seems to differ more by degree than by kind. The great turkey of the traditional American feast is as popular in Florida as in Vermont. The difference lies in the preparation and the setting. Sitting in the sunlight, one can be just as festive at a picnic table on the patio as at a traditional dining room table set with bayberry candles and an autumnal arrangement of dried flowers.

Eating outdoors implies a wider menu range that might include more warm weather foods. It also suggests the possibility of an expanded guest list. There's something about an open-air feast that says "the more the merrier" without undue fuss about seating arrangements.

## Cherry-Cranberry Pie

1 21-ounce can cherry pie filling
1 16-ounce can whole cranberry sauce
¼ cup sugar
2 tablespoons quick-cooking tapioca

1 teaspoon lemon juice
¼ teaspoon ground cinnamon
Pastry for 2-crust 9-inch pie (see recipe, page 124)
2 tablespoons butter *or* margarine

Combine pie filling, cranberry sauce, sugar, tapioca, lemon juice, and cinnamon; let stand 15 minutes. Line 9-inch pie plate with pastry; fill with fruit mixture. Dot with butter. Adjust top crust; seal and flute edges. Cut slits in top crust for escape of steam. Bake at 400° for 35 to 40 minutes. If edges brown too rapidly, cover with foil during last few minutes.

## Whole Grilled Potatoes (see photo, pages 140-141)

*Include these tasty grilled potatoes in your Thanksgiving menu if you live in an area where the November weather is warm enough to permit an outdoor meal.*

6 potatoes
Cooking oil

Shredded Swiss cheese
Sliced green onion

Brush potatoes with some cooking oil. Wrap each in a square of heavy foil. Place on covered grill over *medium-slow* coals for 1½ to 2 hours, turning occasionally. When tender, open with tines of fork and push ends to fluff. Top with shredded cheese and sliced green onion. Makes 6 servings.

## Hickory-Smoked Turkey (see photo, pages 140-141)

> 1 12-pound turkey
> 1 tablespoon salt
>
> ¼ cup cooking oil
> Damp hickory chips

Salt turkey cavity. Skewer neck skin to back. Tuck wing tips behind shoulder joints. Push drumsticks under band of skin or tie to tail. In covered grill, have *medium-slow* coals at back and sides of firebox. Place bird, breast up, on foil drip pan directly on grill. Brush with oil. Insert meat thermometer into thigh being sure it doesn't touch bone. Lower grill hood. Roast till thermometer registers 185°, 3½ to 4½ hours; sprinkle damp hickory chips over coals every 20 to 30 minutes. Brush bird often with oil and add more coals, if needed. Let stand 15 minutes before carving. Serves 12.

*For a Thanksgiving treat, hickory-smoke the traditional turkey. The good smoke flavor comes from using the hickory chips that have been soaked in water atop coals. A covered grill is necessary to keep the heat and smoke circulating.*

## Broccoli in Foil

> 2 10-ounce packages frozen
>   broccoli spears
> Seasoned salt
>
> 3 tablespoons water
> 2 tablespoons butter *or*
>   margarine

Place broccoli on 18x18-inch square of double-thickness foil. Sprinkle generously with seasoned salt and pepper. Sprinkle with water and top with butter. Bring edges of foil up and, leaving a little space for expansion of steam, seal tightly. Cook over *medium-slow* coals till done, about 60 minutes; turn often. Garnish with lemon slices, if desired. Makes 6 servings.

## Fresh Fruit Salad (see photo, pages 140-141)

> ½ cup sugar
> ¼ cup tarragon vinegar
> 2 tablespoons water
> 1 teaspoon celery salt
> 1 teaspoon paprika
> 1 teaspoon dry mustard
> 1 cup salad oil
> 2 medium oranges, chilled
>
> 1 medium grapefruit, chilled
> 1 ripe medium banana
> 4 cups torn lettuce
> 2 cups torn escarole
> 1 avocado, peeled and thinly
>   sliced
> 1 cup red grapes, halved
>   and seeded

Heat and stir sugar, vinegar, and water just till sugar dissolves; cool. Combine vinegar mixture, celery salt, paprika, and mustard. Add oil in slow stream, beating with electric mixer till thick. Chill. Peel and section oranges and grapefruit, reserving juices. Peel and slice banana; brush with reserved citrus juices. Set aside. Combine lettuce and escarole in large salad bowl; arrange orange and grapefruit sections, banana, avocado slices, and grapes atop. Serve with the dressing. Makes 6 to 8 servings.

*A tasty sweet-sour dressing makes this colorful fruit salad a delight to eat. Serve the fruit atop the greens in a large bowl or make individual salads with the fruit on lettuce leaves or escarole.*

## Orange-Tomato Cocktail (see photo, pages 140-141)

Mix 1½ cups orange juice and 1½ cups tomato juice. Chill well. Stir before serving. Garnish glasses with orange slices. Makes 6 (4-ounce) servings.

# Thanksgiving Recipes

## Turkey Breast Italian-Style

| | |
|---|---|
| 1 4-pound ready-to-cook turkey breast | 1 16-ounce can tomatoes, cut up |
| 4 slices bacon | 1 3-ounce can sliced mushrooms |
| • • • | ¼ cup pitted ripe olives, sliced |
| ½ cup chopped onion | ¼ cup dry white wine |
| ½ cup chopped celery | ½ teaspoon salt |
| 1 clove garlic, minced | ½ teaspoon dried oregano, crushed |
| ¼ cup butter *or* margarine | Hot cooked rice *or* spaghetti |
| 3 tablespoons all-purpose flour | |

Place turkey breast in foil-lined roasting pan, bone side down. Place bacon slices over breast. Insert meat thermometer, being careful to avoid bone. Roast, uncovered, at 350° till meat is easily pierced and meat thermometer registers 185°, about 2 hours. Cook onion, celery, and garlic in butter or margarine till tender. Blend in flour. Add undrained tomatoes, undrained mushrooms, olives, wine, salt, and oregano. Cover. Cook and stir till sauce thickens and bubbles. Remove meat thermometer. Place turkey breast on platter. Spoon some sauce over. Pass remaining sauce. Serve with hot rice or spaghetti. Makes 6 to 8 servings.

## Rolled Flounder Kiev

*If you are looking for a change from turkey for Thanksgiving, try Rolled Flounder Kiev. This elegant dish is a variation of the famed Chicken Kiev. Both recipes include the same method of wrapping poultry or fish around a butter mixture.*

| | |
|---|---|
| ¼ cup butter *or* margarine | Pepper |
| 1 tablespoon chopped parsley | 1 beaten egg |
| 1 tablespoon lemon juice | 1 tablespoon water |
| ½ teaspoon Worcestershire sauce | ¼ cup fine dry bread crumbs |
| ¼ teaspoon garlic salt | ¼ teaspoon paprika |
| 4 fresh *or* frozen flounder fillets (about 1¼ pounds) | 2 tablespoons all-purpose flour |
| Salt | • • • |
| | 2 slices Swiss cheese |

In bowl combine butter or margarine, chopped parsley, lemon juice, Worcestershire, and garlic salt. Place butter mixture on waxed paper and form into an 8-inch roll. Chill till butter mixture is firm. Thaw frozen fish. Sprinkle flounder fillets with salt and pepper. Cut butter roll into 4 pieces. Place one piece of the butter roll at the end of each flounder fillet. Roll as for jelly roll, tucking in sides. Fasten fish with wooden picks or tie securely. Combine egg and water. Combine crumbs and paprika. Coat each fish roll with flour and dip in egg-water mixture; then dip in crumb mixture. Place rolled fillets in shallow baking pan. Bake, uncovered, at 350° till fish flakes easily when tested with a fork, about 20 minutes. Halve the Swiss cheese slices diagonally; place one half slice atop each rolled fillet. Broil 4 inches from heat just till the cheese melts. Makes 4 servings.

## Glazed Turkey Roast

| | |
|---|---|
| 1 2½-pound frozen boneless turkey roast | ½ cup Italian salad dressing |
| 1 cup plum preserves | ½ envelope onion soup mix |
| | 1 tablespoon cornstarch |

Remove roast from foil pan; wrap in heavy foil. Place in shallow roasting pan and roast at 350° for 2 hours. Combine preserves, salad dressing, and soup mix. Loosen foil; pour preserve mixture over turkey and reseal. Insert meat thermometer. Roast till meat thermometer registers 185°, 1¾ to 2 hours more. Transfer roast to plate; reserve drippings. Combine cornstarch and 2 tablespoons water; stir into drippings. Cook and stir till thickened. Spoon some of the sauce over turkey; pass remaining. Makes 8 to 10 servings.

*Glazed Turkey Roast features the boneless turkey roll. This convenient roast comes frozen in your choice of all light meat or a combination of light and dark meat. It is ideal for cutting into attractive, even slices, and the leftovers work well in recipes that call for cooked turkey.*

## Pheasant with Wild Rice

| | |
|---|---|
| ½ cup chopped onion | ½ teaspoon ground sage |
| ¼ cup butter *or* margarine | 2 1½- to 3-pound ready-to-cook pheasants |
| ⅔ cup wild rice, rinsed | |
| 1 6-ounce can sliced mushrooms | 6 to 8 slices bacon |

Cook onion in butter till tender; add rice, 2 cups water, and 1 teaspoon salt. Cover; cook till rice is tender, 35 to 40 minutes. Drain mushrooms; stir mushrooms and sage into rice. Season cavities of pheasants with salt; stuff with rice mixture and tie legs to tails. Place bacon over breasts. Roast at 350° for 1 to 2½ hours, depending on size of birds. Serves 6 to 8.

For a colorful as well as appetizing Thanksgiving main dish serve *Glazed Turkey Roast.* Garnish the roast with canned or poached fresh plums. As an accompaniment try scoops of cooked mashed sweet potatoes garnished with parsley.

## Cherry-Almond Glazed Pork

| | |
|---|---|
| 1 3-pound boneless pork loin roast | 2 tablespoons light corn syrup |
| Salt | ¼ teaspoon salt |
| Pepper | ¼ teaspoon ground cinnamon |
| 1 12-ounce jar cherry preserves | ¼ teaspoon ground nutmeg |
| | ¼ teaspoon ground cloves |
| ¼ cup red wine vinegar | ¼ cup slivered almonds, toasted |

Rub pork roast with a little salt and pepper. Place the meat on a rack in a shallow roasting pan. Insert meat thermometer. Roast, uncovered, at 325° for 2 to 2½ hours. Meanwhile, in saucepan combine cherry preserves, red wine vinegar, corn syrup, salt, cinnamon, nutmeg, and cloves. Cook and stir the mixture till it boils; reduce the heat and simmer 2 minutes more. Add the almonds. Keep the sauce warm. Spoon some of the sauce over the pork roast to glaze. Continue cooking the roast till meat thermometer registers 170°, about 30 minutes more. Baste roast with sauce several times. Pass remaining sauce with roast. Makes 8 servings.

## Lamb with Plum-Apricot Sauce

| | |
|---|---|
| 1 4-pound boneless lamb leg | 1 tablespoon cornstarch |
| Salt | ¼ teaspoon ground nutmeg |
| Pepper | ¼ teaspoon ground allspice |
| 1 17-ounce can whole, unpitted purple plums | Dash ground cloves |
| | • • • |
| 1 17-ounce can unpeeled apricot halves | ⅓ cup Madeira *or* dry sherry |

Sprinkle the lamb leg with salt and pepper. Place leg on a rack in a shallow roasting pan. Insert meat thermometer. Roast at 325° for 2 hours. Drain syrup from plums and apricots, reserving 1½ cups syrup. Combine cornstarch, nutmeg, allspice, and cloves. Stir in reserved syrup. Cook and stir till syrup mixture is thickened and bubbly. Reserve 1 cup for fruit sauce. Use remaining syrup mixture to baste lamb. Continue roasting meat till the meat thermometer registers 175° to 180°, about 1 hour more, basting occasionally. Combine reserved syrup mixture, drained plums, and apricots. Heat sauce through. Stir in Madeira or sherry. Serve with lamb. Makes 6 servings.

## Harlow House Mulled Cider

*Each Thanksgiving, Plymouth, Massachusetts, entertains visitors at its historic houses. One of these, Harlow House, said to be built with lumber from the original Pilgrim Fort, serves mulled cider.*

| | |
|---|---|
| 12 cups apple cider (3 quarts) | 1½ teaspoons whole cloves |
| ⅓ cup packed brown sugar | ⅛ teaspoon salt |
| 5 inches stick cinnamon, broken | Dash ground ginger |
| | Dash ground nutmeg |

In large saucepan or Dutch oven combine cider, brown sugar, cinnamon, cloves, salt, ginger, and nutmeg. Bring to boiling; reduce heat. Cover; simmer 15 minutes. Strain. Serve hot. Makes 24 (4-ounce) servings.

## Cucumber-Lime Salad

1 6-ounce package lime-
   flavored gelatin
2½ cups boiling water
2 tablespoons lemon juice
1 cup dairy sour cream

2 cups shredded unpeeled
   cucumber (2 medium)
1 cup shredded carrot
½ cup sliced pimiento-stuffed
   green olives

Dissolve gelatin in water; stir in lemon juice and ½ teaspoon salt. Beat in sour cream. Chill till partially set. Fold in remaining ingredients. Turn into 6½-cup mold. Chill till firm, about 6 hours or overnight. Serves 8.

*For a fresh new taste for your Thanksgiving dinner, try serving Cucumber-Lime Salad. To avoid the confusion of having another plate to pass, prepare the salad in fancy individual molds. Unmold the salads and place them on the table before guests are seated.*

## Double Cranberry Salad

2½ cups cranberry-apple drink
2 3-ounce packages lemon-
   flavored gelatin
1 10-ounce package frozen
   cranberry-orange relish

½ cup chopped celery
½ cup chopped pecans
1½ cups cream-style cottage
   cheese
¼ cup mayonnaise

Bring cranberry drink to boiling. Stir in gelatin till dissolved; stir in relish. Chill till partially set; stir in celery and nuts. Pour *half* into an 8x8x2-inch dish. Combine cheese and mayonnaise; spread over gelatin. Top with remaining gelatin. Chill till firm. Cut into squares. Serves 9.

## Salade Flan

2 3-ounce packages lemon-
   flavored gelatin
3 cups boiling water
½ cup mayonnaise *or* salad
   dressing
1 3-ounce package cream cheese

½ of a 6-ounce can frozen
   lemonade concentrate
• • •
2 cups sliced fresh strawberries
1 small banana, sliced
   diagonally

Dissolve gelatin in boiling water. Reserve ¾ cup gelatin mixture; let stand at room temperature. Pour remaining gelatin in blender container. Add mayonnaise, cream cheese, and lemonade concentrate; cover. Blend till smooth. Chill till partially set. Pour into 9-inch springform pan. Chill till almost firm. Arrange strawberries and banana atop. Chill reserved gelatin till slightly thickened. Spoon over fruits. Chill till set. Serves 8.

## Acorn Squash with Pineapple

Wash, halve, and seed 3 medium acorn squash. Place, cut side down, in a shallow baking pan. Bake at 350° for 40 to 45 minutes. Turn cut side up; sprinkle with salt. Combine one 8¼-ounce can crushed pineapple, drained; 1 medium apple, chopped; and 2 tablespoons packed brown sugar. Fill squash. Dot each squash half with 1 teaspoon butter *or* margarine. Return to oven. Bake till squash is tender, about 30 minutes more. Makes 6 servings.

When deep-fat frying foods—such as Dauphine Potatoes, be careful to use cooking oils or all-purpose shortenings. These are best because they can be heated to a high temperature without smoking. To keep the fat temperature constant, be sure to use a thermometer.

## Dauphine Potatoes

| | |
|---|---|
| 2 potatoes (about 1 pound) | ¼ cup all-purpose flour |
| 2 tablespoons butter | 1 egg |
| ⅛ teaspoon ground nutmeg | Fat for frying |

Peel potatoes; cook in enough boiling salted water to cover till tender. Drain potatoes; mash. In a saucepan combine butter, nutmeg, ¼ cup water, and ¾ teaspoon salt; bring to boiling. Stir in flour; cook and stir till mixture forms a ball. Cool slightly; beat in egg. Add to mashed potatoes; mix well. Shape into 16 balls. Fry, a few at a time, in deep hot fat (375°) till potatoes are golden brown, 2 to 3 minutes. Makes about 4 servings.

## Raisin-Filled Sweet Potatoes

| | |
|---|---|
| 1 17-ounce can sweet potatoes, drained | 2 tablespoons butter, melted |
| 2 tablespoons butter, softened | ¼ cup sugar |
| 1 egg | 2 teaspoons cornstarch |
| Dash ground cinnamon | 1 teaspoon grated orange peel |
| Dash ground ginger | ½ cup orange juice |
| | ½ cup raisins |

Beat together potatoes, softened butter, egg, spices, and ½ teaspoon salt. Spoon into 6 mounds on a greased baking sheet. Make hollows in centers with spoon. Brush with melted butter. Bake at 350° for 15 to 20 minutes. Combine sugar, cornstarch, and peel. Stir in orange juice and raisins. Cook and stir till thickened. Spoon into hollows in potato mounds. Serves 6.

## Holiday Asparagus

| | |
|---|---|
| 2 10-ounce packages frozen cut asparagus | 1½ cups milk |
| 3 tablespoons butter | 1 tablespoon lemon juice |
| 3 tablespoons all-purpose flour | ¼ cup chopped canned pimiento |
| | ¼ cup chopped pitted ripe olives |

Cook asparagus according to package directions; drain well. Meanwhile, in saucepan melt butter; stir in flour, ¾ teaspoon salt, and dash pepper. Add milk. Cook and stir till mixture is thickened and bubbly. Stir in lemon juice, then asparagus, pimiento, and olives. Heat through. Makes 8 servings.

## Tangy Green Beans

In a small skillet cook 2 slices bacon, diced, and 2 tablespoons chopped onion till bacon is crisp and onion is tender. Stir in ¼ cup red wine vinegar, 1 teaspoon sugar, ½ teaspoon salt, and ½ teaspoon celery seed. Simmer, covered, 5 minutes. Meanwhile, cook two 9-ounce packages frozen, cut green beans according to package directions. Drain thoroughly. Combine cooked beans and bacon-vinegar mixture. Makes 6 to 8 servings.

## Whole Wheat-Pumpkin Seed Muffins (see photo, page 154)

| | |
|---|---|
| 1½ cups whole wheat flour | 1 egg |
| ½ cup all-purpose flour | ¾ cup milk |
| ¾ cup shelled pumpkin seeds, chopped | ⅓ cup cooking oil |
| 2½ teaspoons baking powder | ⅓ cup light molasses |

Stir together whole wheat flour, all-purpose flour, pumpkin seeds, baking powder, and ¾ teaspoon salt. Combine egg, milk, oil, and molasses. Make a well in dry ingredients; pour in egg mixture. Stir just till dry ingredients are moistened. Pour batter into greased muffin cups, filling about ⅔ full. Bake at 400° for 20 to 25 minutes. Makes 12 muffins.

*Whole Wheat-Pumpkin Seed Muffins are a quick and easy bread to make for a busy Thanksgiving Day meal. To rewarm leftover muffins, wrap them in foil and heat at 400° for 15 to 20 minutes.*

## Royal Rye Rolls (see photo, page 154)

In a mixing bowl combine 3½ cups rye flour, 2 packages active dry yeast, and 2 tablespoons caraway seed. In a saucepan heat together 2¼ cups milk, ½ cup sugar, 3 tablespoons shortening, and 1 tablespoon salt just till warm (115°-120°), stirring constantly. Add to dry mixture in mixing bowl; add 2 eggs. Beat at low speed of electric mixer for ½ minute, scraping sides of bowl constantly. Beat at high speed for 3 minutes. By hand, stir in ½ cup rye flour and enough of 3 cups all-purpose flour to make a soft dough. Place in a greased bowl, turning once to grease surface. Cover and chill at least 2 hours. Shape dough into 24 oval rolls. Let rise in warm place till dough is almost double (about 1 hour). Brush roll tops lightly with water; sprinkle with coarse salt and additional caraway, if desired. Bake at 375° till done, 20 to 25 minutes. Makes 24 rolls.

## Wheat Germ Bread (see photo, page 154)

| | |
|---|---|
| 6 to 6¼ cups all-purpose flour | 1 package active dry yeast |
| ½ cup whole wheat flour | 2¾ cups water |
| ½ cup nonfat dry milk powder | ¼ cup sugar |
| ¼ cup wheat germ | 3 tablespoons shortening |
| | 2 teaspoons salt |

In mixing bowl combine *2½ cups* of the all-purpose flour, the whole wheat flour, dry milk powder, wheat germ, and yeast. In saucepan heat together water, sugar, shortening, and salt just till warm (115°-120°), stirring constantly. Add to flour mixture. Beat at low speed of electric mixer for ½ minute, scraping sides of bowl constantly. Beat 3 minutes more at high speed. By hand, stir in enough of the remaining flour to make a moderately stiff dough. Turn dough out onto lightly floured surface; knead till smooth (5 to 7 minutes). Place in a greased bowl; turn once to grease surface. Cover and let rise in warm place till double (40 to 50 minutes). Punch down; divide dough in half. Cover; let rest 10 minutes. Shape each half into a loaf; place each loaf in a greased 8½x4½x2½-inch loaf pan. Cover; let rise till almost double (30 to 40 minutes). Bake at 400° for 30 to 35 minutes. Remove from pans; cool on rack. Makes 2 loaves.

Choose the bread for your Thanksgiving feast from this rich harvest of homemade breads. Clockwise, beginning at left rear: *Wheat Germ Bread* (see recipe, page 153), *Royal Rye Rolls* (see recipe, page 153), *Whole Wheat-Pumpkin Seed Muffins* (see recipe, page 153), and *Molasses-Oatmeal Bread.*

## Molasses-Oatmeal Bread

*To keep Molasses-Oatmeal Bread fresh throughout the Thanksgiving weekend, wrap it in foil or clear plastic wrap or place it in a plastic bag. Store the bread in a cool dry place, but not in the refrigerator, since refrigerator storage causes bread to stale quickly.*

5¼ to 5½ cups all-purpose
    flour
2 packages active dry
    yeast
1 tablespoon salt
2 cups hot water (not
    boiling)

¼ cup molasses
2 tablespoons cooking oil
1½ cups regular rolled oats
1 beaten egg white
2 tablespoons regular rolled
    oats

In a large mixing bowl combine *2 cups* of the all-purpose flour, the yeast, and salt. Add hot water, molasses, and cooking oil. Beat at medium speed of an electric mixer for 2 minutes, scraping sides of bowl occasionally. Add *1 cup* of the remaining flour. Beat at high speed 1 minute more. By hand, stir in the 1½ cups rolled oats. Then gradually stir in enough of the remaining flour to make a soft dough. Turn dough out onto a lightly floured surface. Knead till smooth and elastic (about 5 minutes). Place dough in a lightly greased bowl, turning once to grease surface. Cover; let rise in a warm place till almost double (1½ to 2 hours). Punch down. Turn dough out on a lightly floured surface again and divide in half. Cover; let rest 10 minutes. Shape each half into a round loaf. Place on a greased baking sheet. Cover and let rise in a warm place till almost double (45 to 60 minutes). Brush each loaf with egg white. Sprinkle each loaf with *1 table-spoon* of the remaining rolled oats. Bake at 375° for 35 to 45 minutes. If the crust browns too quickly, cover with foil during the last 5 minutes of baking. Remove from baking sheet. Cool on rack. Makes 2 loaves.

## Grandma's Pumpkin Pie

3 eggs
1 16-ounce can pumpkin
½ cup sugar
1 teaspoon ground cinnamon
½ teaspoon ground ginger
½ teaspoon ground nutmeg

½ teaspoon salt
1¼ cups milk
1 5⅓-ounce can evaporated milk
1 unbaked 9-inch pastry shell with edges crimped high

Beat eggs slightly with fork. Mix pumpkin, sugar, spices, and salt. Blend in eggs and the milks. Pour into pastry shell. Bake at 400° till knife inserted off-center comes out clean, about 50 minutes. Cool.

*Everybody's grandmother undoubtedly had a favorite "receipt" for pumpkin pie—often made with sorghum, sometimes made with more spices, sometimes less—but this recipe typifies what we think of as good old-fashioned "punkin" pie. Nothing fancy, just plain good eating.*

## Mocha Meringue Tarts

2 egg yolks
2 cups milk
1 3¾- *or* 4-ounce package *regular* chocolate pudding mix
2 tablespoons packed brown sugar

½ of a 1-ounce square unsweet-ened chocolate, melted
2 to 3 teaspoons instant coffee crystals
2 tablespoons butter
Meringue Shells

In saucepan combine egg yolks, milk, pudding mix, sugar, chocolate, and coffee crystals; blend well. Cook and stir till mixture boils. Remove from heat; stir in butter. Cover surface with clear plastic wrap. Chill at least 2 hours. Beat till smooth. Spoon into Meringue Shells. Serve at once. Serves 6.

*Meringue Shells:* Beat together 2 egg whites, ½ teaspoon vanilla, ⅛ teaspoon cream of tartar, and dash salt till frothy. Gradually add ⅔ cup granulated sugar, beating till stiff peaks form and sugar is dissolved. Cover baking sheet with ungreased brown paper; draw 6 circles, 3½-inches in diameter. Spread each circle with ⅓ cup meringue, using back of spoon to shape shells. Bake at 275° for 1 hour. For crisper meringues, turn off heat; let meringue shells dry in oven (door closed) about 1 hour.

## Cranberry-Eggnog Cheesecake

Cream together 3 tablespoons butter *or* margarine and 3 tablespoons sugar; beat in 1 egg. Stir in 1 cup all-purpose flour, ¼ teaspoon baking powder, and ⅛ teaspoon salt. For crust, press mixture evenly over bottom and 1½ inches up sides of ungreased 9-inch springform pan. Cream together one 8-ounce package cream cheese, softened; ½ cup sugar; and 2 egg yolks. Slowly stir in 1½ cups canned *or* dairy eggnog, 1 tablespoon all-purpose flour, 1 teaspoon lemon juice, and 1 teaspoon vanilla. Fold into 2 stiffly beaten egg whites. Pour into crust. Bake at 350° till knife inserted just off-center comes out clean, about 45 minutes. Cool completely. Combine 1 cup chopped fresh cranberries, ½ cup sugar, and ⅓ cup water. Bring to boiling. Reduce heat; cook gently, uncovered, 5 minutes, stirring occasionally. Soften 1½ teaspoons unflavored gelatin in ¼ cup cold water; stir into hot cranberries till dissolved. Chill till partially set. Spoon atop cheesecake. Chill several hours or overnight. Makes 8 to 10 servings.

# Ring in the New Year

Good wishes for health, wealth, happiness, and a winning football team fill the air at New Year's get togethers. Even though midnight is the traditional time for shouting, the sentiments translate well into a New Year's Eve party or a New Year's Day open house.

This section is packed with recipes and serving suggestions for year's end entertaining at its best. You'll find guest-pleasing dips, spreads, and tasty tidbits to serve around the punch bowl. There are sandwiches and main dishes when heartier fare is wanted.

Fewer customs are associated with New Year's than some other holidays. The exception is the Chinese celebration which is not on January 1 at all. It is included here for you to enjoy its unique foods and its sincere wish for a prosperous year ahead.

Homey foods have New Year's associations too. Some families won't start the year without *Ham Hocks and Black-Eyed Peas* for luck. (See recipe on page 164.) Others prefer *Oyster Stew*. (See recipe on page 166.) And, traditional or not, *Bridge Scramble* is a customary snack to nibble while watching TV bowl games. (Recipe on page 174.)

# New Year's Eve

New Year's Eve has been traditionally a time for "cutting loose," sending the old year on its way and beckoning the incoming year with noise, fun, and hilarity. Parties, noisemaking, ringing bells, carousing, eating, drinking, and dancing have been part of the American year-end celebration scene in one region or another for decades on end.

In ancient cultures, the new year was the time when evil spirits of the previous years were banished, paving the way for the good forces of the coming year. In certain European countries witches were expelled between Christmas and New Year's. In Russia a housewife would beat the corners of her house to evict Satan. Hooting, drums, tin pan beating, horns, noisemakers, all were part of the ancient expulsion ceremony.

It has long been an American custom to give or attend a New Year's Eve party. Sometimes the party is given individually by a single host couple, sometimes it is a group function with various couples contributing different courses. At midnight a beverage—alcoholic or nonalcoholic—is poured and all guests merrily toast the coming year. Often a post-midnight supper is served, as simple or elaborate as the hostess decrees.

Since the advent of television, at most parties the TV set is turned on as the hour approaches midnight. Guests enjoy the countdown till midnight. Then at the witching hour, noisemakers are clacked, everyone's health is drunk to, kisses often are exchanged, dancing, and/or supper begins.

In New York City, many who are not attending a party go to Times Square to join the jubilant throngs gathered to watch the New Year announced on the moving neon sign atop the New York Times Building.

For some, New Year's Eve is more solemnly regarded as Watch Night. Dating back to a Methodist custom started in 1770, many churches hold services early in the evening and then receive participants afterwards with refreshments and conversation. Some services begin about 11 P.M. with a candlelight ceremony, music, and hymn singing. Bells ring at midnight to announce the New Year's arrival to one and all.

Whichever way you choose to celebrate, chances are that food will play a role in the evening's events, whether as a casual, informal midnight supper for a few (such as ours featuring Sausage-Egg Scramble or Hash and Eggs Casserole) or as an elaborate party buffet for a multitude, with all kinds of tempting nibbles, dips, chips, puffs, and punch.

## *Menu*

*Hash and Eggs Casserole*
*or*
*Sausage-Egg Scramble*
*New Year's Lemon Rolls*
*Orange-Apricot Coffee Cake*
*Doughnuts*
*New Year's Sparkler*
*Lemonade*

## New Year's Sparkler

| | |
|---|---|
| 2 32-ounce bottles cranberry juice cocktail | ¼ cup sugar |
| 1 6-ounce can frozen orange juice concentrate, thawed | 1 pint vodka (optional) |
| | 2 7-ounce bottles carbonated water, chilled |

Combine cranberry juice cocktail, orange juice concentrate, and sugar; stir till sugar dissolves. Chill well. To serve, pour juice mixture into pitcher or punch bowl; add vodka, if desired. Carefully pour carbonated water down side of container. Serve over ice. Makes 24 (4-ounce) servings.

## New Year's Lemon Rolls

4¼ to 4½ cups all-purpose flour
1 package active dry yeast
1 cup milk
1 cup granulated sugar
9 tablespoons butter, softened

3 eggs
1½ teaspoons grated lemon peel
¼ teaspoon ground cardamom
1½ cups sifted powdered sugar
2 tablespoons milk

In large bowl mix *2 cups* flour and the yeast. Heat 1 cup milk, ½ *cup* granulated sugar, *3 tablespoons* butter, and ½ teaspoon salt till warm (115-120°), stirring constantly. Add to dry mixture with eggs. Beat at low speed of electric mixer for ½ minute, scraping bowl. Beat 3 minutes at high speed. Stir in enough remaining flour to make moderately soft dough. Knead on floured surface till smooth (3 to 5 minutes). Place in greased bowl; turn once. Cover; let rise till double (1 to 1½ hours). Punch down; divide in half. Cover; let rest 10 minutes. Roll each half to 12x8-inch rectangle. Mix remaining granulated sugar and butter with lemon peel and cardamom; spread over dough. Roll up jelly roll fashion, starting with long side; seal seams. Slice each into 12 rolls. Place, cut side down, in greased 2½-inch muffin pans. (Or use two 9x1½-inch round baking pans for softer rolls.) Cover; let rise till almost double (30 to 45 minutes). Bake at 375° for 15 to 20 minutes. Remove from pan. Combine powdered sugar and remaining milk for glaze. Drizzle glaze over warm rolls. Makes 24 rolls.

*Lemon peel gives these rich sweet rolls a delightful tang. If you like a lot of lemon, use lemon juice instead of milk to make the glaze topping.*

Dress your New Year's Eve table with food. For your midnight supper include *Hash and Eggs Casserole* (see recipe, page 160), *New Year's Lemon Rolls, Orange-Apricot Coffee Cake* (see recipe, page 160), and purchased sugared doughnuts. For the punch and drink serve *New Year's Sparkler* and lemonade.

## Hash and Eggs Casserole (see photo, page 159)

*For your midnight lunch, use either the Sausage-Egg Scramble or Hash and Eggs Casserole for the main dish. Both are packed with extra goodness from meat and eggs.*

6 cups frozen loose-pack hash brown potatoes, thawed
¼ cup butter *or* margarine
1 beef bouillon cube
1 8-ounce can tomato sauce
¼ cup catsup
4 teaspoons instant minced onion

1 tablespoon prepared mustard
1 teaspoon prepared horseradish
4 cups coarsely chopped, cooked roast beef

• • •

12 eggs

Cook potatoes in butter till browned; sprinkle with 1 teaspoon salt. Dissolve bouillon in ⅓ cup *boiling* water; combine with tomato sauce, catsup, onion, mustard, and horseradish. Add to potatoes along with beef. Spread in 13x9x2-inch baking pan. With spoon, make 12 depressions in hash. Break an egg into each. Bake at 375° till eggs set, 30 to 35 minutes. Serves 12.

## Sausage-Egg Scramble (see photo, page 159)

1 8-ounce package brown-and-serve sausage links
¼ cup chopped green pepper
¼ cup chopped onion

8 eggs
½ cup milk
¼ cup chopped canned pimiento
½ cup shredded Cheddar cheese

Quarter sausage links; cook with green pepper and onion till sausage is browned and vegetables are tender. Beat together eggs and milk; stir in pimiento, ¾ teaspoon salt, and dash pepper. Pour over sausage; cook till mixture starts to set on bottom and sides. Lift and fold over so uncooked part goes to bottom (avoid breaking up eggs). Cook till eggs are done but still glossy and moist, 5 to 8 minutes. Sprinkle cheese atop. Serves 4 to 6.

## Orange-Apricot Coffee Cake (see photo, page 159)

*This quick coffee cake uses a convenience muffin mix with a crumb and fruit preserve topping.*

3 tablespoons sugar
3 tablespoons all-purpose flour
2 tablespoons butter *or* margarine

3 tablespoons chopped walnuts
1 14-ounce package orange muffin mix
2 tablespoons apricot-pineapple preserves

Mix sugar and flour; cut in butter. Stir in nuts; set aside. Prepare muffin mix following package directions. Pour into greased 8x8x2-inch baking pan. Cut up large fruit in preserves; spread on batter. Sprinkle with crumb mixture. Bake at 400° for 20 to 25 minutes. Serve warm. Makes 9 servings.

## Creamy Chive Dip (see photo, pages 138-139)

Mix 1 cup dairy sour cream, ⅓ cup mayonnaise *or* salad dressing, ¼ cup snipped chives, 1 tablespoon tarragon vinegar, ½ teaspoon salt, and dash white pepper. Chill. Serve with vegetable dippers. Makes 1⅔ cups.

## Appetizer Beef Patties (see photo, pages 138-139)

| | |
|---|---|
| 1 egg | ¼ teaspoon ground nutmeg |
| 2 tablespoons finely chopped onion | 2 pounds ground beef |
| 1 tablespoon Worcestershire sauce | 1 11-ounce can condensed Cheddar cheese soup |
| 1½ teaspoons salt | ¾ cup light cream |
| | 2 teaspoons prepared mustard |

Mix egg, onion, Worcestershire, salt, nutmeg, and ¼ teaspoon pepper; mix in beef. Shape into 60 patties. Bake in shallow pan at 400° for 10 to 12 minutes. Heat remaining ingredients; serve with patties. Makes 60.

## Pickled Shrimp Appetizer (see photo, pages 138-139)

| | |
|---|---|
| 2 pounds fresh *or* frozen shrimp in the shells *or* 1¼ pounds shelled shrimp | 1½ cups cooking oil |
| Boiling water | ¾ cup white wine vinegar |
| ½ cup celery leaves | 1 tablespoon sugar |
| ¼ cup mixed pickling spice | ½ teaspoon dried dillweed |
| 2 medium onions, sliced | ½ teaspoon mustard seed |
| | 3 medium tomatoes, cut in wedges |

Cover shrimp with boiling water; add celery leaves, spice, and 1 teaspoon salt. Cover and simmer 5 minutes; drain. Peel and devein shrimp in shells under cold water. Place shrimp and onions in deep bowl. Mix 1 teaspoon salt and remaining ingredients *except* tomatoes; pour over shrimp. Cover. Chill several hours or overnight; baste occasionally with marinade. Add tomatoes before serving. Serve in a bowl over ice. Makes about 5 cups.

## Party Chicken-Hamwiches (see photo, pages 138-139)

| | |
|---|---|
| 12 slices firm-textured whole wheat bread | 2 hard-cooked eggs, chopped |
| Butter, softened | ¼ cup mayonnaise |
| 6 slices firm-textured white bread | 2 tablespoons finely chopped celery |
| Dijon-style mustard | 2 tablespoons sweet pickle relish |
| 1 4-ounce package thinly sliced ham | 1 tablespoon sliced green onion |
| 1 cup chopped cooked chicken *or* turkey | 1 teaspoon lemon juice |
| | ¼ teaspoon salt |

Spread one side of whole wheat slices with butter; spread one side of white bread slices with mustard. Trim crusts. Divide ham among *six* slices whole wheat bread. Top with white bread, mustard side down. Combine chicken, eggs, mayonnaise, celery, relish, onion, lemon juice, and salt. Spread about ¼ cup chicken mixture over each slice white bread. Cover each with slice of whole wheat bread, buttered side down (for a total of 6 sandwiches). Quarter sandwiches diagonally. Makes 24 party sandwiches.

### *Menu*
(see photo, pages 138-139)

*Appetizer Beef Patties*
*Party Chicken-Hamwiches*
*Pickled Shrimp Appetizer*
*Cheese Puffs*
*Creamy Chive Dip*
*with*
*Vegetable Dippers*
*Deviled Popcorn*
*Cupcakes*
*Orange-Eggnog Punch*

*When you want heartiness, serve Party Chicken-Hamwiches at your New Year's Eve buffet. Guests will savor the two fillings in these miniature Dagwoods.*

## Orange-Eggnog Punch (see photo, pages 138-139)

(see photo, pages 138-139)

**4 cups dairy eggnog,
  chilled**
**1 6-ounce can frozen orange
  juice concentrate**

**1 28-ounce bottle lemon-lime
  carbonated beverage,
  chilled**
**1 pint vanilla ice cream**

*Remember eating the
creamy orange sherbet on
a stick? Orange-Eggnog
Punch will bring back those
memories — an eggnog with
the zip of orange.*

In punch bowl combine eggnog and orange juice concentrate. Slowly add carbonated beverage. Top with scoops of vanilla ice cream. Sprinkle with nutmeg, if desired. Makes about 20 (4-ounce) servings.

## Deviled Popcorn (see photo, pages 138-139)

Mix ½ cup melted butter, 1½ teaspoons chili powder, ½ teaspoon garlic salt, and ⅛ teaspoon cayenne; toss with 12 cups popped corn. Makes 12 cups.

## Cheese Puffs (see photo, pages 138-139)

**1 4-ounce container whipped
  cream cheese**
**1 egg**
**1 teaspoon lemon juice**
**1 teaspoon frozen chives**

**½ cup shredded sharp
  Cheddar cheese**
**4 slices bacon, crisp-cooked,
  drained, and crumbled**
**4 frozen patty shells, thawed**

*Use a frozen puff pastry to
make delicate Cheese Puffs
for a buffet of appetizers.
These are easy to make
ahead — ready to pop in the
oven just before serving.*

Combine cream cheese, egg, lemon juice, chives, and dash pepper; beat well. Stir in Cheddar cheese and crumbled bacon. Chill. Roll *one* patty shell to 8x4-inch rectangle. Cut into 2-inch squares. Top each square with teaspoon filling. Brush edges with milk. Fold square to triangle; seal edges. Place on baking sheet. Repeat with remaining shells and filling. Chill till ready to bake. Place in 450° oven. Immediately reduce temperature to 400°; bake 12 to 15 minutes. Makes 32 appetizers.

## Strawberry-Champagne Punch

**1 10-ounce package frozen
  strawberries, thawed**

• • •

**2 tablespoons lime juice**

**1 ⅘-quart bottle sparkling
  Burgundy, chilled**
**1 ⅘-quart bottle dry
  champagne, chilled**

Press strawberries through sieve. Stir lime juice into pulp; chill. In punch bowl carefully pour Burgundy and champagne into chilled berry pulp, stirring with an up-and-down motion. Makes 14 (4-ounce) servings.

## Ginger Dip

Mix ¾ cup dairy sour cream; ½ cup mayonnaise; ¼ cup shredded coconut, toasted; and 2 tablespoons finely chopped candied ginger. Cover; chill. Garnish with more toasted coconut. Serve with fruit. Makes 1½ cups.

*Strawberry-Champagne Punch* is a good menu starter for a New Year's Eve snack table. Add *Corn and Nut Crumbles* and *Ginger Dip* with skewered fruit. And for hot appetizers, make *Individual Chicken Quiches*. Finally stuff cherry tomatoes with purchased smoked oysters for color contrast.

## Individual Chicken Quiches

| | |
|---|---|
| 2 sticks piecrust mix | ½ of a 4¾-ounce can chicken |
| 2 eggs | spread (about ¼ cup) |
| ¼ cup light cream | 3 1-ounce wedges Gruyère |
| Dash pepper | cheese, shredded |

Prepare piecrust following package directions. Roll dough thin. Cut into twenty-four 2½-inch rounds. Fit into twenty-four 1½-inch muffin cups. Mix eggs, cream, and pepper. Fill each cup with ½ teaspoon chicken spread, a small amount cheese, and 1½ teaspoons egg mixture. Bake at 400° till golden, 18 to 20 minutes. Cool 1 minute; remove from pans. Makes 24.

## Corn and Nut Crumbles

| | |
|---|---|
| 1 8-ounce package corn | ½ cup grated Parmesan cheese |
| muffin mix | 1 teaspoon garlic powder |
| 1 cup coarsely chopped salted | 3 tablespoons butter *or* |
| peanuts (6 ounces) | margarine, melted |

Prepare mix following package directions; spread batter in well-greased 15½x10½x1-inch baking pan. Sprinkle with nuts, cheese, and garlic powder; drizzle butter atop. Bake at 375° till lightly browned, 20 to 25 minutes. Immediately cut in squares; cool slightly. Remove from pan. Makes 48.

*Menu*

*Individual Chicken Quiches*
*Corn and Nut Crumbles*
*Ginger Dip   Fruit Dippers*
*Cherry Tomatoes*
*with*
*Smoked Oysters*
*Strawberry-Champagne*
*Punch*

# New Year's Day

*Pictured opposite:* Keep the New Year's Day activities simple. Complete a day of watching the parades and football games with a soup supper. All three of these creamy soups begin with canned soups so they're a snap to stir together. Choose (from top left): *Ham-Vegetable Soup, Dilly Vegetable Chowder,* and *Shrimp and Rice Soup* (see recipes, page 166). For a crunchy texture, serve *Bread and Butter Sticks* (see recipe, page 167).

Celebrating New Year's Day in America is an old custom. In pre-colonial America the Iroquois inaugurated the New Year with a Festival of Dreams — days of feasting, dancing, and general merry-making.

When the Puritans arrived, they limited their celebrations to the harvest feast, Thanksgiving. But as settlers from European countries landed on our shores, they brought their own ways of celebrating. The French, Spanish, and non-Puritan English all festively welcomed the New Year.

But no one celebrated this holiday as merrily as the Dutch of New Amsterdam (later New York). The fun-loving Dutch persuaded their English neighbors to celebrate January 1st, instead of the English day, March 25, and they introduced the idea of a New Year's open house, a custom we still enjoy today. The unmarried ladies stayed home New Year's Day and the single men of their acquaintance paid social calls. Visiting hours usually ran from 11 a.m. until dark. The ladies offered refreshments to their callers, generally an assortment of sweets including cookies and honey cakes. Beer, punch, and steaming hot coffee were accompaniments.

Even Presidents followed this genial Dutch custom. George Washington opened his own house to the public the first New Year's after his inauguration and continued the practice throughout his term of office. Other Presidents followed suit and as the crowds grew, so did the damage to the Executive Mansion. The custom persisted until 1934, when Franklin Roosevelt discontinued it as too fatiguing to his fragile health.

Still, open house remains a popular notion throughout the country. A hostess will plan a cold buffet with perhaps two or three hot dishes, kept warm in a chafing dish or over an electric warmer. Often a turkey and/or ham is cooked ahead, then sliced and left on the buffet table for guests to help themselves to assorted sandwich makings. This is especially true for New Year's Day football watchers. A single hot casserole or a hearty soup might be the one piping hot dish on the table. With all the snack foods are trays of cookies, cupcakes, and slices of fruitcake. A large punch bowl filled with eggnog or mulled wine is usually the focal point of the table. There is something special about the New Year a'coming, and Americans traditionally look forward to it with expectations and high hopes.

## Ham Hocks and Black-Eyed Peas (see photo, pages 156-157)

*Legend has it that if you eat Ham Hocks and Black-Eyed Peas on New Year's Day you will have good health and happiness all year long. Whether the legend is true or not, good friends and families enjoy this traditional Southern dish on January 1.*

3 cups dry black-eyed peas
3 pounds smoked ham hocks (10 small)
1¼ cups chopped onion
1 cup chopped celery

1 bay leaf
1 teaspoon salt
⅛ teaspoon cayenne
1 10-ounce package frozen cut okra

Rinse black-eyed peas. Place in 6-quart Dutch oven; add 12 cups water and soak overnight. Stir in ham hocks, onion, celery, bay leaf, salt, and cayenne. Bring to boil. Cover; reduce heat and simmer till ham hocks are tender and beans are done, about 1½ hours. Stir in okra; cook till okra is very tender, 10 to 15 minutes. Remove bay leaf. Season to taste. Makes 6 servings.

## Oyster Stew (see photo, pages 156-157)

For a traditional
observance of the holiday
season serve rich and
buttery Oyster Stew
steaming hot in warmed
bowls. Not to be reserved
just for the holidays, the
stew is a hardy cold-
weather favorite and can
help make any
bitter winter day bearable.

| | |
|---|---|
| 2 tablespoons all-purpose flour | Dash bottled hot pepper sauce |
| 1½ teaspoons salt | 1 pint shucked oysters |
| 1 teaspoon Worcestershire sauce | ¼ cup butter *or* margarine |
| | 4 cups milk, scalded |

In saucepan blend flour, salt, Worcestershire, hot pepper sauce, and 2 tablespoons water. Stir in undrained oysters and butter. Simmer over very low heat and stir gently till edges of oysters curl, 3 to 4 minutes. Add hot milk; remove from heat and cover. Let stand 15 minutes. Reheat briefly. Float pats of butter and oyster crackers atop, if desired. Serves 4 or 5.

## Ham-Vegetable Soup (see photo, page 165)

| | |
|---|---|
| ½ of a 24-ounce package frozen stew vegetables | 1 11¼-ounce can condensed split pea with ham soup |
| 1 cup cubed fully cooked ham | ½ cup milk |

In large saucepan cook stew vegetables, covered, in 1¼ cups boiling salted water till tender, about 20 minutes. Remove potatoes and other large vegetables; cut up and return to pan. Stir in ham, soup, and milk. Heat to boiling. Reduce heat; simmer 5 minutes. Makes 4 servings.

## Dilly Vegetable Chowder (see photo, page 165)

In saucepan blend one 10½-ounce can condensed cream of potato soup with 1½ soup cans milk (about 2 cups); heat through. Stir in one 10-ounce package frozen Danish-style vegetables and ¼ teaspoon dried dillweed. Bring to boiling; reduce heat to low. Beat 1 egg yolk. Gradually stir a moderate amount of the hot soup into egg yolk. Return egg yolk mixture to soup, cook 2 minutes, stirring constantly. Garnish with fresh dill and chopped green onion. Ladle into soup bowls or mugs. Makes 4 servings.

## Shrimp and Rice Soup (see photo, page 165)

| | |
|---|---|
| 2 cups water | 1 10½-ounce can condensed chicken with rice soup |
| 1 teaspoon instant chicken bouillon granules | 1 10½-ounce can condensed cream of shrimp soup |
| ½ cup diced celery | 1 4½-ounce can shrimp, drained |
| 2 tablespoons long grain rice | ½ cup dairy sour cream |
| 1 cup milk | |

Combine water and bouillon granules. Stir in celery and rice. Simmer till celery is tender, 12 to 15 minutes. Stir in milk, soups, and shrimp. Heat through. Just before serving, stir small amount soup mixture into sour cream; return to saucepan and blend well. Heat *but do not boil*. Garnish with lemon wedges and parsley sprigs, if desired. Makes 4 servings.

## Oatcakes

| | |
|---|---|
| 1 cup quick-cooking rolled oats | 2 tablespoons butter *or* margarine, melted |
| 2 tablespoons all-purpose flour | ¼ cup hot water |
| ¼ teaspoon baking powder | ¼ cup quick-cooking rolled oats |
| ¼ teaspoon salt | Butter *or* margarine |

Place ½ *cup* of the rolled oats in blender container; cover and blend till oats are a fine powder. Repeat with another ½ *cup* rolled oats. Combine blended oats, flour, baking powder, and salt. Stir in melted butter. Stir in water. Sprinkle board with remaining ¼ cup rolled oats; place dough on oat-covered board. Roll to a 10-inch circle, about ⅛ inch thick; cut into 12 wedges. Place wedges on ungreased baking sheet. Bake at 350° for 15 minutes. Turn off heat and open oven door. Leave oatcakes in the oven till firm and crisp, 4 to 5 minutes. Serve with butter. Makes 12 wedges.

*The Scottish New Year's festival called Hogmanay is the oldest and one of the biggest and best of the Scottish celebrations. Scottish oatcakes are traditionally served with soup during Hogmanay. Of Celtic origin, oatcakes are typically cut into wedges. Each wedge is known as a farl.*

## Kraut-Pork Pinwheel

| | |
|---|---|
| 1 egg | 1 pound ground pork |
| 2 tablespoons milk | 1 16-ounce can sauerkraut, drained and snipped |
| ½ cup fine dry bread crumbs | ¼ cup chopped onion |
| 1 teaspoon salt | 5 slices bacon, partially cooked |
| 1 teaspoon Worcestershire sauce | |
| Dash pepper | |

Combine egg, milk, bread crumbs, salt, Worcestershire, and pepper. Add meat and mix thoroughly. On waxed paper pat meat mixture to a 10x7-inch rectangle. Combine drained and snipped sauerkraut and onion; spread evenly over meat. Starting with narrow side, roll up meat jelly-roll fashion. Seal ends. Place loaf in a shallow baking dish. Arrange bacon slices across top. Bake at 350° for 45 to 50 minutes. Makes 5 or 6 servings.

*In many cultures the pig was a symbol of good luck and a fitting feast for New Year's Day. It was believed that a pig rooted forward and was thus an omen of a fat and prosperous future, unlike turkeys, ducks, and geese, which scratched in a backward direction. In the southern United States pork and sauerkraut together, as in our recipe, is a fortuitous choice for New Year's dinner.*

## Bread and Butter Sticks (see photo, page 165)

| | |
|---|---|
| 3 tablespoons butter *or* margarine | 1 teaspoon sugar |
| 1 cup packaged biscuit mix | ¼ cup milk |

Melt butter or margarine in 8x8x2-inch baking pan. In mixing bowl combine packaged biscuit mix, sugar, and milk. Stir with fork till a soft dough forms. Beat vigorously 20 strokes till dough is stiff but still sticky. Turn out onto board lightly dusted with biscuit mix or flour; knead gently about 10 times. Roll to an 8x6-inch rectangle. With floured knife, cut dough in half lengthwise; then cut each half crosswise into 8 strips. In the pan used to melt butter, dip each strip in the melted butter, turning to coat both sides. Arrange strips in two rows in pan. Bake at 425° till golden brown, 10 to 12 minutes. Serve bread sticks warm. Makes 16 bread sticks.

# Chinese New Year

Chinese New Year begins and ends with a bang as fireworks explode through the night air of the nation's Chinatowns. It is the high point of the year for Chinese-Americans, a time of visiting, feasting, and celebrating. Chinese-Americans observe the New Year by the lunar calendar. It begins on the day of the first moon after the sun has left the sign of Capricorn and entered Aquarius—between January 21 and February 19. The calendar is divided into sixty-year cycles designated by a specific animal. Each year has certain astrological omens based on the sign of the year's animal.

All Chinese-American communities celebrate the two weeks of New Year with a variety of food. The New Year is a good excuse to order a banquet which can mean as many as thirty or forty dishes—at a restaurant or, a modified smaller version, at home. The home-served meals always include an elegant array of foods with space reserved for at least one fish dish, one poultry dish, a sweet and sour dish, and a vegetable.

The New Year season also is a time to settle all debts, patch up all quarrels, pay visits to friends and relatives, and wipe the slate clean. At this time, some families traditionally honor their ancestors by hanging up pictures of them and placing special foods before the pictures.

During the New Year celebration, Tsao Wang, the Chinese kitchen god, is believed to leave his place by the stove and report to Sheung Duy, the almighty god, on the past year's behavior of his family. Many families still smear the lips of a picture of the god with molasses or sweets so that he will make only a favorable report. The picture then is burned to send him heavenward. On the final day of the holiday a new picture is placed above the stove—signifying he is back ready to oversee familial goings-on.

New Year is also a time of special indulgences and gift-giving. Gifts of money, always tucked into red (good fortune) wrappers, are presented by parents to their children. Families exchange gifts too, usually food—perhaps a home cured ham, a whole swordfish, or baskets of apples and pears.

*Pictured opposite:* The Chinese New Year's table is adorned with pink cherry blossoms. Begin the meal with the popular hors d'oeuvre, *Tea Leaf Eggs* (far right). For the main course, serve (counterclockwise from top right) *Pork-Shrimp Meatball Soup, Grand Old Man, Stir-Fried Pea Pods,* and *Sweet-Sour Glazed Riblets.* And be sure to include a bowl of tangerines for a year of good luck. (See recipes, pages 170 and 171.)

## Sweet-Sour Glazed Riblets

| | |
|---|---|
| 2½ pounds pork spareribs, sawed in half crosswise | 1 tablespoon cornstarch |
| 1 13¼-ounce can pineapple chunks | ⅛ teaspoon salt |
| 2 tablespoons packed brown sugar | 2 tablespoons vinegar |
| | 1 tablespoon soy sauce |
| | 1 small green pepper, cut in 1-inch squares |

Cut meat in 2-rib portions; season with salt and pepper. Place, meaty side down, in large shallow roasting pan. Bake at 450° for 30 minutes. Drain off excess fat. Turn meaty side up. Reduce heat to 350°; bake 30 minutes more. Meanwhile, drain pineapple, reserving ⅓ cup syrup. In saucepan combine brown sugar, cornstarch, and salt. Blend in reserved syrup, vinegar, soy, and ½ cup cold water. Cook and stir till thickened and bubbly. Stir in green pepper and drained pineapple. Cover; cook 5 minutes. Drain fat from ribs. Spoon sauce over ribs. Bake 15 minutes more. Makes 8 servings.

## Menu

*Tea Leaf Eggs*
*Pork-Shrimp Meatball Soup*
*Grand Old Man*
*Sweet-Sour Glazed Riblets*
*Rice*
*Stir-Fried Pea Pods*
*Eight-Treasure Pudding*
*Tea*

## Tea Leaf Eggs (see photo, page 169)

(see photo, page 169)

*These unusual appetizers are designed to be decorative as well as appetite-inducing. Tapping the egg shells allows the tea liquid to seep through and flavor the eggs. It also forms a network of tea lines.*

In saucepan cover 8 to 10 eggs with cold water to at least 1 inch above eggs. Rapidly bring to boiling; cover pan tightly. Reduce heat; simmer 15 minutes. Rinse quickly in cold water till eggs are cool enough to handle; drain. Tap eggs gently all over till shells are network of fine cracks (do not remove shells). Return eggs to saucepan; add 2 cups cold water, 2 tablespoons soy sauce, 4 teaspoons aniseed, 2 inches stick cinnamon, 2 teaspoons loose black tea, 1 teaspoon sugar, and 1 teaspoon salt. Bring to boiling; reduce heat. Simmer, covered, *2 hours.* (Add boiling water to keep eggs covered, if needed.) Drain; chill eggs well. Before serving, roll eggs between palms to loosen shell. Peel, starting from large end of egg. Makes 8 to 10.

## Pork-Shrimp Meatball Soup (see photo, page 169)

| | |
|---|---|
| 1 egg | ½ pound ground pork |
| 2 tablespoons soy sauce | 10 teaspoons instant chicken |
| 2 tablespoons fine dry |    bouillon granules |
|    bread crumbs | 1 medium onion, chopped |
| 1 tablespoon finely chopped | 1 bay leaf |
|    onion | ½ teaspoon dried rosemary, |
| ¼ teaspoon ground ginger |    crushed |
| 1 4½-ounce can shrimp, drained | Few sprigs parsley |
|    and finely chopped | 1½ cups shredded lettuce |

In bowl thoroughly combine egg, soy, bread crumbs, 1 tablespoon onion, and ginger. Add shrimp and pork; mix well. Shape into 60 small balls using about 1½ teaspoons mixture for each. In Dutch oven mix bouillon granules, onion, bay leaf, rosemary, parsley, 10 cups water, and ½ teaspoon salt; bring to boiling. Add meatballs; return to boiling. Cover; simmer 15 minutes. To serve, remove bay leaf and stir in lettuce. Makes 16 to 20 servings.

## Stir-Fried Pea Pods (see photo, page 169)

*Pea pods, or Chinese peas, are picked before maturity and used, pods and all, in Chinese cooking. They add color and crispness to many dishes. Since they are very tender, they require little cooking. Stir-frying, a quick-cooking method, preserves the delicate color and insures the desired crisp texture.*

| | |
|---|---|
| 1 10-ounce can bamboo shoots | 2 6-ounce packages frozen |
| 1  8-ounce can water |    pea pods, thawed |
|    chestnuts | 1½ teaspoons instant chicken |
| 1 6-ounce can whole mushrooms |    bouillon granules |
| 1 small clove garlic, minced | ⅓ cup boiling water |
| 1 tablespoon soy sauce | 2 tablespoons cold water |
| 1 tablespoon cooking oil | 2 teaspoons cornstarch |

Drain bamboo shoots, water chestnuts, and mushrooms; thinly slice water chestnuts. In a preheated large skillet or wok cook garlic in soy sauce and oil over low heat till garlic is browned; add bamboo shoots, water chestnuts, mushrooms, and pea pods. Toss and cook over high heat for 1 minute. Dissolve bouillon granules in the boiling water; add to mixture. Cover; cook over medium heat for 2 minutes. Blend cold water into cornstarch. Stir into pea pod mixture. Cook, uncovered, over high heat till thickened, about 1 minute. Garnish with cashew nuts, if desired. Makes 8 servings.

## Grand Old Man (see photo, page 169)

| | |
|---|---|
| 1 3-pound fresh *or* frozen red snapper, dressed, head and tail on | Dash white pepper |
| | 1 cup chicken broth |
| 3 tablespoons snipped parsley | ⅓ cup light cream |
| 1 bay leaf | 1 beaten egg yolk |
| 3 whole peppercorns | ½ cup chopped green onion |
| 2 tablespoons butter *or* margarine | 1 green pepper, chopped |
| | 1 teaspoon lemon juice |
| 2 tablespoons all-purpose flour | Dash ground nutmeg |
| | ¼ cup grated fresh ginger root |
| | 2 tablespoons cooking oil |

Thaw frozen fish. Pour water into fish poacher to depth of ½ inch. Add parsley, bay leaf, peppercorns, and 1 teaspoon salt. Bring to boiling. Place fish on greased rack; set into poacher. Cover; steam till fish flakes easily with fork, about 15 minutes. Meanwhile, melt butter in saucepan; blend in flour, white pepper, and ¼ teaspoon salt. Add chicken broth. Cook and stir till thickened; stir in cream. Gradually stir about ½ *cup* hot mixture into egg yolk; return to hot mixture. Add ¼ *cup* onion and the green pepper. Cook and stir over low heat till slightly thickened. Add lemon juice and nutmeg. Remove fish to warm platter; sprinkle remaining onion and ginger root over fish. Heat oil; pour over all. Garnish fish with green onion and parsley or Chinese parsley, if desired. Pass sauce. Serves 6.

*An entire red snapper is indeed a Grand Old Man of the Sea—and of the banquet table as well. The Chinese cook fish and chicken whole since cutting them in any manner is symbolic of a lack of food in the New Year. This fish, steamed and served whole, is a magnificent sight.*

## Eight-Treasure Pudding

| | |
|---|---|
| 2½ cups milk | 6 pitted dates, split lengthwise |
| 1 cup long grain rice | |
| ½ cup sugar | 10 to 12 walnut *or* pecan halves |
| 1 teaspoon vanilla | 1 *each* red and green candied cherry, halved |
| ¼ teaspoon ground cinnamon | |
| 3 beaten eggs | Almond Glaze |

In saucepan combine milk, rice, sugar, and ½ teaspoon salt. Bring to boiling. Reduce heat; cover. Cook over very low heat till rice is tender and milk is absorbed, 45 to 50 minutes; stir often. Stir in vanilla and cinnamon. Stir moderate amount hot mixture into eggs; return to hot mixture. Cook and stir over low heat, 2 minutes. Remove from heat. Cool slightly.

Meanwhile, place a ring of date halves, spaced about 1-inch apart, around the side of a buttered 1½-quart round bowl. Lay nut halves side by side in circle inside ring of dates. Cut red cherry halves from top almost to bottom in thin slices to form petals. Place cut cherries on bottom of bowl, spreading petals to form flowers. Add thin strips from green cherry to form stems. Spoon rice mixture into bowl; be careful not to disturb design. Chill 5 to 6 hours or overnight. Carefully unmold. Pour about *3 tablespoons* hot Almond Glaze over pudding. Pass remaining. Serves 8 to 10.

*Almond Glaze:* In saucepan combine 2 tablespoons sugar and 1½ teaspoons cornstarch. Blend in ½ cup cold water. Cook over medium heat, stirring constantly, till thickened and bubbly. Remove from heat; stir in 1 tablespoon butter *or* margarine and ¼ teaspoon almond extract.

*Sometimes called eight-precious pudding or eight-jewel pudding, this is an elegant banquet dessert, especially suitable for the Chinese New Year. It is named for Confucius' belief that the number eight symbolized the eight fundamental elements which represented perfection in the universe. And perfection is a fitting word for this dessert.*

# New Year's Recipes

## Chicken Liver-Pimiento Rolls

8 ounces chicken livers, chopped
1 tablespoon butter *or* margarine
2 hard-cooked eggs, diced
¼ cup chopped canned pimiento
¼ cup mayonnaise *or* salad dressing

1 teaspoon finely chopped onion
1 teaspoon prepared mustard
¼ teaspoon salt
Dash Worcestershire sauce
• • •
20 tiny party rolls

In skillet cook chopped chicken livers in butter or margarine till pink is just gone, about 5 minutes. Combine cooked liver with hard-cooked eggs, pimiento, mayonnaise or salad dressing, onion, prepared mustard, salt, and Worcestershire sauce. Chill. Split tiny party rolls. Spread the bottom half of each party roll with about 1 tablespoon of the chicken liver mixture; replace the top. Makes 20 small party sandwiches.

## Italian Sausage Rolls

1 pound Italian sausage in casing
¼ cup water
2 medium green peppers, cut in strips

2 medium onions, thinly sliced
• • •
5 hard rolls, split and buttered

In covered skillet cook whole Italian sausage in water for 5 minutes. Drain. Continue cooking sausage over low heat 12 minutes more to brown, turning often. Drain excess fat, reserving 2 tablespoons drippings; drain sausage well on paper toweling. Cook green pepper strips and onion slices in reserved drippings, covered, over medium-low heat till tender, about 10 minutes; stir occasionally. Cut sausage into 5 portions. Return sausage to skillet; heat through. Place one sausage portion in each roll; top each with some of the cooked green pepper and onion. Makes 5 sandwiches.

## Green Pepper Pinwheels

1 unsliced loaf white sandwich bread, cut lengthwise into ¼-inch-thick slices

1 5-ounce jar cream cheese spread with Roquefort
1 medium green pepper

Trim the crusts from bread slices. Spread each slice with cream cheese spread. Cut green pepper into ⅛-inch strips. Place strips of green pepper across each bread slice at 1-inch intervals. Beginning at narrow end, roll up each slice jelly roll fashion. Wrap sandwich rolls in foil or clear plastic warp; chill thoroughly. To serve, cut each roll in ⅜-inch-thick slices.

## Big Top Sandwich

1 unsliced round loaf rye
bread (9 inches in
diameter)
Butter *or* margarine,
softened
Chicken Filling

Leaf lettuce
2 medium tomatoes,
thinly sliced
2 tablespoons creamy Italian
salad dressing
Egg Filling

Cut bread crosswise into four round slices. Spread with butter. Spread bottom slice with Chicken Filling. Add next bread slice. Cover with lettuce and tomatoes. Drizzle with salad dressing. Add third bread slice; spread with Egg Filling. Top with last bread slice. Insert wooden picks through loaf to secure. Chill thoroughly. Cut into wedges. Makes 8 servings.

*Chicken Filling:* Combine 1 cup finely diced cooked chicken *or* turkey, ⅓ cup mayonnaise, ¼ cup shredded sharp Cheddar cheese (1 ounce), ¼ cup finely chopped celery, and 2 tablespoons finely chopped green pepper. Chill.

*Egg Filling:* Combine 3 hard-cooked eggs, finely chopped; ¼ cup finely chopped dill pickle; 3 tablespoons finely sliced green onion; 3 tablespoons mayonnaise; ¼ teaspoon salt; and dash bottled hot pepper sauce. Chill.

*The festive Big Top Sandwich gets its name from its appearance which resembles a circus tent. Spread the bread layers with fillings of diced chicken, lettuce and tomatoes, and egg salad.*

## Country Grilled Sandwiches

1½ cups chopped cooked chicken
*or* turkey
1 8¾-ounce can whole kernel
corn, drained
½ cup chopped celery

½ cup mayonnaise
½ teaspoon salt
16 slices whole wheat bread
8 slices American cheese
Butter, softened

Combine chicken, corn, celery, mayonnaise, salt, and dash pepper. Spread *8 bread slices* with mixture. Top each sandwich with cheese slice and a slice of bread. Butter top and bottom of sandwich. Brown sandwiches on both sides in a skillet till golden and cheese melts. Makes 8 sandwiches.

*If your New Year's Day festivities include outdoor winter activities or just a quiet day in front of the television, serve a simple but hearty hot grilled sandwich. Easy to make, it starts with cooked chicken, corn, and celery, and is topped with slices of American cheese.*

## Bologna-Cheese Club Sandwiches

6 ounces bologna
4 slices Swiss cheese
(4 ounces)
¼ small onion
3 small sweet pickles
• • •
3 tablespoons mayonnaise *or*
salad dressing

2 tablespoons chopped green
pepper
2 teaspoons prepared mustard
18 slices sandwich-style rye
bread
Butter *or* margarine
Lettuce
2 tomatoes, sliced

Grind together bologna, cheese, onion, and pickles. Stir in mayonnaise, green pepper, and mustard. Spread bread slices with butter on one side. Spread bologna-cheese filling on buttered side of *half* the bread slices; top with 6 more bread slices. Arrange lettuce and tomatoes atop. Cover with remaining 6 bread slices, buttered side down. Makes 6 sandwiches.

## Bridge Scramble (see photo, pages 156-157)

(see photo, pages 156-157)

6 cups puffed oat cereal
3 cups pretzel sticks
3 cups mixed salted nuts
½ cup butter, melted

¾ cup grated Parmesan cheese
1 tablespoon garlic salad
    dressing mix

In 13x9x2-inch baking pan heat cereal in 300° oven till warm, about 5 minutes. Remove from oven. Stir in pretzel sticks and the mixed nuts. Pour the melted butter over cereal mixture. Sprinkle with Parmesan cheese and dry garlic salad dressing mix. Stir thoroughly. Return the cereal mixture to oven and heat for 15 to 20 minutes more. Makes about 12 cups.

## Shrimp-Cheese Balls

2 3-ounce packages cream
    cheese, softened
1½ teaspoons prepared mustard
1 teaspoon grated onion
1 teaspoon lemon juice
Dash cayenne

Dash salt
1 4½-ounce can shrimp
    (about 1 cup)
⅔ cup chopped mixed salted
    nuts

Combine cream cheese, mustard, onion, lemon juice, cayenne, and salt; blend well. Drain shrimp; break into pieces. Stir shrimp into cheese mixture. Chill. Form into ½-inch balls. Roll in nuts. Makes 40 appetizers.

## Curried Appetizer Meatballs

½ cup crushed herb-seasoned
    stuffing mix
⅓ cup evaporated milk

1½ to 2 teaspoons curry powder
¼ teaspoon salt
1 pound ground beef

Thoroughly combine stuffing mix, milk, curry, and salt; add beef and mix well. Shape into about 40 small balls. Place in large shallow baking pan. Bake at 400° for 15 minutes. Keep warm in chafing dish. Makes 40.

## Pimiento Cheese Dip

2 cups shredded pimiento
    cheese (8 ounces)
½ cup dairy sour cream
1 3-ounce package cream
    cheese, softened
½ cup hot-style tomato juice

2 canned mild green chili pep-
    pers, seeded and chopped
3 slices bacon, crisp-cooked,
    drained, and crumbled
Raw vegetable dippers
Assorted crackers

In small mixing bowl combine pimiento cheese, the sour cream, cream cheese, hot-style tomato juice, and green chilies. Beat with rotary beater till light and fluffy. Stir in crumbled bacon. Chill. Serve the dip with raw vegetable dippers and assorted crackers. Makes 2 cups dip.

## Three-Way Cheese Appetizer

| | |
|---|---|
| 1 8-ounce package cream cheese, softened | 1 tablespoon snipped parsley |
| ½ cup dairy sour cream | 1 teaspoon steak sauce |
| ¼ cup butter *or* margarine, softened | Almonds *or* salmon *or* smoky Cheddar cheese and seasonings as desired |

To prepare the basic cheese mixture combine cream cheese, sour cream, and butter; beat till fluffy. Stir in parsley and steak sauce. Basic cheese mixture is used to make Cheese Ball, Salmon Spread, or Smoky Dip.

*Cheese Ball:* Chill basic cheese mixture. Shape into ball and coat with ⅓ cup finely chopped toasted almonds and ⅓ cup snipped parsley.

*Salmon Spread:* Stir one 7¾-ounce can salmon, drained and flaked, and ¼ teaspoon dried dillweed into basic cheese mixture. Chill.

*Smoky Dip:* Have 1 cup shredded smoky Cheddar cheese (4 ounces) at room temperature. In small mixing bowl beat Cheddar cheese into basic cheese mixture with 1 to 2 tablespoons milk and 1 teaspoon prepared mustard to make dipping consistency. Chill. Stir before serving.

*Dips and spreads which have become very popular with the American people are soft, creamy cheese mixtures that can be scooped up or spread on crackers, chips, raw vegetables, or fresh fruit. With this cheese appetizer you can choose just one of the variations or go three ways by tripling the basic cheese recipe.*

*Looking for an appetizer with lots of possibilities? Three-Way Cheese Appetizer begins with a basic cheese mixture, to which you add a variety of ingredients. You can make the Cheese Ball, Salmon Spread, or Smoky Dip. All are delicious with an assortment of crackers.*

## Oliebollen (olee' bowl len)

These Dutch fritters were sometimes called olykoeks or raised doughnuts. In the 18th century, the Dutch in New York considered their "oily cakes" absolutely necessary to the New Year festivities. Washington Irving described them as "balls of sweetened dough fried in hog's fat, and called dough nuts or oly-koeks." We have eliminated the "hog's fat" for a more digestible olykoek.

| | |
|---|---|
| 3¼ cups all-purpose flour | 3 egg yolks |
| 2 packages active dry yeast | ½ cup raisins |
| 1 cup milk | ½ cup chopped mixed candied |
| ⅓ cup sugar | fruits and peels |
| ¼ cup shortening | Fat for frying |
| 1 teaspoon vanilla | ½ cup sugar |
| 2 eggs | 1 teaspoon ground cinnamon |

Combine *2 cups* of the flour and yeast. In saucepan heat milk, ⅓ cup sugar, shortening, and 1 teaspoon salt just till warm (115-120°), stirring constantly. Stir in vanilla. Add to dry ingredients; add eggs and egg yolks. Beat at low speed with electric mixer for ½ minute, scraping bowl. Beat 3 minutes at high speed. Stir in remaining flour, raisins, and candied fruits and peels. Cover; let rise till double (about 30 minutes). Carefully drop by tablespoonsful into deep hot fat (375°); fry about 3 minutes, turning to brown all sides. Drain on paper toweling. While still warm, dust with mixture of ½ cup sugar and the ground cinnamon. Makes 36.

## Potato Bread With Sour Cream and Chives

In mixing bowl combine 2½ cups all-purpose flour and 2 packages active dry yeast. Heat together 1½ cups milk, 2 tablespoons sugar, 2 tablespoons butter, and 2 teaspoons salt just till warm (115-120°), stirring constantly. Add to dry ingredients. Add one 10½-ounce can condensed cream of potato soup, ½ cup dairy sour cream, ¼ cup snipped chives, and 1 teaspoon dried tarragon, crushed. Beat at low speed of electric mixer for ½ minute, scraping sides of bowl constantly. Beat 3 minutes at high speed. By hand, stir in enough of 4 cups all-purpose flour to make moderately stiff dough. Turn out onto lightly floured surface and knead till smooth (5 to 8 minutes).

Place in lightly greased bowl; turn once. Cover; let rise till double (50 to 60 minutes). Punch down. Cover; let rest 10 minutes. Divide dough in half; shape into two loaves. Place in two greased 9x5x3-inch loaf pans. Let rise again till double (about 30 minutes). Bake at 400° till done, about 30 minutes. Remove from pans. Cool on rack. Makes 2 loaves.

## Pimiento-Bacon Sandwich Rolls

| | |
|---|---|
| 8 individual French rolls | 1 teaspoon lemon juice |
| ½ cup butter *or* margarine, | 1 teaspoon prepared |
| softened | horseradish |
| 1 tablespoon chopped green | 8 slices pimiento cheese |
| onion | 8 slices bacon, crisp-cooked |
| 1 tablespoon prepared mustard | and crumbled |

Split rolls. Combine butter, onion, mustard, lemon juice, and horseradish. Spread on cut surfaces of rolls. Place *one* cheese slice on bottom half of each roll, folding to fit. Sprinkle bacon over cheese; cover with roll tops. Bake on ungreased baking sheet at 350° for 12 to 15 minutes. Makes 8 servings.

## Marinated Brussels Sprouts Appetizers

2 10-ounce packages frozen
   Brussels sprouts
• • •
½ cup tarragon vinegar
½ cup cooking oil
1 small clove garlic,
   minced

1 tablespoon sugar
1 teaspoon salt
   Dash bottled hot
    pepper sauce
2 tablespoons thinly
   sliced green onion

In saucepan cook the Brussels sprouts according to package directions; drain. Combine the tarragon vinegar, cooking oil, garlic, sugar, salt, and hot pepper sauce. Add the drained Brussels sprouts and sliced green onion; toss. Cover the vegetable mixture and chill thoroughly 8 hours or overnight, stirring often. Drain the vegetable mixture to serve.

## Julienne Vegetable Plate

½ cup mayonnaise *or*
   salad dressing
¼ cup crumbled blue cheese
   (1 ounce)
• • •
1 tablespoon milk
1 teaspoon lemon juice

1 cup celery sticks cut
   2 inches long
1 cup carrot sticks cut
   2 inches long
1 cup cherry tomatoes
1 cup zucchini sticks cut
   2 inches long

In small mixing bowl blend together mayonnaise and blue cheese. Add the milk and lemon juice, beating till mixture is smooth. Chill thoroughly. Arrange celery, carrot sticks, cherry tomatoes, and zucchini on platter. Serve mayonnaise mixture as dip for vegetables. Makes 4 servings.

## Zesty Vegetable Salad

3 medium turnips, peeled and
   sliced (2 cups)
3 medium carrots, peeled and
   sliced (1½ cups)
½ small cauliflower, broken
   in flowerets (1½ cups)
1 small green pepper, cut in
   strips (½ cup)

2 cups water
1 teaspoon salt
½ cup vinegar
⅓ cup sugar
¼ cup salad oil
2 teaspoons curry powder
1 teaspoon salt
¼ teaspoon pepper

Halve turnip slices. In saucepan combine the turnips, carrot slices, cauliflower, green pepper strips, water, and 1 teaspoon salt. Bring mixture to boiling; cover the saucepan and simmer vegetables till crisp-tender, about 5 minutes. Drain and cool. In screw-top jar combine the vinegar, sugar, salad oil, curry powder, 1 teaspoon salt, and the pepper. Cover the jar and shake vigorously. Pour the curry dressing over the vegetables; toss lightly. Refrigerate the vegetable salad several hours or overnight, stirring the mixture occasionally. Makes 8 servings.

*Plan a buffet supper for a New Year's party and include Zesty Vegetable Salad in the menu. Or if serving a full meal isn't exactly what you had in mind, prepare an interesting appetizer buffet and choose Marinated Brussels Sprouts Appetizer and Julienne Vegetable Plate for flavor and texture contrasts. Regardless of the type of party you are planning, choose foods you can make ahead. It's easier than having several last minute jobs to do. All three of these recipes are geared to be made ahead, chilled overnight, and served with no final preparation necessary.*

## Bishop's Wine

| | |
|---|---|
| 2 tablespoons whole cloves | 16 cups dry red wine |
| 3 oranges | 1½ cups sugar |
| 3 lemons | 6 inches stick cinnamon |

*Bishop's Wine is an excellent warm-up beverage after a cold New Year's sledding or skiing party. Prepared hours ahead of the planned activity, this variation of the Wassail Bowl is a mulled wine. Within minutes the punch is ready to be served your guests piping hot. Before serving, be sure to remove the clove-studded fruit.*

About 3 hours before serving the wine, stick whole cloves into the unpeeled oranges and lemons. In large kettle combine *6 cups* of the wine, sugar, and cinnamon; add clove-studded fruit. Cover; let mixture stand until shortly before serving. Remove cover; bring mixture just to boiling. Remove from heat; cover and let steep 15 minutes. Remove clove-studded fruit and stick cinnamon, squeezing fruit gently (don't break peel). Add remaining wine; heat through. Serve hot. Makes 25 (5-ounce) servings.

## Alexandras

| | |
|---|---|
| 4 jiggers vodka (6 ounces) | 2 cups ice cubes |
| 4 jiggers coffee liqueur (6 ounces) | 1 pint vanilla ice cream |

Pour vodka and coffee liqueur into blender container. Add ice cubes, one at a time, blending at low speed till slushy. Add ice cream by spoonsful and blend just till combined. Serve immediately. Makes 8 (4-ounce) servings.

## Spicy Cranberry Punch

| | |
|---|---|
| ¼ cup red cinnamon candies | 1 6-ounce can frozen limeade concentrate |
| 4 cups water | 1 6-ounce can frozen orange juice concentrate |
| 2 32-ounce bottles cranberry juice cocktail, chilled | |

In small saucepan heat cinnamon candies and water, stirring till candies melt. Chill. At serving time combine candy liquid, cranberry cocktail, and frozen concentrates in punch bowl. Stir to dissolve the frozen concentrates. Float ice in punch bowl, if desired. Makes about 20 (5-ounce) servings.

## Ambrosia Cake

| | |
|---|---|
| 1 10-inch sponge cake | 1 3½-ounce can flaked coconut |
| • • • | ¼ cup packed brown sugar |
| 2 cups dairy sour cream | 1 11-ounce can mandarin orange sections, drained |
| 1 20-ounce can crushed pineapple, drained | |

Cut cake crosswise into 3 layers. Combine sour cream, drained pineapple, coconut, and brown sugar. Place bottom cake layer on plate; top with ⅓ *of pineapple mixture.* Add second cake layer; top with another ⅓ of mixture. Add last cake layer and remaining pineapple mixture. Decorate the top with orange sections. Chill till serving time.

## Daiquiri Pie

| | |
|---|---|
| 1 envelope unflavored gelatin | 3 to 4 drops green food |
| 1 cup sugar | coloring |
| ½ teaspoon salt | 2 tablespoons light rum |
| 3 slightly beaten egg yolks | 3 egg whites |
| ⅓ cup lime juice | 36 vanilla wafers |

In saucepan combine gelatin, ⅔ cup of the sugar, and salt. Stir in egg yolks, lime juice, and ½ cup water. Cook and stir till mixture thickens and gelatin dissolves. Remove from heat; stir in food coloring. Cool to room temperature. Stir in rum. Chill till mixture begins to thicken. Beat egg whites till soft peaks form. Gradually add remaining ⅓ cup sugar, beating till stiff peaks form. Fold in gelatin mixture. Chill till mixture mounds. Line bottom of 9-inch pie plate with vanilla wafers, filling in spaces with broken pieces of wafers. Line sides of pie plate with whole vanilla wafers. Pour in gelatin mixture. Chill till firm, several hours or overnight.

*Dazzle family and friends at your New Year's party with a luscious pie reminiscent of the classic Daiquiri cocktail.*

## Chocolate-Coconut Crunch Parfaits

| | |
|---|---|
| 1 4¼- *or* 4½-ounce package | 2 tablespoons packed |
| *instant* chocolate | brown sugar |
| pudding mix | 2 tablespoons butter *or* |
| 1¾ cups milk | margarine, melted |
| ¼ cup crème de cacao | • • • |
| ⅓ cup all-purpose flour | Frozen whipped dessert |
| ¼ cup flaked coconut | topping, thawed |

Prepare pudding mix according to package directions *except* use the 1¾ cups milk and the ¼ cup crème de cacao in place of liquid called for. Chill. Meanwhile, stir together flour, coconut, and brown sugar; stir in butter. Crumble coconut mixture into shallow baking pan. Bake at 350° for 10 to 12 minutes, stirring often. Cool. In 4 parfait glasses layer crumb mixture and pudding. Chill 1 to 2 hours. Top with dessert topping. Serves 4.

*Glamorize the good old-fashioned flavor of chocolate pudding by adding crème de cacao. And for the finishing touch, splash on a dollop of whipped dessert topping. These delicious parfaits are the perfect ending to a New Year's Eve buffet.*

## Butterscotch-Marble Cake

| | |
|---|---|
| 1 package 2-layer-size | 1 cup water |
| white cake mix | ½ cup cooking oil |
| 1 3⅝- *or* 3¾-ounce package | 4 eggs |
| *instant* butterscotch | ½ cup chocolate syrup |
| pudding mix | Powdered sugar |

In mixing bowl combine cake mix, dry pudding mix, water, and oil. Beat at medium speed of electric mixer till smooth, about 2 minutes. Add eggs, one at a time, beating well after each. Pour ⅔ *of the batter* into well-greased and floured 10-inch fluted tube pan. Mix remaining ⅓ of the batter with chocolate syrup; pour evenly over batter in pan. Bake at 350° till cake tests done, about 1 hour. Cool 25 to 30 minutes in pan. Remove from pan; cool on wire rack. Sift powdered sugar lightly over cake.

# Make Your Own Own Christmas

Special gifts from your kitchen—clockwise from back: *No-Cook Mint Patties, Easy Chocolate Truffles, Seasoned Coating Mix, Strawberry-Port Jam, Triple-Cheese Spread, Homemade Horseradish Mustard, Gingered Pear Sauce, Spiced Tea Mix,* and *Chocolate-Covered Cherries.* (See index for pages.)

# Christmas Food Gifts

*Pictured opposite:* Tasty preserves are dressed up for giving. Choose from bright *Cranberry jelly, Mint-Apple Jelly, Orange Marmalade* (see recipe, page 184), *Kumquat Marmalade* (see recipe, page 184), or *Winter Preserves* (see recipe, page 184). To pretty-up the jars for gifts, create a tree from yarn-covered plastic foam; gather a cluster of foam snowballs and stud with holly; wrap tiny foam scraps with shiny paper and burlap ravelings; or make colorful fruits of papier-mâché.

No matter what the calendar says, it's never too soon to start thinking about Christmas—especially if you plan to give gifts from your kitchen. Jams and jellies bottled in the summer or early autumn, unique containers, breadboards, or extra pans bought throughout the year—all are stored with the Christmas gift-giving season in mind.

To help you in your choice of Christmas food gifts, this section has selected recipes that are ideal for gift-giving—special jars of homemade jams and jellies, flavorful cordials and liqueurs, and tempting sweets. Create some of these specialty gifts and delight relatives and friends.

Food gifts to be mailed take special thought. Send moist quick breads instead of yeast breads, as they will stay fresh longer. And choose moist cookies or bar cookies rather than thin sugar cookies or tender spritz. When wrapping, pack cookies individually or pair them, back to back. The best candy choices for mailing include fudge and caramels. Be sure to line the box with waxed paper and put a cushion of crumpled tissue paper on the bottom and between each layer to protect the gift.

Besides the assortment of recipes on the following pages, many of the breads, cookies, and candies in the other sections of this book are also great to make for December gift-giving. So this year, treat those special friends on your Christmas gift list to personalized kitchen-made gifts.

## Mint-Apple Jelly

4 cups canned apple juice
1 1¾-ounce packaged powdered
  fruit pectin
1 cup fresh mint leaves
6 drops green food coloring
4½ cups sugar

In 8- to 10-quart kettle or Dutch oven combine apple juice, pectin, mint, and food coloring. Bring mixture to full rolling boil. Stir in sugar. Bring again to full rolling boil; boil hard, uncovered, 1 minute, stirring constantly. Remove from heat. Remove mint. Quickly skim off foam with metal spoon. Pour at once into hot sterilized jars; seal with metal lids and screw bands or ⅛-inch layer of paraffin. Makes 6 half-pints.

## Cranberry Jelly

3½ cups cranberry juice
  cocktail
1 1¾-ounce packaged powdered
  fruit pectin
4 cups sugar
• • •
¼ cup lemon juice

In 8- to 10-quart kettle or Dutch oven combine cranberry juice and pectin. Bring to full rolling boil. Stir in sugar. Bring again to full rolling boil. Boil hard, uncovered, 1 minute, stirring constantly. Remove from heat. Stir in lemon juice. Quickly skim off foam with metal spoon. Pour at once into hot sterilized jars; seal with metal lids and bands or paraffin. Makes 6 half-pints.

## Orange Marmalade (see photo, page 183)

(see photo, page 183)

4 medium oranges
1 medium lemon
• • •
1½ cups water

¼ teaspoon baking soda
6 cups sugar
½ of a 6-ounce bottle liquid
  fruit pectin

Remove peel from oranges and lemon; scrape off excess white membrane. Cut peels into very fine strips. Combine peel, water, and baking soda. Bring to boiling; cover and simmer 10 minutes. Remove white membrane from fruit. Section fruit, working over a bowl to catch the juice. Combine sections, juice, and undrained peel. Cover and simmer 20 minutes.

Measure 3 cups cooked fruit mixture; stir in sugar. Bring to full rolling boil; boil, uncovered, 5 minutes. Remove from heat; stir in pectin. Skim off foam with metal spoon. Pour at once into hot sterilized jars; seal with metal lids and screw bands or ⅛-inch paraffin. Makes 6 half-pints.

## Kumquat Marmalade (see photo, page 183)

1 pint fresh kumquats
4 cups water

2 cups sugar
1 tablespoon lemon juice

Slice kumquats into paper-thin slices, removing seeds as needed, to measure 2½ cups slices. Cover with the 4 cups water; let stand overnight. In 8- to 10-quart kettle or Dutch oven bring the kumquat mixture to boiling. Reduce heat; boil gently, uncovered, for 30 minutes.

Pour mixture into 3-quart saucepan. Stir in sugar. Bring mixture to full rolling boil. Boil hard, uncovered, stirring constantly till mixture sheets off a metal spoon, 4 to 5 minutes. Stir in lemon juice. Remove from heat; quickly skim off the foam. Pour at once into hot sterilized jars; seal with metal lids and screw bands or ⅛-inch paraffin. Makes 3 half-pints.

## Winter Preserves (see photo, page 183)

1½ cups dried prunes
1½ cups dried apricots
• • •
5 cups water

1 large orange
5 cups sugar
1 8½-ounce can crushed
  pineapple

Rinse prunes and apricots; place in medium saucepan and cover with water. Cover pan; simmer mixture 15 minutes. Drain, reserving cooking liquid. Cool. Pit and cut up prunes. Cut up apricots. Peel orange, reserving peel. Section orange, working over bowl to catch juice. Dice orange sections. Scrape peel; discard white membrane. Slice peel into thin slivers.

In 8- to 10-quart kettle or Dutch oven combine cooked prunes, apricots, reserved cooking liquid, orange peel, reserved orange juice, diced orange, sugar, and undrained pineapple. Boil mixture gently, uncovered, till of desired thickness, about 20 minutes. Stir occasionally. Remove from heat; quickly skim off foam. Pour at once into hot sterilized jars; seal with metal lids and screw bands or ⅛-inch paraffin. Makes 3 half-pints.

*If you haven't made your jams and jellies in September and stored them away for December gift-giving, it's not too late. You can purchase many of the fruits and ingredients called for in these recipes any time. Be sure to make enough of these colorful jams, jellies, marmalades, and preserves so that you'll have a variety to give away or to keep for your family.*

## Strawberry-Port Jam (see photo, pages 180-181)

| | |
|---|---|
| 1 20-ounce bag frozen whole unsweetened strawberries, thawed | ½ teaspoon grated lemon peel |
| | ¼ teaspoon ground nutmeg |
| • • • | 1 1¾-ounce package powdered fruit pectin |
| 1½ cups ruby port | 4 cups sugar |

Chop berries; reserve juice. Add water to berries and juice to measure 2½ cups. In 8- to 10-quart kettle combine berry-juice mixture, port, lemon peel, and nutmeg; mix well. Add pectin; mix well. Bring to full rolling boil; stir constantly. Stir in sugar. Bring again to full rolling boil. Boil hard, uncovered, 1 minute, stirring constantly. Remove jam from heat; quickly skim off foam. Stir and skim for 10 minutes to cool slightly and to prevent floating fruit. Ladle strawberry-jam mixture into hot sterilized jars. Seal jars with metal lids and screw bands or ⅛-inch paraffin. Makes 6 half-pints.

*Jelly isn't the only food gift you can make. Why not prepare Homemade Horseradish Mustard or Triple-Cheese Spread, or fix Seasoned Coating Mix? Any of these is great for a gourmet friend of yours or someone who is hard to buy for. Who knows, you may launch a new tradition this year by giving your friends one of these unusual gifts.*

## Homemade Horseradish Mustard (see photo, pages 180-181)

| | |
|---|---|
| 2 vegetable bouillon cubes | 2 teaspoons ground turmeric |
| 1½ cups hot water | ¼ cup white wine vinegar |
| 4 teaspoons cornstarch | 4 teaspoons prepared |
| 4 teaspoons sugar | horseradish |
| 4 teaspoons dry mustard | 2 slightly beaten egg yolks |

Dissolve bouillon cubes in water. In small saucepan blend cornstarch, sugar, mustard, and turmeric. Stir in vinegar and horseradish. Slowly blend in bouillon. Cook and stir over low heat till thickened and bubbly; gradually stir a moderate amount into egg yolks. Return to saucepan. Cook and stir about 1 minute. Store, covered, in refrigerator. Makes 1½ cups.

## Triple-Cheese Spread (see photo, pages 180-181)

| | |
|---|---|
| 2 cups shredded sharp Cheddar cheese (8 ounces) | 1 3-ounce package cream cheese |
| ½ cup crumbled blue cheese | 2 tablespoons milk |

Bring cheeses to room temperature. Combine cheeses; beat well with electric mixer. Blend in milk. Keep refrigerated. Makes about 2 cups.

## Seasoned Coating Mix (see photo, pages 180-181)

| | |
|---|---|
| 1 cup fine dry bread crumbs | 4 teaspoons onion powder |
| 4 teaspoons curry powder (optional) | 1½ teaspoons salt |
| | ½ teaspoon garlic powder |
| | Dash cayenne |

In mixing bowl combine all ingredients; mix well. Store in tightly covered container. Use to coat chicken pieces or fish fillets. Makes 1 cup.

## Marzipan

*Marzipan is a legacy of medieval times. Crusaders reportedly brought the first marzipan back to Europe from the Middle East. It was fashioned in the shape of the medieval coin of the realm called Mawthaban, and became a great favorite of European royalty. For New Year's Queen Elizabeth I once received a chessboard, a replica of St. Paul's Cathedral, and the figure of St. George — all modeled in marzipan.*

*Fruits are the most popular shapes today, but part of the fun of making your own marzipan is the creation of special shapes for gifts. Marzipan pigs have always been special treasures in German and Scandinavian households — symbols of good fortune in the next year's harvest.*

| | |
|---|---|
| 1 cup sugar | Food coloring |
| ¾ cup boiling water | Whole cloves |
| 1 tablespoon light corn syrup | Unsweetened cocoa powder |
|    *or* dash cream of tartar | Light corn syrup |
| 1 8-ounce can almond paste | Red sugar |

Butter sides of heavy 1-quart saucepan. In it combine sugar, water, and corn syrup or cream of tartar. Cook and stir over medium heat till sugar dissolves and mixture boils. Cook *without stirring* to soft-ball stage (240° on candy thermometer). Pour onto platter. *Do not scrape pan.* Cool till slightly warm, about 30 minutes. *Do not move.* With spatula, scrape candy from edge of platter toward center; continue working with spatula till creamy and stiff. Knead till smooth. Store in covered container for 24 hours to soften. Warm mixture in bowl over hot water; work till smooth (add a few drops of water, if needed). Work in almond paste till smooth. Place in bowl, then cover with damp cloth; let stand several hours. Divide candy in half; tint one half red and remaining half yellow. Shape candy into fruits as directed below. Lay fruits on waxed paper; let dry, uncovered, overnight. Next day, add blushes or sugar coating as directed. Makes about ¾ pound.

*Pears:* Mold pears, using 1½ teaspoons candy tinted yellow for each. Add a whole clove for the blossom end. Let dry overnight. Next day, brush with a pink blush, using red food coloring and water.

*Bananas:* Mold bananas, using 1½ teaspoons candy tinted yellow for each. Let dry overnight. Next day, tint one end with green food coloring; streak banana with a mixture of equal parts cocoa and water.

*Apples:* Mold balls, using 1½ teaspoons candy tinted red for each. Add a whole clove for the blossom end. Let dry overnight. Next day, add a red blush to the apples, using red food coloring.

*Strawberries:* Mold balls, using 1 teaspoon candy tinted red for each. Shape a point at one end and flatten the other. Let dry overnight. Brush strawberries with light corn syrup and roll each in red sugar. Dry thoroughly.

## Malted Fruit Bars

| | |
|---|---|
| ½ cup packed brown sugar | ½ cup chocolate malted milk |
| ¼ cup granulated sugar |    powder |
| 6 tablespoons butter *or* | ½ teaspoon baking powder |
|    margarine, softened | ½ cup chopped mixed candied |
|       • • • |    fruits and peels |
| 2 eggs | ½ cup chopped walnuts |
| 1 teaspoon vanilla | Malted Sugar |
| ¾ cup all-purpose flour | |

Cream together sugars and butter till fluffy. Add eggs and vanilla; beat well. Stir together flour, milk powder, and baking powder; stir into creamed mixture. Stir in fruits and nuts. Bake in greased 9x9x2-inch baking pan at 350° for 30 to 35 minutes. Cool; top with Malted Sugar. Makes 24.

*Malted Sugar:* Combine 2 teaspoons *each* powdered sugar and chocolate malted milk powder. Sift over cooled cookies.

## Easy Toffee

1 cup chopped walnuts
¾ cup packed brown sugar
½ cup butter *or* margarine

½ cup semisweet chocolate
pieces

Butter an 8x8x2-inch pan; sprinkle walnuts on bottom. In a 1½-quart saucepan combine brown sugar and butter or margarine; cook over medium heat to soft-crack stage (290° on candy thermometer), stirring often. Remove from heat and spread over nuts in pan. Sprinkle chocolate pieces atop; let stand 1 to 2 minutes. When chocolate is softened, spread evenly over toffee. Chill thoroughly; break into pieces. Makes about 1 pound.

*For those on your gift list who enjoy chocolate, make Easy Toffee, Apple-Peanut Butter Fudge, or Mallow-Nut Fudge. The toffee needs chilling so reserve it for those close-by. Both types of fudge are easy to pack for long distance shipping or traveling.*

## Apple-Peanut Butter Fudge

1 6-ounce package semisweet
chocolate pieces (1 cup)
½ of a 7-, 9-, or 10-ounce
jar marshmallow creme

½ cup peanut butter
1 teaspoon vanilla
2 cups sugar
⅔ cup apple juice

Combine chocolate, marshmallow creme, peanut butter, and vanilla; set aside. Butter sides of heavy 2-quart saucepan. In it combine sugar and apple juice. Stir over medium heat till sugar dissolves and mixture boils. Cook to soft-ball stage (240° on candy thermometer), stirring often. Remove from heat; quickly add chocolate mixture. Stir just till blended. Pour into buttered 9x9x2-inch pan. Cut in squares when firm. Makes 36 pieces.

## Mallow-Nut Fudge

1 10-ounce package tiny
marshmallows
1 12-ounce package semisweet
chocolate pieces
2 cups broken walnuts

4½ cups sugar
1 13-ounce can evaporated
milk
1 cup butter *or* margarine
1 tablespoon vanilla

In large bowl mix marshmallows, chocolate, and nuts. In large saucepan mix sugar, evaporated milk, and butter or margarine; bring to boiling. Cook and stir over medium heat to soft-ball stage (236° on candy thermometer). Stir in vanilla; pour over marshmallow-nut mixture. Beat till chocolate and marshmallows melt. Pour into greased 15½x10½x1-inch pan. Cool; cut in squares. Makes about 70 pieces.

## Plum Cordial

Mix 3 pounds fresh purple plums, halved and pitted; 4 cups sugar; and 4 cups gin in large jar. Cover tightly. Turn jar end over end till sugar is in suspension (sugar will not dissolve). Let stand at room temperature for 2 days. Invert; let stand 2 days more. Repeat turning every other day for 6 weeks. Strain out plums; serve cordial in liqueur glasses. Makes 8 cups.

## Homemade Cranberry Cordial

*Pictured opposite:* Choose from *Orange-Flavored Liqueur, Homemade Cranberry Cordial,* or *Coffee-Flavored Liqueur* for the perfect finale to an elegant holiday meal.

| | |
|---|---|
| 1 16-ounce package cranberries (4 cups) | 3 cups sugar 1 pint gin (2 cups) |

Coarsely chop cranberries. Place fruit in a ½-gallon jar or crock. Add sugar and gin. Seal jar with a screw-top lid, or cover crock tightly with foil. Store mixture in a cool place. Turn the jar over each day for 3 weeks. (If in a crock, stir gently.) Transfer to quart jars; cover tightly. Strain cordial before serving. Serve well chilled. Makes about 3¼ cups cordial plus 3 cups drained cranberries, which can be used as a relish.

## Coffee-Flavored Liqueur

*Surprise your Christmas guests by serving them delicious cordials such as Orange-Flavored Liqueur. Or give these special gifts to some of the people on your Christmas list. For an extra-special touch, present these cordials in pretty glass decanters.*

| | |
|---|---|
| 2 cups water 1½ cups granulated sugar 1½ cups packed brown sugar | ⅓ cup instant coffee granules 1 ⅘-quart bottle vodka 2 teaspoons vanilla |

In a saucepan combine water and sugars. Simmer gently, uncovered, for 10 minutes. Remove mixture from heat. Stir in coffee granules. Cool. Pour *half* into each of two 1-quart jars. Stir *half* of the vodka and vanilla into each jar. Cover; let stand at room temperature 2 weeks. Makes 5½ cups.

## Orange-Flavored Liqueur

| | |
|---|---|
| 4 medium oranges Water | 2 cups sugar 2 cups vodka *or* rum |

Squeeze juice from the oranges; reserve the peel from 1 orange. With a sharp knife scrape the white membrane from the reserved peel; cut the peel into thin strips. Add enough water to orange juice to make 2 cups. In a saucepan combine orange juice mixture, orange peel, and sugar. Bring to boiling; reduce heat and simmer over low heat 5 minutes. Cool mixture and pour into a large jar. Stir in vodka or rum. Cover with lid; let stand at room temperature for 3 to 4 weeks. Strain liqueur. Serve in cordial glasses or in cocktail glasses over ice. Makes about 5 cups liqueur.

## Cherry Bounce

| | |
|---|---|
| 8 cups fresh unpitted tart red cherries (2 pounds) 2 cups sugar 1½ teaspoons whole allspice | 1½ teaspoons whole cloves 2 inches stick cinnamon • • • 4 cups bourbon |

Wash and stem cherries. Place *half* of the cherries in each of two 1-quart jars. Then, layer *half* of the sugar and *half* of the spices in each jar. Pour *2 cups* bourbon in each jar; cover tightly. Stir cherry mixtures daily till all of the sugar is dissolved. Screw on jar tops and store in a cool, dark place for at least 2 months. Strain before serving. Makes 4 cups.

## Gingered Pear Sauce (see photo, pages 180-181)

(see photo, pages 180-181)

*If you are looking for an unusual gift, try Gingered Pear Sauce. Your friends will be able to use the sauce as a topper for pancakes and waffles or over fruit or ice cream. Dress up your gift by sealing the spicy fruit sauce in fancy canning jars.*

2½ pounds pears (6 to 8 medium)
Ascorbic acid color keeper
3¼ cups sugar

½ teaspoon grated lemon peel
⅓ cup lemon juice
2 tablespoons finely chopped candied ginger

Peel and core pears; slice into bowl of cold water and color keeper. Drain well. Measure 5 cups pears into saucepan. Add sugar. Cook and stir over low heat till sugar is dissolved. Simmer till fruit is translucent, stirring often. Add lemon peel and juice and ginger. Boil 15 minutes, stirring frequently. Pour sauce into hot sterilized jars; seal. Makes 4 half-pints.

## Spiced Tea Mix (see photo, pages 180-181)

8 ounces orange pekoe tea leaves (3 cups)
¼ cup shredded orange peel
1 tablespoon finely chopped candied ginger

4 inches stick cinnamon, coarsely crushed
2 teaspoons whole cloves, coarsely crushed

Combine tea leaves, orange peel, ginger, cinnamon, and cloves in a 1-quart casserole. Cover; heat in a 300° oven, for 15 to 20 minutes, stirring once or twice. Place tea mix in a jar with a tight-fitting lid; seal. Store in a cool place at least 1 week. Use 1 to 2 teaspoons tea mix for each 6 cups boiling water. Strain tea before serving. Makes about 3 cups tea mix.

## Candied Coconut Chips

*Don't let the leftover coconut discourage you from making Candied Coconut Chips. You can shred the coconut and use it in many types of baked goods such as Cherry Christmas Pie (see recipe, page 124). Or save the coconut milk and meat to make the delicious Christmas drink, Coconut Milk Punch (see recipe, page 27).*

Remove the shells from 2 coconuts. Chip pieces from coconuts, leaving a thin layer of white meat attached to brown skin. (Refrigerate remaining coconut for future use.) In a saucepan bring 2½ cups water and 1½ cups sugar to boiling. Boil rapidly, uncovered, till mixture resembles corn syrup, about 25 minutes. Add coconut pieces; mix well. Drain. Roll pieces in additional sugar. Dry, uncovered, on rack for 1 to 2 days. Makes 2 cups.

## No-Cook Mint Patties (see photo, pages 180-181)

⅓ cup light corn syrup
¼ cup butter, softened
1 teaspoon peppermint extract

1 pound powdered sugar, sifted (4¾ cups)
1 drop *each* red and green food coloring

Blend corn syrup, butter, extract, and ½ teaspoon salt. Add sugar; mix with spoon and hands till smooth. Divide into thirds; knead red food coloring into one third and green food coloring into another third. (Leave remaining third white.) Shape into small balls; flatten with fork on waxed paper-lined baking sheets. Let dry several hours. Makes 72 patties.

## Chocolate-Covered Cherries (see photo, pages 180-181)

60 maraschino cherries with
  stems
3 tablespoons butter, softened
3 tablespoons light corn syrup

2 cups sifted powdered sugar
1½ pounds dipping chocolate
  *or* white chocolate
  (for coating candy)

*The dipping chocolate used to coat homemade Chocolate-Covered Cherries comes in large pieces and is sold by the pound. Purchase it at a local candy store or in some large supermarkets.*

Drain cherries well; place on paper toweling. Combine butter, corn syrup, and ¼ teaspoon salt; stir in powdered sugar. Knead till smooth. (Chill if mixture is too soft.) Shape 1 teaspoon of sugar mixture around each cherry. Place on a waxed paper-lined baking sheet; chill. In a small, heavy saucepan, melt chocolate, stirring constantly. *Do not add any liquid.* Holding cherries by stems, dip one at a time, into chocolate. Spoon chocolate over cherries to coat. Place on waxed paper-lined baking sheet, and chill till chocolate is hardened. Store in a covered container in a cool place. Let candies ripen a week or two. Makes 60 chocolate-covered cherries.

## Easy Chocolate Truffles (see photo, pages 180-181)

8 ounces milk chocolate, cut
  in pieces
8 ounces semisweet chocolate,
  cut in pieces
1 egg

2 egg yolks
2 tablespoons butter *or*
  margarine, softened
½ cup multicolored decorative
  candies

Melt chocolate in top of double boiler over boiling water. Remove from heat; add egg and egg yolks, one at a time, beating smooth after each. Add butter; beat smooth. Chill till firm enough to hold shape. Shape into 1-inch balls; roll in candies. Refrigerate or freeze. Makes 36.

## Caramel Divinity Dreams

2½ cups granulated sugar
½ cup light corn syrup
½ cup water

2 egg whites
1 teaspoon vanilla
Dipping Caramel

In saucepan combine sugar, corn syrup, water, and ¼ teaspoon salt. Cook to hard-ball stage (260° on candy thermometer), stirring only till sugar dissolves. Beat egg whites to stiff peaks. Slowly pour sugar mixture over whites, beating at high speed of electric mixer. Add vanilla; continue beating till candy holds its shape. With buttered hands, shape into ¾-inch balls. Dry on waxed paper till firm. Drop balls, one at a time, into Dipping Caramel; turn with fork till thinly coated. Lift out; cool on waxed paper. Makes 72.

*Dipping Caramel:* In a large, heavy saucepan blend 1⅓ cups granulated sugar, 1 cup evaporated milk, ¾ cup packed brown sugar, and ⅛ teaspoon baking soda. Cook and stir till sugars dissolve. Boil, stirring often, till candy reaches soft-ball stage (234° on candy thermometer). Remove from heat. Cool to 110° without stirring. Beat till mixture is thick and creamy and loses its gloss. Beat in an additional ¼ cup evaporated milk. (If caramel becomes too stiff, stir in additional evaporated milk, a teaspoonful at a time.)

## Puffed Trees

12 regular marshmallows
8 cups puffed rice cereal
1 cup sugar
¾ cup water
¼ cup light corn syrup

12 drops green food coloring
2 to 3 drops oil of
  peppermint
Confectioners' Icing
Red cinnamon candies

Let marshmallows stand uncovered overnight. Place cereal in 325° oven for 10 minutes; keep warm while making syrup. Butter sides of saucepan; combine sugar, water, syrup, and ¼ teaspoon salt. Cook and stir over medium heat till mixture comes to boiling; reduce heat and continue cooking till mixture reaches hard-ball stage (250° on candy thermometer). Stir in green food coloring and oil of peppermint. Pour syrup slowly over warm cereal, stirring just enough to coat thoroughly. Butter hands lightly and shape cereal mixture into 12 cone shapes for trees, using ½ cup for each. Put Confectioners' Icing into cake decorator; pipe around trees. Decorate with candies. Attach marshmallows to bottoms with wooden picks. Makes 12.

*Confectioners' Icing:* Add enough light cream to 2 cups sifted powdered sugar to make mixture that will hold shape but can be piped easily.

## Jingle Popcorn Balls

12 cups popped corn
2 cups snipped gumdrops
1 cup snipped pitted dates
1 cup light corn syrup
½ cup honey

1½ teaspoons vinegar
¾ teaspoon salt
1 tablespoon butter *or*
  margarine
1½ teaspoons vanilla

In large bowl combine popped corn, gumdrops, and dates. In heavy saucepan combine corn syrup, honey, vinegar, and salt. Bring to boiling. Cook mixture over medium heat to hard-ball stage (260° on candy thermometer). Add butter and vanilla, stirring till butter is melted. Pour over popcorn mixture; stir to coat evenly. Form into 2-inch balls. Makes about 30 popcorn balls.

## Caramelized Fruit and Nuts

1 cup packed brown sugar
½ cup granulated sugar
½ cup milk
1 tablespoon light corn syrup
1 tablespoon butter
1 tablespoon vanilla

½ cup walnut halves
½ cup pecan halves
¼ cup blanched almonds,
  toasted
¼ cup snipped pitted dates
¼ cup candied cherries

Combine brown sugar, granulated sugar, milk, and corn syrup. Cook and stir over medium heat till sugars dissolve and mixture boils. Continue cooking to soft-ball stage (236° on candy thermometer). Add butter and vanilla. Let cool 10 minutes. Beat *just till mixture begins to lose its gloss,* 3 to 4 minutes. Quickly stir in nuts and fruits till coated. Drop immediately from spoon onto buttered baking sheet. Makes about 24 candy clusters.

## Glazed Cashew Clusters

| | |
|---|---|
| 2 cups cashew nuts | ¼ teaspoon cream of tartar |
| 2 cups sugar | 1 teaspoon vanilla |

Spread cashews on baking sheet; toast in 350° oven till golden brown. Cook and stir sugar and cream of tartar with 1 cup water till sugar dissolves. Bring to boiling; boil to hard-crack stage (300° on candy thermometer). Remove from heat; stir in nuts and vanilla. Set pan in hot water to keep soft. Drop tablespoonsful onto greased baking sheet. Makes 1 pound.

*Finding containers for nut gifts shouldn't be a problem. Use odd goblets, vases, small glasses, covered cans, or boxes — tie with colored ribbons or gold cord and the gift is complete.*

## Filbert Fancies

| | |
|---|---|
| 1 cup shelled, unblanched filberts, coarsely chopped | 1 beaten egg |
| 2 cups sifted powdered sugar | 2 1-ounce squares unsweetened chocolate, melted and cooled |
| 3 tablespoons butter *or* margarine, softened | 1 6-ounce package tiny marshmallows (about 4 cups) |
| 1 teaspoon vanilla | 1 cup shredded coconut |
| Dash salt | |

Spread filberts on baking sheet. Toast in 350° oven till golden brown, about 10 minutes. Cool. Beat sugar, butter, vanilla, and salt into egg till very light and fluffy. Stir in cooled chocolate. Fold in marshmallows and nuts. Drop teaspoonsful into bowl of coconut; roll to coat evenly. Place on waxed paper-lined baking sheets. Let stand till set. Makes 48.

## Spicy Sherried Walnuts

| | |
|---|---|
| 1½ cups packed brown sugar | 1 teaspoon pumpkin pie spice |
| ¼ cup sherry | 5 cups walnut halves |
| 2 tablespoons light corn syrup | Granulated sugar |

In saucepan mix brown sugar, sherry, syrup, spice, and ¼ teaspoon salt. Heat till sugar is dissolved. Stir in walnuts; coat well. Roll in granulated sugar. Dry on baking sheet. Store in loosely covered container.

## Herbed Pecans

| | |
|---|---|
| 3 tablespoons butter | ¼ teaspoon garlic powder |
| 3 tablespoons Worcestershire sauce | ¼ teaspoon cayenne |
| 1 teaspoon salt | Dash bottled hot pepper sauce |
| ½ teaspoon ground cinnamon | 1 pound pecan halves |

In heavy skillet melt butter. Stir in remaining ingredients *except* pecans. Add pecans; toss till nuts are well coated. Place in single layer in 15½x 10½x1-inch baking pan. Toast pecans in 300° oven till nuts are brown and crisp, 20 to 25 minutes, stirring frequently. Makes about 4 cups.

# Centerpieces and Arrangements

Part of the fun of the holidays is coming up with new ideas for decorating your home—especially your dining table. Use mid-November to January as a time to experiment with centerpieces and arrangements. For Thanksgiving, fill a wicker cornucopia with fall fruits, Indian corn, and colorful gourds. Or layer colored dried beans in a large glass brandy snifter. At Christmas, keep the theme red and green. Try an arrangement as traditional as apples and evergreens or as offbeat as radishes and artichokes. For New Year's Day, decorate a cake as a clock, or for the football-family, set up a buffet arrangement with football favors. The traditional can be fun, but the 'new' often is more exciting. Use the ideas on the following pages as beginning themes for your own smashing centerpieces and arrangements.

**Cornhusk tree:** For a festive holiday buffet, feature this attractive cornhusk tree as a centerpiece. The tree requires the following *materials:* a 24-inch plastic foam cone, a 16- or 17-ounce metal can, masking tape, cornhusks, cardboard, spool wire, about 450 ⅜-inch red wooden beads, a 2½-inch plastic foam ball, an 8-inch piece of ¼-inch dowel, heavy white glue, small hairpins or floral stems made into hairpin shape, and a basket or container for the base of the tree. You will need the following *equipment:* heavy rubber bands, pins, a knife, and scissors.

Set the foam cone on the metal can. Press down and mark the outline of the can on the cone. Cut with a knife an indentation 1 inch deep. Cover can with masking tape. Fit can into indentation.

Place cornhusks in boiling water till pliable. Remove from water and drain. Wrap in a towel. Spread glue on cone and covered can. Cover with cornhusks, laying them flat; overlap and pin to hold, if necessary.

To cover ball, insert the dowel 3 inches into ball. Tear more softened cornhusks into 1-inch strips. Glue strips onto ball, starting and ending at dowel and overlapping as necessary. When the ball is covered, wire the ends of the cornhusks to the dowel tightly. Set ball and dowel aside to dry.

Mark the cone from bottom to top into alternating 2¾-inch and 1½-inch inter-vals. Place rubber bands around cone to mark the intervals.

For cornhusk puffs, soften husks in boiling water and wrap in a towel. Tear off thin outer edges. Tear husks into 1½-inch-wide strips. Cut cardboard guide 2¾x2 inches. Fold a husk strip in half over the 2-inch side of cardboard guide. Pinch ends of husk together at edge of cardboard; wire husk guide. Cut wire; trim cornhusk close to wire. Remove cardboard guide. Put thumbs inside husk at fold; puff out husk.

To pin puffs to tree, begin at bottom of cone. Turn puff so wired end is down. Pin to cone. Working from left to right, slip edge of next puff into first puff; pin to cone. Continue around cone. Pin a second row with the wired end up at rubber band. Make a third row, using puffs made by folding husks over the 2¾-inch side of cardboard guide. Pin this row between the two rows of larger puffs. Repeat these 3 rows on each 2¾-inch section. Remove rubber bands.

To add ball, cover the top two inches of the dowel by gluing on cornhusks. Insert remainder of dowel into cone.

To add beads, thread beads on pieces of wire cut to fit cone. Fit rows of beads around cone between rows of puffs. Twist ends of wire together. Hold beads in position with hairpins or floral stems pushed in between beads.

To finish tree, insert trunk end of tree into a basket or other container.

**Cornhusk tree centerpiece for a holiday buffet table**

**Lantern centerpiece for table arrangement**

**Lantern centerpiece:** Lanterns are reminiscent of English and American colonial Christmases when lamplighters provided light for coach-and-four who brought guests to inns and great houses for celebrations. Lanterns also made light possible for carolers who sang their way from door to door.

Renew thoughts of these old times by using an antique lantern or reproduction for a holiday centerpiece. Enhance an open-bottom lantern with a candle arrangement, using real or artificial flowers. Then, group 4 more arrangements without the candle around the lantern.

Or use the kerosene lamp—empty—you keep on hand for power outages. Purchase plastic foam in a wreath shape or large flat disk. Put lamp inside the wreath or on the disk and use the rest of the plastic foam to anchor greens. Holly leaves and berries give contrasting red and green colors. For a special touch, add pine cones and dried flowers to complete the centerpiece.

**Balsa creche:** This scene, although simplistic in design, brings the Christmas message home when displayed on a table. The designs are outlined with felt marking pens. The whole family can help with this project, and each member will gain satisfaction from contributing to what might someday be an heirloom.

To make the freestanding creche, you need the following: balsa wood—2 pieces 36x4x⅛-inch, 1 piece 36x3x⅛-inch, 2 pieces 36x1x1-inch, 3 pieces 36x1x¼-inch, and 1 piece 36x1x⅛-inch; contact cement; brown fine-point permanent felt-tip pen; sandpaper; scissors; knife; and clear matte protective coating.

Make patterns by enlarging drawings at right (1 square=1 inch). Cut out figures following patterns, using 36x4x⅛-inch pieces of balsa for the 3 arches, angel, crib, sheep, and cow and the 36x3x⅛-inch piece for Mary, Joseph, and the lamb. Sand smooth; then, copy designs on the figures with the felt-tip pen.

To assemble the base and figures, cut

**Natural balsa-wood creche for indoor use**

three 15-inch strips from the 36x1x1-inch pieces of balsa and five 15-inch strips from the 36x1x¼-inch pieces. Carefully build the base from back to front as follows, sandwiching the figures between layers of the above balsa strips.

Glue the largest arch to the center front of a 15x1x1-inch strip. Fill in each side of arch with 1x⅛-inch strips cut to fit. Glue another 15x1x1-inch strip in front of arch and fill-in-pieces. Glue the two remaining arches to this strip, and fill in spaces. Then, glue a 15x1x¼-inch strip of balsa in front, and glue an angel and Joseph to front of the strip.

Continue filling in spaces. Glue two 15x1x¼-inch strips in front of angel and Joseph. On last layer glue Mary, sheep, and cow. Fill in spaces. Glue on two 15x 1x¼-inch strips. Glue on crib and lamb and fill in spaces.

Before gluing remaining 15x1x1-inch strip on, draw border design on front of it. Then, glue to front of creche. Sand edges and spray on coating.

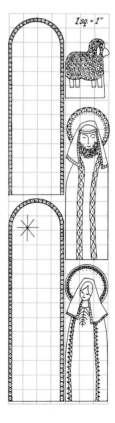

**Shiny wreath and ornaments:** When you want decorations that can be used both indoors and out, waterproof Mylar is a practical solution. To make the shiny wreath, you'll need an 18-inch piece of lightweight cardboard, 1 yard silver Mylar (available at most art supply stores), and a stapler and staples.

Trim the cardboard to a circle 18 inches in diameter, then cut a 7-inch circle from the center to form a wreath. Cut about 100 seven-inch leaves from the Mylar. Make a slit in stem end of each leaf and staple one side of slit over the other to give three-dimensional effect. Staple leaves to cardboard in overlapping fashion till all cardboard is covered and wreath is formed.

Hang the wreath above a table of snacks, and arrange shiny geometric ornaments with greens. You can make the ornaments by gluing leftover pieces of Mylar to shaped cardboard bases.

For an outside door arrangement, dangle the geometric shapes from the wreath—rain or snow won't destroy these delightful waterproof decorations.

**Pomander balls:** An arrangement of pomander balls will add both fragrance and eye-appeal to your Christmas decor. Use them later as party favors or door prizes at your holiday fling. Guests will remember you all year long when they use the pomander balls to freshen closets. However you use them, plan to make them 3 to 4 weeks ahead.

Wash and dry thick-skinned limes, lemons, and oranges. Start holes in the skins with a skewer, then insert whole cloves. Cover the entire surface of the fruit with the cloves.

**Shiny silver wreath and geometric ornaments**

For each ball mix 1 teaspoon ground cinnamon and 1 teaspoon orrisroot (find this in the spice section of the supermarket or at a pharmacy). Place the spices in a small plastic bag with the clove-covered fruit. Shake to coat the fruit well. Wrap the fruit loosely or place in a foil-covered tray or basket. Keep in a dry place till the fruit shrinks and hardens (about 3 to 4 weeks). Turn the fruit every few days. Tie each ball with bright-colored ribbons and they're ready to use.

**Children's table setting:** Children always appreciate festive parties and especially decorations created just for them. Here are a few festive suggestions.

An essential part of a successful party is the table setting. First, coordinate the napkins and tablecloth in a bright color and use contrasting colored runners. You might want to choose runners that match your dishes, as in the photo below. Since it's the holiday season, you probably have lots of homemade cookies and candies on hand. Put them in see-through jars and group them under a tabletop Christmas tree for the centerpiece.

Wrap inexpensive toys and favors, and put one or two packages at each child's place. And to top off the holiday look, put a candy cane on each plate.

If you want a Santa theme, use St. Nick as the centerpiece and group the wrapped packages around him—or in a bag that's spilling over in front of him. Put a chocolate-covered Santa or Santa lollipop on each plate.

Near the end of the party, let each child open his packages. As the children leave, let each choose a favorite cookie or piece of candy from the jars.

**Pomander balls**

**Children's table setting**

**Patchwork place mats and napkins:**
Setting your table for Christmas entertaining needn't involve a lot of work. Instead of using a fancy tablecloth, adapt simple-to-make patchwork place mats and napkins to the holiday season by adding tiny silver bells to the place mat tabs. And use evergreens, ornaments, and candles as a centerpiece.

To make four place mats, you'll need 16 small silver bells and ¾ yard of each of three 45-inch-wide cotton prints in colors that complement each other. (For four napkins, buy an extra ¾ yard of fabric.) Cut eight 18x13-inch rectangles from the cotton prints. To make the tab pattern, fold a 7x5-inch paper rectangle lengthwise and measure up 3½ inches on outside edge. Cut from that point diagonally to the top of the center fold creating a point. Open the pattern and use to cut 32 tabs from the cotton prints.

Pin two contrasting print tabs right sides together and stitch, using a ½-inch seam; leave the end opposite the point open for turning. Turn and press. Repeat to make a total of 16 tabs.

Pin 4 tabs to the right side of a large rectangle, with open ends on the edge and points facing in. Make sure end tabs are ½ inch from either side to allow for the side seams of the place mats. Baste.

Place a contrasting rectangle right side down atop rectangle with tabs inside. Stitch around, leaving an opening for turning. Turn and blindstitch opening. Attach one bell to point of each tab.

If you want a more Christmasy look for your table but still want to use the place mats and napkins during the rest of the year, use a holiday print for one side and an everyday print for the other side. The tiny bells are easily attached and removed according to the season.

To make the napkins, cut four 13-inch squares from the remaining fabric. Make a narrow hem and machine-stitch. For the double-duty napkins, you can use the holiday print or a solid color that goes well with the print. If you use a solid color, choose one that goes well with either side of the place mats.

**Patchwork centerpiece:** Whether you sew a great deal or just occasionally, you're likely to have quite a few scraps of leftover lightweight fabric on hand. Use these scraps to make a centerpiece that will delight your guests—both young and old. (You can also use scraps that are left over from the patchwork place mats and the napkins.)

To make the centerpiece, cut various shaped pieces from several colors and patterns of fabric. Purchase plastic foam balls in an assortment of sizes, and glue the fabric pieces to them. Use several colors and patterns of fabric on one ball for a patchwork effect, or cover the whole ball with one fabric. Surround a stack of the balls with real or artificial holly and evergreens. Add a brightly colored candle or two and you have a centerpiece that's fun to look at and easy to store.

If you like the look of different shapes, purchase and cover other plastic foam articles. Stars, cones, flat disks, and other small shapes can be interestingly arranged in a centerpiece and later used on your tree.

**Evergreen arrangement:** In a dilemma over what to use to give your house a festive look? Let nature come to your aid. No matter what part of the country you're from, a trip outdoors can often produce the items needed for an effective centerpiece or arrangement. Evergreens and other green leaves make good beginnings—pine boughs, holly leaves and berries, mistletoe, and magnolia leaves make excellent borders or underliners in arrangements. If your Christmas tree is full and pruning helps the shape, use the pruned boughs by arranging them with extra ornaments and candles on an end table or any bare surface.

When you're dining, cover a soup tureen underliner with bright-colored glass ornaments and use evergreen as a border (see photo at right). If you really like the natural look, use pinecones, pyracantha, and bittersweet berries instead of glass ornaments for colorful additions to your Christmas decor.

**Patchwork place mats, centerpiece, and evergreen arrangement**

**Small table trees:** Small trees made from unique materials create just the right decorative touch for a coffee table or an end table. The festive tree at the left is made entirely of holly sprigs. For this tree, you'll need four 9x4½x3¼-inch plastic foam blocks, florist wire, fine chicken wire, a shallow compote, and many 6- to 8-inch long holly sprigs.

To form tree, stand three blocks on end and tie together with florist wire. Set fourth block on end on top to get an 18-inch-high tree form. Round off corners. Soak form in water for two hours. When thoroughly soaked, wrap form securely with fine chicken wire.

Stand wet form on the compote and stick holly sprigs through wire and into foam. Cover thickly with holly, shaping into a tree shape as you add holly.

To keep tree fresh, add water daily. Pour it carefully over top block so the excess will soak into lower blocks. You can use this same idea to make small trees of long-stemmed fresh flowers, mistletoe, or winter greenery.

Also use pinecones and bows for a small Christmas tree. Start with a plastic foam cone sprayed brown or dark green. Drill holes in the ends of small pinecones and insert wires dipped in glue; dry. Stick wire-stemmed cones into the plastic foam cone; spray with gold paint. Make small bows from ½-inch-wide velvet ribbon. Pierce the bow with a nail, insert it into the foam, and glue a jewel to the head of the nail. Add small wire-stemmed balls as desired.

**Needlepoint posies:** The materials needed for three flowers—one large and two small flowers, each with five petals: 1 yard No. 10 penelope canvas, 1 tapestry needle, 5 skeins 3-ply Persian needlepoint yarn—one white and *one each* of four shades of pink or the desired color, ¾-yard medium-weight fabric for backing, tiny beads, bead wire, 1-inch green plastic tape, permanent felt-tip pen, and copper household wire—a 14-inch piece for each small petal and a 17-inch piece for each large petal.

**Small holly table tree**

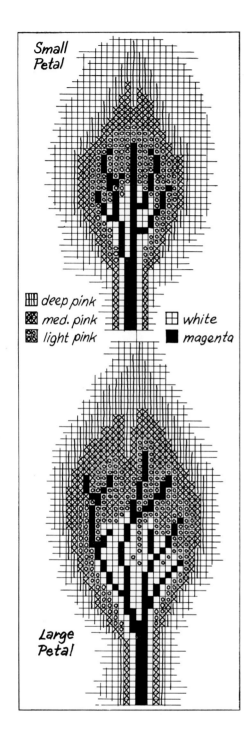

Small
Petal

⊞ deep pink
⊠ med. pink
▨ light pink
⊞ white
■ magenta

Large
Petal

## Needlepoint posies

Cut a 7x4-inch piece of canvas for each small petal and a 8x5-inch piece for each large petal. (You'll need 5 small *or* 5 large petals for each flower.) Use the felt-tip pen to copy the petal designs on the canvas. Following the color-coded diagrams, work petal in basket weave stitch. Work outer edges of petal first.

Next, stitch center veins in the darkest color and then fill in the rest as indicated in the diagram.

Trim around completed needlepoint, leaving ½-inch margin of unstitched canvas. Fold canvas edges to underside of petal; press flat. Insert the cut piece of copper wire under edges and bind wire to canvas using several plys of yarn and an overcast stitch. Cut a bias fabric piece slightly larger than petal and slip-stitch to back of petal.

To make center for each flower, cut a 36-inch piece of bead wire; tie knot 3 inches from one end. String beads onto wire; tie knot 3 inches from end. Loop wire into 8 circles and secure at bottom with a few twists of wire ends.

To assemble the flower, arrange 5 small *or* 5 large petals and fan out. Insert bead loops in center. Twist wire ends of petals and center together. Hold the flower together by wrapping a length of copper wire tightly around outside of petal grouping, beginning just above point where base of petal flares and working down toward the twisted wire stem. Wrap the wire twists at base of flowers with green plastic tape.

**Corrugated paper angels**

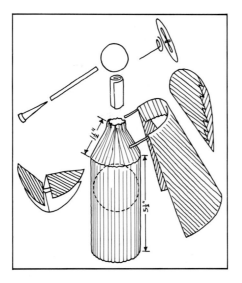

**Corrugated paper angels:** For these attractive angels, you'll need corrugated paper, paper straws, glue, typing paper, golf tees, 1¾-inch paper doilies, gold spray paint, 16-gauge brass wire, thread, 2-inch plastic foam balls, 1½-inch plastic foam balls, and gold cord.

To make angels in the mobile, cut robes, arms, and wings from 2 layers of corrugated paper, back to back. For the neck, glue a flattened piece of paper straw to wrong side of body section. Place typing paper inside arms as backing. Glue body together; glue arms and wings in place. Split end of neck; glue to paper doily. Cover end of straw neck by gluing a 1-inch paper circle onto each side of doily. For the angel's trumpet, glue piece of paper straw to golf tee; spray gold. Feather wings by denting with a spoon handle. Tie angels to brass wire with thread.

To make the standing angels, start with the body. Cut a 7-inch-square piece of corrugated paper. To form neck base at top of body, on wrong side of corrugated square cut a line 1½ inches in from one edge, cutting all the way across the corrugation and only through backing. Slit backing of each corrugation from neck base to cut line.

Form square into cylinder 2 inches in diameter, and glue at overlap. (A 2-inch foam ball inside will help hold body shape.) For neck, roll a short piece of paper to ½-inch in diameter. Bend in top 1½ inches of body to resemble rocket nose cone and glue to neck. Cut arms from heavy paper, score, and bend at elbow. Glue corrugated paper to arms. Glue the arms to body.

For cape, cut 24-inch circle from corrugated paper; cut into eight wedges. Cut off each point 4 inches from tip. Fold under 1 inch on sides and top; dent corrugation with knife back for design.

Run gold cord under neck fold, tie at neck, and glue cape to body. Glue 1½-inch foam ball to neck. Glue piece of thin brass wire to doily circle and push into angel's head for halo. Make wings and trumpets as for mobile angels.

**Advent wreath:** The Advent season begins four Sundays before Christmas. The wreath, symbolic of this four-week period, has four candles—three violet and one rose-colored. Violet symbolizes penitence and preparation of the body and mind for Christmas. Rose denotes the true Christmas spirit—that of joy and anticipation. On the first Sunday of Advent, one candle is lit while the family joins in prayer. On the remaining Sundays, an additional candle is lit till on the final Sunday, all four candles are lit.

The Advent wreath ring shown at right is porcelain, but most people make their own wreaths. To do this, buy a plastic foam wreath and make four indentations equal distances apart. Cut out the holes a little smaller than the size of the candles so the candles will fit securely. Or, purchase four matching candleholders and place them on the plastic foam. Decorate the plastic foam wreath with greenery and other colorful decorations.

**Seed ornaments and obelisk:** (see photo, page 43): Materials you'll need: 16-inch plastic foam obelisk and 3-inch plastic foam balls; white glue; hairpins; assorted dried seeds—pumpkin, sunflower, watermelon, cantaloupe, kidney beans, white navy beans, black-eyed peas, lentil beans, split peas, and coffee beans; and star-shaped pasta.

For the ornaments, have some sort of design in mind before you start (you can be fairly abstract about it and design the ornament as you go along) and decide on the combination of seeds you want to use. For most ornaments, it is advantageous to start at a given point on the foam ball and glue on a single, round seed, such as a lentil bean, as your beginning point. From this, glue seeds encircling the single seed until you have covered the ball. Use a nozzle-type applicator for the glue, and apply glue to only a small area at a time. To make a loop for hanging, insert a hairpin and glue in place.

Use the same technique for the obelisk, starting at the base and working toward the point. The basic materials

**Advent wreath**

are the same. You can obtain obelisk forms from any art supply store. They come in various sizes and also in cone-shapes. Again, the possibilities for the design are unlimited. Design all four sides the same, or make a different design on each side.

The seed ornaments often are used for Christmas decorations. They look especially attractive on a table tree, in a glass container, or in an arrangement (see photo, page 43). They require reasonably gentle handling but are more durable than standard glass ornaments. Each takes a bit of time and patience to make, but the result is spectacular.

**An easy-to-assemble tiered crepe paper tree**

**Tiered crepe paper tree:** This modernistic tree is ideal for decorating buffets and sideboards. It can also serve as the main Christmas tree in homes or apartments where space is limited. You'll find this lightweight decoration is appropriate for office parties, too. Best of all, you can make it yourself.

To make this tree, assemble one 3-inch, one 2½-inch, and one 2-inch plastic-foam ball; a 32x⅝-inch dowel; green and gold spray paint; a paper-covered 1-pound coffee can; a large lump of florist's clay; heavy green crepe paper; artificial red berries; artificial white fruits; and a gold treetop ornament.

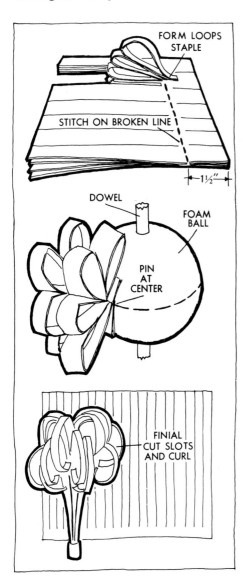

FORM LOOPS
STAPLE

STITCH ON BROKEN LINE

←1½"→

DOWEL

FOAM BALL

PIN AT CENTER

FINIAL
CUT SLOTS AND CURL

Carefully cut a point at one end of the dowel. Paint the dowel and the three plastic foam balls with green spray paint. Spray the paper-covered can with gold paint. Set aside to dry.

When the dowel, can, and plastic foam balls are completely dry, thread the 3-inch ball on the dowel, using the pointed end to make the hole. (Make sure the hole isn't too large or the ball will slide on the dowel.) Position the largest ball near the bottom. Repeat with the 2½-inch ball, placing it about halfway up the dowel. Place the 2-inch ball about 5 to 6 inches from the top. Anchor the blunt end of the dowel in a large lump of florist's clay, and place the clay inside the gold-painted can.

Cutting on the cross grain of the crepe paper, cut four 10x9-inch rectangles, four 9x7½-inch rectangles, and five 8x6-inch rectangles. (Be careful to use a double thickness of paper if you use a lightweight crepe paper.)

To make crepe paper loops, stack the four 10x9-inch pieces of crepe paper. Sew or staple 1½ inches from longest edge. Cut the wider part into 1-inch strips up to stitches or staples. Loop each strip back to stitching as shown in diagram at left; staple loops in place. Pin strip of loops around 3-inch ball.

Repeat for the other two tiers, using the four 9x7½-inch pieces of paper on the 2½-inch ball and four of the 8x6-inch pieces for the 2-inch ball. Cut the strips ¾ and ½ inch wide respectively.

Cut the remaining 8x6-inch piece of crepe paper into ¼-inch strips to within ½ inch of longest edge. Curl each strip with scissors. Glue strip around dowel, as shown in the photo at left.

To finish tree, arrange artificial red berries and artificial white fruits in between loops of crepe paper, fastening with pins. Position the gold treetop ornament on pointed end of dowel.

To add an extra special touch to your centerpiece, arrange evergreen branches around the base of the tree, and don't forget to include a few ornaments and gaily wrapped packages.

**New Year's Eve midnight supper buffet party**

There's more to the holiday season than Christmas. Thanksgiving begins it and New Year's Eve is the climax. But while each holiday deserves special decorations, you can keep them simple and inexpensive and still create a festive mood.

**Thanksgiving decorations:** During autumn, nature provides a bounteous supply of fruits, vegetables, and other natural materials that can be used in decorations. So, when Thanksgiving rolls around, you shouldn't have trouble giving your table and home the look of fall.

Often, you can use ordinary objects you have around the house as containers for the decorations. For example, put cattails, wheat, pyracantha, or bittersweet in a wooden bucket or butter churn for a large table or floor arrangement. Or, fill a wooden bowl or small apple basket with bright-colored vegetables such as dark green acorn squash, orange Hubbard squash, eggplant, green and red sweet peppers, and amber winter onions. Or, fill it with fresh fruits such as red and golden apples, oranges, tangerines, bananas, and pears. Later, when everyone's hungry again, the fruit centerpiece becomes a bowl of snacks.

How about using pinecones for a Thanksgiving centerpiece scene? Make pilgrims using a big cone for the body and a small cone or piece for the head. For hands, face, and hats, cut pieces of black and white construction paper. For turkeys, use chenille stems (from a craft store) for combs and feathers and attach wire to the stems for legs.

Arrange some Indian corn, hedge apples, and decorative gourds around a smiling scarecrow for the harvest look. Or, use Fuji and pompon mums with daisies or wheat for a fall centerpiece that lasts for weeks. Then, as you move closer to the Christmas season, keep the look of nature, but use brighter colors.

**New Year's party:** Welcome the New Year with a party that's brimming with color and good fun. If an intimate gathering is your way of hosting on New Year's Eve, a midnight supper will cap the evening pleasingly. Have your guests arrive around eleven and plan to serve the meal just after midnight. Whether you serve buffet or sit-down style, be sure to have make-ahead food dishes that let you spend time with your guests.

Decorations can range from a simple centerpiece, such as the one at left, to entire wall coverings. For the centerpiece, group tapers around flowers, greens, and large pieces of quartz or other sparkling rock. Any fresh or dried flowers are appropriate for New Year's.

A New Year's Eve party wouldn't be complete without noisemakers. You might want to make a variety of noisemakers and use them in your centerpiece. Start with empty ribbon spools or small boxes and fill with marbles, dried peas and beans, or tiny bells. Attach dowel sticks for handles and decorate with pastel paper and streamers.

To make a centerpiece or arrangement, cover the edge of a piece of plastic foam with ribbon and stick the handles of the noisemakers into the foam. Just before midnight, let guests select noisemakers from the centerpiece.

When table space is limited, hang a clock mobile overhead instead of using a centerpiece. Cut felt in different shapes and colors for clocks and faces. Glue additional felt in other colors to the faces for numbers and hands. (Sequins are useful as number substitutes.) Be sure that the clock hands say that midnight is near! Gather old necklace chains and gold braid and attach to felt clocks. Put two ¼-inch dowel sticks or 2 heavy pieces of wire together by crossing and tying with gold cord. Use a long enough piece of cord to suspend the wire or dowels from the ceiling. Attach clocks so that they dangle from the chains. Use leftover felt to make clock-faced coasters.

New Year's is likely to be the end of a busy holiday season. It's a time to relax after the Christmas rush and to look forward to a busy new year. So, plan decorations around your time and energy—don't wear yourself out!

# INDEX

## A-B

# D-G

# N-Q

# T-Z

We gratefully express our thanks
to the Gorham Company for the
use of two illustrations found in
the *Christmas-Time Cook Book*.